MANAGEMENT AN
EDUCATION

Series Editors: PET.
JOHN SAYER

**Leaders and Leadership in the
School, College and University**

Leaders and Leadership in the School, College and University

PETER RIBBINS

CASSELL
for British Educational Management and Administration Society

Cassell
Wellington House
125 Strand, London WC2R 0BB

PO Box 605
Herndon, VA 20172

First published 1997

British Library Cataloguing-in-Publication Data
A catalogue record for this book is available from the British Library.

ISBN 0-304-33887-7 (hardback)
      0-304-33888-5 (paperback)

Typeset by Kenneth Burnley at Irby, Wirral, Cheshire.
Printed and bound in Great Britain by Redwood Books, Trowbridge, Wiltshire.

Contents

Acknowledgements

This book had its origins in the National Conference of the British Educational Administration Society which took place in Balliol College in the University of Oxford in September 1995. I am grateful to the members of the National Council for making the conference and this book possible, the members of the West Midlands Association who organized the conference, and all those who contributed to and attended the conference. I must also acknowledge my colleagues from higher education Lesley Anderson, Hugh Busher, Len Cantor, Peter Earley, Viv Garrett, Agnes McMahon, Janet Ouston and Steve Rayner who worked with me on that part of the conference concerned with the conversations which constitute the heart of this book. I am also grateful to each of the educational leaders, Roy Blatchford, Keith Bovair, Mick Brown, Bernard Clarke, Ken Edwards, Mary Gray, Helen Hyde, Mary Marsh and Rosemary Whinn-Sladden for finding the time and patience in impossibly busy lives to speak to us and to check the texts which we sent to them.

Contributors

Lesley Anderson is Education Services Manager and Senior Lecturer at Oxford Brookes University. Before that Lesley worked as an education adviser, a researcher and development officer and a secondary school teacher. Having been co-opted on to the Council of BEMAS in 1992, she became Hon. Secretary in 1993 and was elected Vice-Chairman in 1994. She has been a key activist in the relaunch of the Society.

Roy Blatchford was headteacher of Bicester Community College between 1986 and 1996. He was previously a deputy head of two schools in inner London. On graduating, his first post was in publishing and he has maintained a strong interest in writing ever since. He is author of a number of books and articles. He worked with Peter Earley on the production of the Henley Distance Learning 'Management in Education' materials. He was a member of the SCAA working party in English. In 1996 he took up a post as UK Director of 'Reading is Fundamental'.

Keith Bovair is headteacher at Durants School, Enfield – a special school for pupils with moderate learning difficulties. This is his second headship. Before Durants, Keith was a lecturer in special education including curriculum theory and development and counselling in schools and is working on a book on the management of special education. He has wide experience of special education within the UK and the USA.

Mick Brown is Principal of South East Derbyshire College in Ilkeston. After school he worked for National Westminister Bank for four years before going to university to study Economics. He then trained as a teacher and decided to seek a post in further education. He has worked in a number of colleges becoming Head of Department and then, for three almost idyllic years, Vice-Principal before, in 1992, being appointed to his present position.

Hugh Busher is a Lecturer in Education, University of Sheffield. After teaching in comprehensive schools for many years, much of his work is now on policy making and management in education. His publications include studies of teachers' professional development, the management of evaluation and staff development, the process of change in schools. He is a member of the Research Committee of BEMAS and co-ordinator of the BERA task group on autonomous schools and colleges.

Len Cantor is Emeritus Professor of Education at the Department of Education, Loughborough University of Technology. He has written widely on education and is the author of standard books on further education in England and Wales, including *Further Education Today*, and on Comparative Education and Training.

Bernard Clarke has been Head of Peers School, Oxfordshire since January 1988. He was a bank clerk, lorry driver, social worker and a teacher in India and Bristol before moving to Burleigh Community College, as Vice-Principal. At Burleigh, he worked with two remarkable Principals, John Gregory and Keith Foreman. For him, leadership is about trying to practise what you preach. He is married to a health visitor. They have four children, all of whom have attended the schools at which he has worked.

Peter Earley is Principal Lecturer at Oxford Brookes University. He has also worked for the Management Development Centre at the London Institute of Education. Before that he was, for many years, a researcher at the NFER. He has researched and published widely and his writings include an influential examination of the first three years of headship. More recently, he has been involved in studies of the management of staff development, of the role of school governing bodies and of school management competences.

Kenneth Edwards has been Vice-Chancellor of the University of Leicester since 1987, having spent the previous 21 years at the University of Cambridge where he was Head of the Genetics Department and Chairman of the Council of the School of Biological Sciences, and then Secretary General of the Faculties (one of the three principal administrative offices). Currently, he Chairs the Advisory Committee of the Leicester Common Purposes Initiative. He has published widely in the field of genetics.

Viv Garrett is a Lecturer in Educational Management at Sheffield Hallam University. Viv was previously a teacher in comprehensive schools, most recently as a deputy headteacher. She joined the University in 1990 after plucking up courage to jump off the career ladder towards headship. She is an active member of BEMAS, serves as Secretary for the Yorkshire and Humberside Region and is Chair of the national Marketing Committee.

Mary Gray is the Headmistress of a large primary school located within a socially deprived area of Bristol. She has been in post since 1990 in what is her second headship. She was previously headteacher in a large primary school in a middle-class suburb of Essex; a school which she opened and built up over a period of ten years.

Helen Hyde was born and educated in South Africa. At university she studied Theology and Modern Languages and has sustained a lasting passion for both ever since. Helen and her husband came to the United Kingdom in 1970. She worked in two London comprehensive schools as a teacher, a head of department and then, for four years, as a Deputy Head before being appointed in 1987 to her present post as Head of Watford Girls Grammar School. In 1991 the school gained grant maintained status.

Mary Marsh became Head of Holland Park School, London in April 1996. She started her teaching career as a geography teacher at a Luton comprehensive school, and then became deputy head of St Christopher School in Letchworth. Before moving to Holland Park, she was Head of Queen's School, Bushey. Mary was a member of the IT advisory group of the Dearing curriculum review. She has an MBA from the London Business School and is a member of Demos, the independent think tank.

Agnes McMahon is a Senior Lecturer in the University of Bristol, School of Education. Her teaching, research and publications are in the field of educational management and policy and she is currently leading a Leverhulme-funded project about secondary teachers' perceptions of Continuing Professional Development.

Janet Ouston is Head of the Management Development Centre at the Institute of Education. She trained as a psychologist, and worked for many years as an educational researcher. Janet has worked in education management since 1980, and published *Women in Education Management* in 1993. More recently, with Brian Fidler and Peter Earley, she has been researching the impact of OFSTED on the management of schools and is editing a book on the early experience of OFSTED.

Steve Rayner is a Lecturer attached to the Assessment Research Unit in the School of Education, Birmingham University. Before that he was Head of Penwithen School. He has taught in mainstream and special schools, specializing in pupils experiencing emotional and behavioural difficulties. Steve has researched into the management of special education, the psychology of individual difference and teaching and learning styles. He is completing a book on teaching styles and learning enhancement.

Peter Ribbins is Professor of Education Management and Dean of Education at Birmingham University. He has worked in industry, secondary schools and an education office. Much of his research has focused on leadership. His books include *Improving Educational Leaders*, *Headship Matters* and *Radical Educational Policies and Conservative Secretaries of State*. He has edited *Pastoral Care in Education* and is editor of *Educational Management and Administration*.

Rosemary Whinn-Sladden is Headteacher of Parkside, a large primary school within Humberside. Now well into her second headship, at the time of the conversation, Rosemary was attempting to finish her masters' degree in educational management. She is a committee member for BEMAS Yorkshire and Humberside and a champion for improving the quality of teaching to give children a good chance at education.

List of abbreviations

BEMAS	British Educational Management and Administration Society
BERA	British Educational Research Association
CE	chief executive
CEO	Chief Education Officer
CFF	Central Formula Funding
DES	Department of Education and Science
DFE	Department for Education
EFL	English as a Foreign Language
ESL	English as a Second Language
FE	further education
FEFC	Further Education Funding Council
GCSE	General Certificate of Secondary Education
GM	Grant Maintained
GNVQs	General National Voluntary Qualifications
HMI	Her Majesty's Inspector
HoD	Head of Department
IIP	Investors in People
ILEA	Inner London Education Authority
INSET	in-service training
IT	information technology
IT	Intermediate Treatment
LEA	Local Education Authority
LFM	Local Fund Management
LMS	Locally Managed School
LP	leading professional
MBA	Master of Business Administration
MLD	Moderate Learning Difficulty
NACPE	National Association for Pastoral Care in Education
NAHT	National Association of Head Teachers
NFER	National Foundation for Educational Research
NUT	National Union of Teachers

OFSTED	Office for Standards in Education
PGCE	Post-Graduate Certificate in Education
PSE	Personal and Social Education
PTA	Parent–Teacher Association
PVC	Pro-Vice Chancellors
RE	Religious Education
SCAA	School Curriculum and Assessment Authority
SHA	Secondary Headteachers Association
SMT	Senior Management Team
TES	*Times Educational Supplement*
TTA	Teacher Training Agency

PART 1

Introduction

CHAPTER 1

Leaders and leadership in the school, college and university: a prelude

Peter Ribbins

Introduction

In September 1995, after a year of planning, the British Educational Management and Administration Society (BEMAS) held its Annual National Conference. This took place at Balliol College in Oxford and its theme was *Leaders and Leadership in Education*. The membership of the Society contains many who exercise significant leadership functions at all levels within our educational system. Even so it had been some years since the theme of headship or principalship had been thoroughly explored at a National Conference. For reasons which I will attempt to explain below it was felt that this was an appropriate time to revisit this important topic.

The conference used the usual tried and tested methods including a series of keynote lectures and over 40 papers from members. Some of these papers have already been published in *Educational Management and Administration* (e.g. Gronn, 1996) and others are awaiting publication within the journal and elsewhere. In addition, the programme contained a number of novel elements. The most important of these was an opportunity for conference members to read, in preparation for the conference, eight sets of individual and substantial conversations on leaders and leadership between the heads of a variety of different kinds of educational institutions and a researcher from higher education on leaders and leadership (BEMAS, 1995). In addition, and as part of the formal programme, they could attend sessions at which they could discuss three of these conversations with the leaders/researchers who were involved at the conference. Furthermore, those who came to Balliol College had a chance to examine with the eight BEMAS researchers aspects of the talk of the eight leaders. In what follows, I shall say something about two main issues: Why was this a good time to examine leaders and leadership in education? How was this organized before, during and after the conference?

Why is this a good time to examine leaders and leadership in education?

When the organizing committee from the West Midlands Association of BEMAS suggested the theme for this conference, it did so knowing, of course, that there is a huge mass of literature on leaders and leadership in education and a substantial corpus of writing on headteachers and headship, particularly in secondary schools. What, then, was the point of seeking to add to all this? We tackled this by asking ourselves questions about the current state of our knowledge such as: How helpful is it? How relevant is it? Why do we need more research? What forms might this research take?

How helpful is it?

Thomas Greenfield thought much of what is written in this area 'bland and boring' (Greenfield and Ribbins, 1993, p. 164). In a conversation which I once had with Christopher Hodgkinson, he described the extant literature on leadership as a 'swamp' which

> goes on and on and ranges from the sublime to the ridiculous with little in between. Taken as a whole it is a shambles, a mess full of philosophical confusion. If you could burn words at the stake in the same way the Nazis burnt books, the first word I would suggest is leadership. It is full of word magic of the worst kind. I was moved to write a book on leadership (Hodgkinson, 1982) to get this message across. (Ribbins, 1993a, p. 21)

This was not entirely the answer which I had expected from one of the most distinguished *and prolific* of all writers on leadership in recent times but it did make me wonder if I might not give a rather similar answer were I ever asked to comment on the extant literature on secondary, and to a lesser extent primary, headship. It would be more difficult to comment in this way upon what we know of the leaders of other kinds of educational institution since the literature on headship in special education, principalship in further education and vice-chancellorship in universities is much more limited.

How relevant is it?

As I have argued above, there is a substantial literature on heads and headship, especially in secondary education, in the UK and in many other countries as well. This takes the form of many surveys, autobiographies, autobiographical statements, biographies and case studies (Ribbins and Marland, 1994). Sadly, a good deal of this is now of rather doubtful relevance. Much of it draws upon studies conducted in the 1970s and earlier. And, as Reynolds and Parker note,

the complexity of the contemporary situation in which he or she is likely
to be, the overload of pressures – all these are likely to call for a style of
effective headteacher very different from the one-dimensional creatures
that stalk through the present day literature within school effectiveness.
(Reynolds and Parker, 1992, p. 178)

Much of what we 'know' of headship relates largely to a bygone age. If this is
less true of the leadership of other kinds of educational institution this is so essentially because we 'know' much less about this anyway.

Why do we need more of it?

To an extent I have already considered this question. For the record, a number of
reasons might be advanced. First, if we need to know about leadership in education and if there are some areas in which very little research has taken place, it
follows that we require more. Second, if in other areas much of what we know is
no longer relevant, it follows, once again, that we need more. But there are other
reasons why we need more research into this theme. Let me illustrate why I think
this is so by reference to what we know of contemporary secondary headship in
the UK. Let me preface these remarks by stressing that I do not claim that no high
quality research has taken place on this theme over the last decade. On the contrary, a good deal of illuminating work has been undertaken and much, although
by no means all of it, is publicly available. But beyond the claim that the quality
of headship is somehow related to the quality of teaching and the quality of teaching is somehow related to the quality of student learning, there is not much
consensus to be found. Even with regard to the relationships posited above there
is by no means universal agreement. Thus studies in Australia, the Netherlands,
the United States and the UK challenge one or more aspects of such claims. More
specifically, in studies which have taken place in the countries listed above and in
parts of Africa and South-East Asia the idea that headteachers, or principals as
they are more usually described, are significant educational leaders has been con-
tested (Harber, 1992). Let us consider the case of the UK.

A good deal of contemporary writing suggests that in attempting to cope with
the demands of the many innovations contingent on the unrelenting pace of recent
educational reform, many heads have tended to focus upon their 'administrative'
rather than their 'educational' functions. In 1988, Williams predicted

the daily life of English headteachers in the 1990s will be very different
from their predecessors a generation earlier. . . . Heads will become managers of an imposed curriculum rather than partners in curriculum
development . . . at the same time schools and their heads will be given
greater financial autonomy, and they will have to consider economic issues
such as the most effective and efficient ways to deliver a specific curriculum. Financial skills such as drawing up budgets, control of budget

management and management information systems will loom large in the day-to-day life of headteachers. (Williams, 1988, pp. ix, xi)

Many researchers believe that this prediction has come to pass. Evetts (1994), for example, in a study of 20 Midland heads, concludes that 'heads are no longer educational leaders'. In a report drawing on inspections of over 900 schools, Woodhead, Chief Inspector of Schools, is almost as blunt. He concludes 'Relatively few heads . . . spend sufficient time evaluating the quality of teaching and learning. Many should play a stronger part in curriculum development' (OFSTED, 1995, p. 6). It would have been possible to have quoted similar conclusions in further studies drawn from both the UK and in other parts of the world.

My studies of heads and headship within the UK, Malaysia, Australia, the Yemen and elsewhere have, on the whole, led me to a rather more positive view. In the UK, it is certainly possible to discover headteachers who have slipped into an essentially administrative interpretation of their role. They have done so with more or less reluctance. As one said, 'headship is not what it was. It is not just the ever increasing pace of change. Nor the fact that so many of these changes are so poorly thought through . . . I have found myself swamped with administrative and financial responsibilities' (Ribbins, 1993b, p. 24). But as Brian Sherratt, the head of the UK's largest school, has put it:

> If you see yourself essentially as an administrator you can hardly hope to be the leading professional as well [. . .] some heads are more comfortable simply retreating into their administrative duties as a defence from the hard intellectual and personal effort required to make sense of the curriculum. . . . This is not to say heads shouldn't be interested in administrative matters . . . it would be a very strange head who did not have an intense interest in budgetary matters. It is the budget which virtually drives everything. But you need to be clear as a head what your task is within it. Some heads seem to enjoy becoming a kind of financial clerk. It is hard to defend this. (Ribbins and Marland, 1994, p. 191)

But it seems to me that in the circumstances remarkably few have allowed this to happen. On the contrary, my experience as a researcher, teacher, consultant and husband suggests that the commitment which secondary and other heads, but especially those in secondary schools, bring to their work today is mind-boggling. As Bernard Clarke puts it, 'I talk to heads from other parts of the world, and they can't believe what is required of heads in this country. . . . The British system has a tradition of the head as both academic and pastoral leader and that makes it big. . . . If you lay the business manager aspect of the role, the marketer, and all the other things, it becomes a huge job.' An indication of the extent of the overload has been quantified by a survey conducted in 1994 by the Office of Manpower Economics for the School Teachers' Review Body. This found that 'the average for secondary heads was more than 60 (hours a week)' (Passmore, 1995). In the past, studies of this kind in other areas have been viewed with some scepticism since it is usually in the interest of those being surveyed to exaggerate. Astonishingly, in this case, the figures proposed may actually underestimate.

In *Headship Matters*, for example, we report several examples of much greater workload. Peter Downes, for example, confesses 'I probably work too hard, I probably work about 75–80 hours a week.' In the conversations reported in this book it is possible to find similar levels of commitment. Helen Hyde admits that she 'attends every single school function' and there are many of these. Happily, she 'likes working in the evenings' and, presumably, many weekends and some part of every 'holiday' too (Ribbins and Marland, 1994). And Roy Blatchford says he puts in up to 80 hours a week. He 'gets in at a quarter past seven (and is) there most evenings until 7.00 and many through until 9.30'. It is such dedication which may make it possible to take seriously the claim which such heads make that, despite the pressure, they still regard themselves primarily as educative leaders. Whether they should have to work so hard to make this possible is, of course, quite another matter. Indeed there is growing evidence that such workloads lead to stress, disillusionment, illness and the search for early retirement (Cooper and Kelly, 1993; Passmore, 1995; Day and Bakioglu, 1996).

Given such controversy, it is not surprising that, as Grace (1995) puts it in a powerful new book on *School Leadership*, there is a 'renaissance of interest and activity in the study of educational leadership' (p. 1). What has caused this? Grace believes 'the answers to this question are as complex and as contradictory as the phenomenon of leadership itself. The existence of crisis in many societies – legitimation crisis, moral crisis, economic crisis and social and political uncertainties – generate the conditions in which salvationist leadership is looked for' (p.1). In an important keynote paper at the BEMAS conference, which described and examined the various claims of 'transformational leadership', Peter Gronn (1996) looked sceptically at one of the most influential forms of salvationist leadership. Whilst I welcome this renaissance of interest, and the bracing scepticism of writers like Grace and Gronn, I believe that we do not just need more studies of, or new ideas about headship or principalship, but new ways of researching leaders and leadership in education.

What forms might this take?

In developing my thinking on this, I was struck by some of the points which John Rae made in his biography *Delusions of Grandeur: A Headmaster's Life, 1966–1986*. In this he set out to 'explore, through my own experience, the role of the English public school headmaster' (1993, p. 11). He claims that existing biographies and autobiographies 'do not tell you much about what it is really like to do the job' (p. 11). In his view 'fiction has been more successful in entering the headmaster's mind'. But even fictional portraits can be one-dimensional. For Rae:

> Auchincloss is the only author who understands how the master's personality influences the way he will play the role and how the demands of the role draw out particular aspects of his personality. . . . What makes the life

of a public school headmaster interesting is not just how he did the job but what the job did to him. (pp. 11, 12)

Such a view may have as much relevance to the study of heads – headmistresses as well as headmasters – working in state schools as it does to those in public schools. It may also be as pertinent to research into the role of educational leaders at other levels in secondary schools, in primary and special schools, and in colleges and in universities. In addition, what might be of equal interest in all such cases is the dialectic made up of the ways in which the personality of a headteacher or principal shapes how he or she interprets and plays the role and the ways in which headship shapes the personalities of those who hold it.

If we are to develop such an understanding of leadership in schools, colleges and universities we need more and new methods of research. As ever, it is easier to suggest the need for this than to propose what it might look like. In thinking of possible new approaches, I begin from the proposition that the world of the school, the college and the university, and of those who attempt to lead them is a complex one characterized by many realities. Given this, I see no escape from the need for an approach which makes the study of the individual and her or his subjective interpretation of reality one of the 'foundation blocks' of a satisfactory account of life within such institutions. Whilst this requires a broadly interpretivist view, I have come to believe that such an approach, on its own, provides, at best, only a partial explanation of patterns of leader/follower behaviour. As Seddon (1994) has pointed out 'it denies the possibility of causal explanations which do not rest on intentionality' (p. 47). Furthermore, it also tends to neglect power because, to the extent that it fails to distinguish between qualitatively different types, and socially arranged levels of context, interpretism lacks an adequate explanation of inter-contextual relations. If this is correct, then only an approach which has a concern for both agency and structure viewed within a context shaped by the interaction of macro (the societal level), meso (the institutional level) and micro (the individual level) relations is likely to enable the researcher to gain an insight into the life of educational leaders and their institutions which is more complex and may be closer to everyday reality than that which is possible using research methods based on alternative assumptions. In any case discussions such as this have been prominent in recent debates in social and organizational theory and have preoccupied such eminent scholars as Archer (1988) and Giddens (1979). As such, as Peter Gronn and I have argued, they will play an increasingly prominent role in the development of post-positivist approaches not only to the study of leadership but to our understanding of educational management more generally (Gronn and Ribbins, 1996).

In a series of papers I have tried to work out what all this entails for the study of management, organization and leadership in education (Ribbins and Sherratt, 1992; Ribbins, 1993a; Gronn and Ribbins, 1996; Ribbins, 1996). A key aspect has been the definition of a set of five main *propositions* which, taken together, offer a 'new' framework for the study of contemporary leadership in a period of radical educational reform. I put 'new' in inverted commas because I am aware that, taken separately, some of the propositions listed in the *prolegomenon* are not especially novel. But others may be rather more so, and so too, perhaps, is the set taken as a whole. Finally, I have described the set as a *prolegomenon* because it represents a relatively early attempt to produce a framework which may or may not, in due course, prove to be as coherent, logically ordered and comprehensive as I had hoped. However that may be, I suggest that what is needed is data on:

1   the educational reforms and proposals for education reform in their particular historical, social, economic, cultural and values framework;
2   the contemporary scope, dimensions and character of the reforms;
3   the interpretations of, and responses to, the reforms by key national and local stakeholders;
4   the interpretations of, and responses to, the reforms by the professional associations to which headteachers, principals, and vice-chancellors belong;
5   the interpretations of, and responses to, the reforms by headteachers, principals and vice-chancellors in specific schools, colleges and universities.

The first two propositions constitute macro-level, longitudinal and comparative relational contexts. The next three cover actors who are operating in a variety of interpretive contexts at macro (3), meso (4) and micro (5) levels. Much of the rest of my discussion will focus on the fifth of the propositions identified above and as such argues for meso- and micro-level ethnographies of educational leaders. Three elements of interpretive contexts at these levels are implicit in proposition (5): situated, individual portrayals; multi-actor perspectives; and an analysis of multi-actor perspectives in action. I will illustrate what this means for the case of secondary headship but would argue that it is, in principle, of equal relevance to the study of leadership in a wide variety of educational contexts and beyond.

A situated portrayal

Many accounts of headship are based upon surveys which typically claim to some extent to be more or less representative of the views of headteachers in general. From these surveys the researcher extracts composite glossed accounts of key issues which may represent more or less accurately the views of the sample as a whole or the ideas of a particular headteacher on one or more topics. In extreme cases, the data from such research seem to be simply *raided* to demonstrate the validity of a thesis to which the researcher was committed before undertaking the study. But even where the data are treated with respect, it is still hard to see how such an approach can possibly offer a rich and comprehensive understanding of the *perspectives* which heads bring to their work. For this to be possible the reader must be offered a much fuller access to their views across a representative range of *issues*.

   Such an approach would present the reader with a set of portraits of the perspectives of individual heads each reported in some depth. It can take a variety of forms. Mortimer and Mortimer (1991a, 1991b), for example, invited seven primary and nine secondary heads, to respond *in writing* to a set of issues specified by the researchers. These issues dealt with: 'the background of the headteacher and the school; the headteacher's personal philosophy of education; organization and management of the school; organization and management of learning; relation-ships; and personal reflections on headship' (1991a, p. viii). They accept that

> in a collection of such personal contributions, where heads and schools are identified by name, there is bound to be a certain amount of inhibition that affects what is written. On the whole, we think these heads have been remarkably frank but we are conscious, as were they, that the repercus-sions of too much openness can be severe. (1991a, p. ix)

In this aspect of my work on headship I have emphasized the need for greater spon-taneity and a more open and shared process of agenda negotiation than seems possible using the methods employed by the Mortimers. With this in mind, I have derived my accounts from *face to face* interviews. This was the approach used both in preparing for *Headship Matters* and in undertaking the interviews reported for this conference. Later I will describe in more detail how this was organized. Before this, I will say something about the other forms of conceptualization.

Multi-perspective

Traditional reports of headship *decontextualize* in the way which has been described above but also sometimes do so insofar as they do not attempt to locate what heads say within a context of the views of *significant others* (senior and other staff, pupils, parents and governors) within the *community of the school*. A contextualized perspec-tive would seek to give the reader some access to such information.

Multi-perspective in action

Relatively few extant studies explore what headteachers say (as described above) in the context of what they do. I have been aware for some time that to offer a con-textualized perspective of headship (or of any other role) in action the researcher must do at least five things. First, to collect relevant documentary evidence which touches upon the role of a specific head within a particular school. Second, to observe a head as he or she enacts his or her role in practice in relevant situations. Third, to discuss with the head what he or she is trying to do and why. Fourth, to set this account against the views of significant others. Finally, to compare and con-trast all the available evidence in the hope of producing the kind of enriched portrait of heads and of headship called for above. The following examples of such studies are further classified into three categories according to the extent to which the educational leader is their principal focus and his or her status in undertaking the research involved.

Category 1: The educational leader as incidental actor. Such studies do not focus on the perceptions and practices of the educational leader, rather he or she is regarded as one among a number of subjects for investigation (Ball, 1981; Burgess, 1983; Hargreaves, 1967; Lacey, 1970). At 'Rivendell' I was involved in research which in part attempted to examine the characteristics of three regimes of headship at the school in terms of the educational and managerial values and praxis of three successive heads, 'Mr Barber', 'Mrs Sewell' and 'Mr Lucas', claimed to espouse; how these claims were regarded by others within the school; and, to what extent and how each of these three very different headteachers sought to enact their vision and values in practice and with what effect (Best *et al*, 1983).

What made this a Category 1 Study was that in trying to describe these three regimes of headship we did not regard the views and actions of the three headteachers involved as any more central to our understanding of what was taking place than those of other staff. In this context, I would classify in this category many of the ethnographic based studies of schools published over the last 25 years which touch upon the role of the headteacher.

Category 2: Educational leaders in focus. Studies of this type are characterized by a focus on the perceptions and actions of the particular educational leader involved. Elizabeth Richardson's famous on-the-record study of Nailsea School and its headteacher may be an early example of this category (Richardson, 1973). But, perhaps the most interesting example of this category of study currently available is entitled *Looking into Primary Headship.* In this, Geoff Southworth (1995) reports on research in which he studied 'a headteacher by observing him at work inside the school. . . . I investigated the idea of producing a portrait of the subject and saw parallels with biography' (p. 1). Southworth set out to look *into* and not just *at* headship and in doing so sought to do more than just 'describe one head's work, but (to delve) into what this meant for the individual himself' (p. 2). The core of the book is a 'case study and my reflections on it. The subject of the case study is Ron Lacey, headteacher of Orchard Community Junior School' (p. 2). It deals with Lacey's background and context, what he did as a head, how he controlled what happened within the school, a portrait of his headship and with his response to the case study of himself. But Lacey is described as 'the informant' and Southworth emphasizes that 'Ron was the *native* I was studying and the research was aimed to elicit his vision of his world' (p. 38). Lacey is clearly the subject of the research and not a partner within it. As such, Southworth's description of his project as a 'biography' to describe his project is appropriate. It is such considerations which make it a Category 2 and not a Category 3 study of headship, albeit an unusually full, intense and interesting one.

Category 3: Educational leaders as co-researchers. Since 1989 I have been involved in a *third level* research project at Great Barr Grant Maintained Comprehensive School which, with 2400 pupils of between 11 and 18, is the largest school in the UK. At first, this study was informed by the ideas first developed at Rivendell and refined elsewhere. It was originally planned to focus upon an examination of the way in which a large urban comprehensive school was responding to the educational reform agenda initiated by the 1988 Education Act. As such it would have been best described as Category 1 research. But as the research progressed I became more and more interested in the role of the head as an interpreter and enactor of change. As a 'biography' of Brian Sherratt at Great Barr, during this phase, it took a form which was in many respects similar to Southworth's study of Ron Lacey at Orchard Community Junior School and could be classified as a Category 2 Study.

More recently still with Brian Sherratt's active involvement, I have been trying to develop a *novel* third level approach to the study of headship. In this the head is *both* the principal subject of the research *and* a full partner within it. Our research is *autobiographical,* insofar as it requires and enables the head, as *internal researcher,* to reflect systematically and critically upon his praxis during a period of intense reform. He has done this in various ways including 40 interviews and many other conversations with me over the last six years, the production of a *frank diary* of his everyday life as a head, and the collection of relevant documentation. The study is *biographical* insofar as I, as *external researcher,* have recorded over 200 interviews with significant others including teachers, other staff, pupils, parents and governors and have observed a wide variety of events related to the exercise of his leadership in practice. We began the demanding process of writing it up thereafter. In its present form, it has evolved into a Category 3 study of headship.

In terms of the contextual analysis discussed above, *Leaders and Leadership in the School, College and University* represents, to the best of our knowledge, the first Level 1 account of its kind which reports upon the views of a number of heads and principals currently working in a wide range of educational institutions. In the section which follows, the approach which was used to collect this unique series of *Situated Portrayals* is described.

Producing and analysing the nine interviews

Producing the interviews

The Committee charged with managing the Balliol Conference, wished to include something novel for members. This was one of the terms of reference which Hugh Busher and I, in accepting responsibility for organizing the programme, took very much to heart. A second term of reference was that the proceedings would be made publicly available in various ways. This has taken a variety of forms including the distribution to all conference members of a three-volume text running to several hundred pages which included many of the keynotes and members' papers and drafts of eight of the nine interviews reported in the chapters which follow. In addition, twelve papers which examined these interviews in various ways, and which were later to constitute an important source for the final three analytical chapters of this book, were made available at the conference. In planning these interviews and analytical chapters I had it in mind that it would be on this material that any subsequent book would be based. In what follows, I will describe what happened, beginning first with the interviews and then turning to the analytical chapters.

In the first part of this introductory chapter, I have described the theoretical ideas underpinning the production of the interviews reported later. They represent what I have described as a *situated perspective*. How have they been produced?

Initially, Hugh Busher and I identified possible researchers to set up the research, select the interviewees and produce the interviews. Those invited were all people who had been active participants in BEMAS events in the past. Only one of those I sounded out felt too busy to take part. There were to have been nine interviews and therefore nine researchers but for reasons which I will explain shortly, one was forced to drop out at a late stage. Initially, most of the research team met at the University of Birmingham to discuss how the project was to be organized. We decided that we would focus on educational leaders responsible for managing institutions rather than systems. In doing so, we felt it necessary to have representatives from all the main types of educational institutions including the heads of primary schools (two), secondary schools (four), a special school, a further education college and a university. In doing so we had some regard to what we knew of the membership of BEMAS as a whole. Each researcher was allocated a type of institution and invited to select the person they would wish to interview and to agree it with me. Some attempt was made to achieve as wide a variation as possible but we make no claim that the group as a whole is anything like a representative sample.

After an initial, usually telephone, conversation each *interviewee was sent a letter* which, after a preamble saying something about the conference, made the following points:

> You will be involved at a variety of levels as follows:
>
> 1   In an initial interview of 90+ minutes between ourselves. The main themes of our discussion are listed in the interview schedule included with this letter. This is intended as a framework to support our talk, not a straitjacket constraining it. I hope you will agree to me raising supplementary issues as appropriate. If there are issues of particular concern to you not identified in the schedule and which you feel we should discuss, please let me know before or when we meet.
>
> I will tape record our interview and get it transcribed. I will then undertake a preliminary edit to ensure that it reads as well as possible whilst remaining as faithful to what you have said and the way in which you have said it. I will then send you the edited transcript for your suggestions as to additions, revisions, excisions, etc. Since the interview will be on the record our objective will be for us to produce an agreed text with which we are both happy. In this sense we will both have a veto on what is included and what is excluded. You will also be able to withdraw from the whole venture at any time should you feel this to be necessary although should this become a possibility I should be grateful if you could let me know as early as possible in order that I can find someone else to work with. Once the set of interviews has been produced and agreed, we will be putting them together, with an introduction, and sending the set to conference members. We hope they will have been read before people come to Balliol.

2 In attending with me when I make my presentation as my contribution to the seminars on 'Contemporary Leadership in Schools and Colleges: Aspects of Praxis and Practice' planned for Friday 22nd September 1995.

3 In contributing either from the stage or the floor to the Plenary session planned for Friday 22nd September 1995.

4 In leading at least two presentations on the Saturday session entitled 'Case Studies of Leaders and Leadership in Schools and Colleges'. What we envisage here is that you would speak about your interview elaborating and explaining it in ways that you feel appropriate for about 20 minutes and then invite questions and other responses from those who choose to attend your sessions. I will be with you when you make these presentations.

5 During the conference a Conference Rapporteur will be talking to those involved in preparation for making a final presentation on the morning of Sunday 24th. He may wish to talk to you. Also all nine heads and principals and all nine BEMAS researchers with whom they have worked will need to meet with the Rapporteur at 1.45 on Saturday 23rd September to brief him.

6 Finally, we hope there will be a book from the conference. We are not, as yet, in a position to guarantee this. We will need your prior agreement that we can use your agreed interview to produce the text of such a book.

Whilst we hope you will find the whole experience a valuable and interesting one, we are aware of what an obligation all this will entail for you. Please let me know if all this is acceptable to you.

If you need any further points clarified I shall hope that we can achieve this when next we meet.

The *Interview Schedule* identified the following themes:

Interview Schedule

The terms 'headteacher', 'headship', 'school', etc. are used below. These should be amended to 'principal', 'vice-chancellor', 'college', 'university', 'principalship', etc. when appropriate.

1 How would you describe your own education and to what extent and in what ways has this experience influenced what you have tried to achieve as a teacher and headteacher?

2 How and why did you become a teacher and a headteacher?

3 How did you prepare yourself for becoming a headteacher?

4 How well prepared were you for your first headship?

5 What is your vision for your school and how do you go about trying to achieve it?

6 What are your key educational and managerial values? How successful are you in putting them into practice?

7 How do you manage people?

8 How do you manage resources?

9 What part do you play in enabling more effective teaching and learning?

10 How do you manage external relations?

11 Is it harder to be an effective headteacher than it used to be?

12 How do you manage others within the school to lead?

13 What sort of a leader are you?

14 Who manages you? To whom are you accountable?

15 Is there any part of your role you find especially difficult and/or do not like?

16 Do you still enjoy being a headteacher?

17 Is the term 'headteacher' still an accurate description for what you expect of yourself and others expect of you? Is it time we joined much of the rest of the world and called our school leaders 'principals'?

In our letter to interviewees we had stressed that they could withdraw at any time. We felt this to be right at the time and still do. In the event one did exercise this prerogative. This took place after the interview had taken place, been transcribed and received its first draft edit. By the time it was clear that this was going to happen, there was little time to replicate the process. The problem was compounded by the fact that the BEMAS researcher, who did identify a possible alternative interviewee, was committed to being out of the country for several weeks. As such it seemed very doubtful if it would be possible to undertake the required editorial process in the time available. This is why no college principal was included in the original text. Subsequently, it was possible to fill this gap and the interview between Len Cantor and Mick Brown, Principal of South East Derbyshire College, has been added. Hugh Busher, Viv Garrett and Janet Ouston have had access to this interview and have drawn upon it in producing the text of the final analytical chapters of this book.

A brief curriculum vitae for each of the nine institutional leaders and nine BEMAS researchers who were involved in producing the interviews and analytical chapters are included with the 'List of Contributors'. The partnerships are set out below:

Interview partnerships

Institutional leader	*Research partner*
Roy Blatchford	Peter Earley
Keith Bovair	Steve Rayner
Mick Brown	Len Cantor
Bernard Clarke	Lesley Anderson
Kenneth Edwards	Hugh Busher
Mary Gray	Agnes McMahon
Helen Hyde	Peter Ribbins
Mary Marsh	Janet Ouston
Rosemary Whinn-Sladden	Viv Garrett

Most of the conversations were conducted in late 1994 or early 1995 and the process of producing an agreed text took place in the weeks and months that followed. Len Cantor's discussion with Mick Brown was the exception to this rule since this was undertaken in early 1996. Once it became clear in early 1996 that a book was to be published, interviewers were asked if they wanted to make any further revisions or additions to the texts of the conversations presented at Balliol and to check whether those whom they had interviewed wished to do the same. As a result, some changes were subsequently made to some of the conversations which were originally published in the BEMAS Conference Proceedings. In my view, none of these changes has been substantial.

Analysing the interviews

In 1995, once the transcripts of the interviews were available we moved on to attempt some analysis of what had been said. In doing so we took note of the list of topics which had been identified in the original interview schedule and also drew upon a preliminary examination of the text of the eight conversations. From this twelve key themes were identified. Each of the eight BEMAS researchers then agreed to lead one or more of the seminars planned for the conference which were to be based upon a paper or papers analysing the set of interviews in terms of the themes as follows:

Themes and leaders of 1995 BEMAS Conference seminars

Seminar	Theme	Seminar leader
1	What influence did family, friends, early life, etc. have on their experience and views on education?	Janet Ouston
2	How do they describe their careers before becoming a head? Why and when did they decide to become a head?	Lesley Anderson
3	How did they go about this? How difficult was it to achieve? How do they regard the selection processes which they experienced? How well prepared were they for the first days, weeks, years of such leadership?	Peter Earley
4	What is their vision for their institution? How do they seek to share and develop this?	Steve Rayner
5	What part do they play in enabling more effective teaching and learning in their institutions? Are they satisfied with the contribution they make?	Hugh Busher
6	To whom are they accountable? Who manages them? How do they see the role of parents, governors, students, LEAs, DFE, etc? How do they manage external relations?	Viv Garrett

7	How do they remember their own education and what influence did this have on their views as educators/managers?	Janet Ouston
8	What influences have shaped their views as heads? What do they mean by effective leadership? Has this changed? If so, in what ways and why? Is it harder to be an effective leader than it used to be? If so, why?	Peter Earley
9	What are their key educational and managerial values? What sort of leader are they? How do they enable others to lead?	Agnes McMahon
10	How do they manage people and resources?	Hugh Busher
11	How do they cope with stress and when things go wrong? What aspect of their role do they most/least like? Where do they find support?	Viv Garrett
12	Are they necessary? Are they democratic?	Peter Ribbins

Subsequently, for purposes of this book, the minor themes have been consolidated into the three main topics discussed in the final chapters. In producing these Janet Ouston in 'Pathways to headship and principalship', Viv Garrett in 'Principals and headteachers as leading professionals' and Hugh Busher in 'Principals and headteachers as chief executives' have drawn upon the twelve papers identified above and all the nine interviews now available as well as an examination of some of the relevant literature. It could be argued that in analysing the interviews in this way we are engaged in just the kind of decontextualization I criticized earlier. I would say just two things in response. First, such an interpretation of what I have had to say would misunderstand my intentions. I have never wished to argue that an approach which does not seek to contextualize has no merit. On the contrary, some of the most illuminating writing in the field has taken this form. Second, and in any case, since readers have access to the whole of each of the nine interviews it is possible for them to locate any particular claim or interpretation in the context of the views of our interviewers as a whole.

A reprise

In this introduction I have tried to explain why we chose 'Leaders and leadership in the school, college and university' as the theme for the BEMAS Conference of 1995 and for this book. I have also sought to describe the approach we have taken and to locate this within a wider context. As such we have tried to produce a set of fairly detailed individual portraits of nine educational leaders drawn from across the educational system which says something about the kinds of people who become headteachers, principals and vice-chancellors. In doing so I have acknowledged our debt to the ideas of others who have written on the kinds of themes which are the principal subject of this book. John Rae, for example, pointed us to the need to look hard at what it is really like to do the job of educational leadership, and in doing so to examine not just how educational leaders do their job but also to consider what the job does to them. In justifying the need for studies of this kind, I would echo the Mortimers' claim that

> Although a great deal has been written about headship, there are few books that enable heads to speak for themselves. Yet over the last 25 years, in the course of our experience within the education service, we have been struck by the eloquence and, at times, passion, with which headteachers speak about their roles and responsibilities. (1991b, p. vii)

I believe that passion is the right word to use in this context. It is not a word which by any means all heads of schools, colleges and universities would use to describe their work and their attitudes to it. Some would share Ted Wragg's view that 'When teachers show interest in becoming a head, some kindly older hand usually takes them on one side and lets them talk until they get over it' (1995, p. 60). He claims

> demands on heads have escalated in the last few years. Many lament not being able to teach children as often as they used to, or having time to discuss with staff what is happening in the classroom. As business-type demands have grown, so time and energy available for other matters has eroded. (Wragg, 1995, p. 60)

This may be so, and certainly there are echoes of what he says in a number of studies which report the views of headteachers on headship (see Evetts, 1994; Hustler *et al*, 1995). But there are also many expressions to the contrary (Hustler et al, 1995; Mortimer and Mortimer, 1991a, 1991b; Ribbins, 1996) and it is this perspective which predominates among the nine educational leaders whose views are reported in this book. Certainly, a number of them confess to loving the job. Given our approach, the heads really should have the last word. Asked how she feels about headship, Helen Hyde says:

> I really love the job – I love coming to school – I love dealing with the personnel side – I like dealing with my staff – I like to feel I am helpful and I like to feel my school is achieving for the girls. I love the job – I really do.

Rosemary Whinn-Sladden is even more uninhibited:

> I like being in charge. I'm sure it is one of the seven deadly sins. . . . I love being the head. I absolutely love being the head. I love being able to do things and see something happen. I have always been a lousy indian and I have always known I was going to be a head. . . . I simply knew I was going to be a headteacher and I enjoy it.

References

Archer, M. (1988) *Culture and Agency: The Place of Culture in Social Theory*, Cambridge: Cambridge University Press.

Ball, S. (1981) *Beechside Comprehensive*, Cambridge: Cambridge University Press.

BEMAS (1995) *Leaders and Leadership in Schools and Colleges*, Proceedings of the National Conference of the British Educational Administration Society held at Balliol College Oxford in September 1995.

Best, R. *et al* (1983) *Education and Care*, London: Heinemann.

Burgess, R. (1983) *Experiencing Comprehensive Education: A Study of Bishop McGregor School*, London: Methuen.

Cooper, C. and Kelly, M. (1993) 'Occupational stress in headteachers' *British Journal of Educational Psychology*, 63.

Day, C. and Bakioglu, A. (1996) 'Development and disenchantment in the professional lives of headteachers' in Goodson, I. and Hargreaves, A. (eds) *Teachers Professional Lives*, London: Falmer.

Evetts, J. (1994) 'The new headteacher: the changing work culture of secondary school headship' *School Organization*, 14 (1).

Giddens, A. (1979) *Central Problems in Social Theory*, London: Macmillan.

Grace, G. (1995) *School Leadership: Beyond Educational Management*, London: Falmer.

Greenfield, T. and Ribbins, P. (1993) *Greenfield on Educational Administration: Towards a Humane Science*, London: Routledge.

Gronn, P. (1996) 'From transactions to transformations: a new world order in the study of leadership' *Educational Management and Administration*, 24 (1).

Gronn, P. and Ribbins, P. (1996) 'Leaders in context: post-positivist approaches to understanding educational leadership' *Educational Administration Quarterly*, 32 (3).

Harber, C. (1992) 'Effective and ineffective schools: an international perspective on the role of research' *Educational Management and Administration*, 20 (3).

Hargreaves, D. (1967) *Social Relations in a Secondary School*, London: Routledge.

Hodgkinson, C. (1982) *The Philosophy of Leadership*, Oxford: Blackwell.

Hustler, D., Brighouse, T. and Ruddock, J. (eds) (1995) *Heeding Heads: Secondary Heads and Educational Commentators in Dialogue*, London: David Fulton.

Lacey, D. (1970) *Hightown Grammar*, Manchester: Manchester University Press.

Mortimer, J. and Mortimer, P. (1991a) *The Secondary Head; Roles, Responsibilities and Reflections*, London: Paul Chapman.

Mortimer, J. and Mortimer, P. (1991b) *The Primary Head; Roles, Responsibilities and Reflections*, London: Paul Chapman.

OFSTED (1995) *The Annual Report of Her Majesty's Chief Inspector of Schools: Standards and Quality in Education*, London: HMSO.

Passmore, B. (1995) 'Heads call time on long hours' *TES*, 16 June.

Rae, J. (1993) *Delusions of Grandeur: A Headmaster's Life, 1966–1986*, London: HarperCollins.

Reynolds, D. and Parker, A. (1992) 'School effectiveness and school improvement in the 1990s' in Reynolds, D. and Cuttance, P. (eds) *School Effectiveness*, London: Cassell.

Ribbins, P. (1993a) 'Conversations with a *condottiere* of administrative value' *The Journal of Educational Administration and Foundations*, 8 (1).

Ribbins, P. (1993b) 'Telling tales of secondary heads: on educational reform and the National Curriculum' in Chitty, C. (ed.) *The National Curriculum: Is it Working?*, Harlow: Longman.

Ribbins, P. (1996) *Portraying leaders and leadership: new directions in the study of heads and headship*,

Paper delivered at the Fifth National Research Conference of BEMAS held at Robinson College, Cambridge, 25–27 March 1996.

Ribbins, P. and Marland, M. (1994) *Headship Matters: Conversations with Seven Secondary School Headteachers*, Harlow: Longman.

Ribbins, P. and Sherratt, B. (1992) 'Managing the school in the 1990s: a new view of headship' *Educational Management and Administration*, 20 (3).

Richardson, E. (1973) *The Teacher, the School and the Task of Management*, London: Heinemann.

Seddon, T. (1994) *Context and Beyond: Reframing the Theory and Practice of Education*, London: Falmer.

Southworth, G. (1995) *Looking into Primary Headship*, London: Falmer.

Williams, G. (1988) Foreword in Cooper, B. and Shute, W. (eds) *Training for School Management*, London: Bedford Way Paper 35.

Wragg, T. (1995) 'You don't have to be mad to try this. . .' *TES*, 20 October.

PART 2

Conversations

CHAPTER 2

Mary Gray

In conversation with Agnes McMahon

AM: *How do you remember your own education, and to what extent has that experience influenced you in what you want to achieve as a teacher and a headteacher?*

MG: I don't particularly remember being happy at primary school.

AM: *Were you educated in Manchester?*

MG: Yes, then we moved to Oxford and I had two years before secondary education there. Then I went to Notre Dame High School which was a convent-run school in Oxford and I thoroughly enjoyed it. Looking back now I suppose it was quite archaic in its set-up in that it was an all-girls school. It was so gentle, so caring. It did help me to develop within myself a feeling of caring towards other people because of the attitude of the nuns. The Notre Dame nuns at that stage were not a particularly austere order, they were really quite avant garde, and they themselves appeared to be very happy, very loving towards all their pupils, and celebrated their pupils' successes. I have no bad memories of it at all.

AM: *Where did you go to college?*

MG: I went to college in London. (*What was that like?*) It was enjoyable. I can't say I was a dedicated academic at that time.

AM: *Did you start out training for teaching straight away?*

MG: Yes. From the beginning, if I'm honest, I was recognized as a student with great potential in terms of teaching skills, so that was quite successful.

AM: *And you enjoyed teaching practice?*

MG: Yes. It's so long ago I can't think. No one's asked me these questions for years.

AM: *From what you've said already, perhaps the attitude of the nuns at the high school is something that has carried through to your practice as a teacher and as a head. Do you think there are other things you'd like to add?*

MG: I'm trying to recall back. I always felt I wanted to teach. It's very difficult, with hindsight, because it's such a long way back. Was that because at that particular period in time one of the careers that was regarded as the right career was teaching? I really don't know. I can honestly say I've never felt a desperate need for another career. There are times when I would have loved to have had the extra time to develop my own artistic ability but that's the price I've had to pay in order to carry on with this career.

AM: *When did you become a teacher? Did you start teaching straight from college?*

MG: Yes.

AM: *And was that in London?*

MG: No. My first school was in Oxford. It was in the era of 'small is beautiful' in terms of education, it was all hessian and dried flowers – a gorgeous period, and Oxfordshire itself had a forceful impression on me, but I didn't stay long in fact because Lyn and I had met in London and we got married so that's when I started teaching in London. So I moved from the beautiful village of Woodstock and then taught in London, just behind Oxford Street.

AM: *Did you have a career break when you had the boys?*

MG: No. We broke new ground there actually. I didn't have the feeling that I was the kind of person who wanted to stay at home at that stage. Perhaps because we had the children so young, I wasn't ready to stop teaching and I didn't really fancy the ironing and the washing and everything else that went with it. So we had a marvellous compromise. We had a nanny whom the boys called Auntie Sheila and we had her for 12–13 years. She started off with us and we just kept her and she's just 'Auntie' to the boys.

AM: *Are you still in contact with her?*

MG: Yes. She used to come before I left for school and stay until I got back. I think that's why it worked so well, but in those days it was quite a hard thing to do as you had to be back to school within six weeks of the birth. Although looking back now, I suppose I must have been quite certain that I wanted to carry on teaching, because once all the friends I was at college with got married and got pregnant they automatically gave up their careers. And I think perhaps people at the time thought that my husband and I were quite unpaternal and unmaternal.

AM: *Were you in London at this time?*

MG: No. From London we moved up to the north-east.

AM: *Can you sketch out the different stages in your career; when you got your responsibility posts and when you got your deputy headships?*

MG: One thing relating to the children I suppose was that I didn't want to take on extra responsibility too soon. So I taught in Oxford and in London, then when we moved to the north-east I did supply for the first term while we got a house sorted out, then after that I was promoted to a Scale 1 post. And then we were on the move again because my husband got promotion and we moved to Richmond, North Yorkshire, so again I had to start again, and build up my scale posts. Then whilst still in Richmond I got my first deputy headship of a large school in Darlington. Then from there we moved back south to Essex.

AM: *Was it a bigger school?*

MG: No, about the same size. Group 7 – about 650 children. And stayed there for about three years and then I got my first headship.

AM: *And you were there for about ten years?*

MG: Yes. When I was in Richmond I was one of those lucky people who had a year off and went to Durham University. That was in the days when every teacher was going to be released for a year for professional development – that policy was soon abandoned.

AM: *What did you do there?*

MG: I did the Advanced Diploma in Primary Education.

AM: *Was that good experience?*

MG: Yes, in terms of theory and philosophy. In terms of practical understanding with the people who you are working with, no. But as an experience in itself, very positive, very good. We were also used as consultants to other schools who needed help in developing some aspects of their work. That was very useful, because you could look at another establishment to which you were not attached; they indicated what they needed and you tried to plan for them how that could be achieved and work with them.

AM: *How did you prepare yourself for becoming a head? Did you decide when you moved from Richmond to Essex that you could go for headships but you wouldn't because of the children?* (Yes). *But had you decided at that stage that you would like a headship?*

MG: I decided that the second deputy headship was only a very temporary move. It was different in that it was an all-junior school which was something I hadn't actually experienced. That was interesting because it made me decide that I didn't want to be head of a junior school.

AM: *Did you prepare yourself for headship in a conscious way do you think?*

MG: That's very difficult. I suppose there have been so many people in my life who have been involved in education, and I've been used in so many ways by other people that really this helped me develop skills for headship. I suppose I've been asked to run so many courses or to be the practitioner coming in and talking that this helped me in many ways decide both that I did want a headship and the direction I wanted that headship to go once I got one. I don't want to sound arrogant, but having worked for a variety of heads, I think I was astute enough and interested enough to see how other people worked and identify what approaches appeared to be successful and unsuccessful. I felt that with that experience I could succeed. It sounds like boasting but it isn't.

AM: *Not at all, I suppose you've got to feel confident that you can do the job? I was thinking in relation to the HEADLAMP initiative, do new headteachers begin the job thinking I've got loads and loads to learn before I'm going to be able to handle this? Maybe they recognize there are things to learn here, but presumably you've got to feel a reasonable degree of confidence before you put yourself forward?*

MG: Well otherwise you'd be a disaster within the first term, you wouldn't be able to create the right atmosphere and set the right direction for the school. The expectations of the staff will be such that they'll expect you to come in able to cope. They're not going to look very kindly at somebody who's appointed to be a head but has a series of disasters. I also think looking back that, at the time I was involved in deputy headships and headships, there was still an old philosophy working in education that to be a good head and a good deputy all you had to be was an excellent teacher. It was almost a reward for past good teaching service. And I think many of the heads who have subsequently had problems are those who obviously were very gifted teachers, but who within their careers hadn't developed the management side of the role. Some of them were ostriches who just put their heads in the sand and hoped it would go away or somebody else would take on the responsibility. It's now changed even further so that the role of headship that I'm involved in now is entirely different from when I started 14 years ago. Basically I'm a managing director now. I am the curriculum leader, but I'm the curriculum leader who identifies and delegates and that is only one part of the strands of my role as a head.

AM: *In retrospect how well prepared do you think you were for your first headship?*

MG: Very, because I had been deputy of two extremely large establishments, both with heads who were in their final years of headship, where I had a non-teaching role. This was unusual in those days, so I had the opportunity of being selective in developing the skills needed for headship. I could undertake a specific responsibility, fulfil that, then another responsibility and fulfil that.

AM: *I know you opened up a new school. Did you phase in the entry, did you start with 5 year olds and then move up, or did you have a full age range from the beginning?*

MG: Full age range.

AM: *You were in a position to appoint all the staff?*

MG: I was in a position to appoint all the staff, and I was also in the position of working quite closely with the architect.

AM: *It must have been quite an exciting project?*

MG: Yes, it was brilliant.

AM: *Did you have a lead-in period?*

MG: No, I had to carry on with the deputy headship role until the end of the summer and then open the new school in September, so I was actually doing two jobs in the summer.

AM: *What kind of leader do you see yourself as?*

MG: I'd say benevolent and assertive. I suppose I've always got the overall vision of what a school should be in terms of the opportunities, such as offering the children more care. The sort of ethos that leadership fosters, and also the values you have as a person, inevitably impact on the establishment. That's the assertive side. The benevolent bit, is that I enjoy seeing people blossom. I see my role as a facilitator who gives opportunities both to staff and the children. The children to benefit in terms of their growth, the staff in terms of their career. And one of my hidden attributes is that I'm quite perceptive, so when you talk about benevolence, I'm perceptive to other people's needs, and at times put other people's needs before my own.

AM: *Presumably there is a potential tension there between, for example, supporting a member of staff who is going through a period of stress – bereavement or divorce or something like that – supporting them through that, but if there's somebody who's a nice, caring person but not doing the job very well, how long can you be supportive and caring before you say something to them?*

MG: That's when I think I'm quite Machiavellian, I would start working on them straight away, if I felt they were a very caring person but that the quality of education that was being offered to the children was not of a standard that I found acceptable, I would find various ways of taking action because usually if people are not performing well, they're not aware of it, or if they are aware of it they try to shut it away because they don't know what to do, so therefore I would work with those people. There is a limit in how far you can take them, but you can take them from being a poor operator to an acceptable operator. It would be naïve of me to think I could take them any further than becoming competent.

AM: *Do you think it's harder now to be an effective school leader than it used to be, and if so why?*

MG: I think it is harder now because the expectation is greater, because the role has changed into all these diverse parts that you have to be involved in. There's the finance; management of staff; demands of government. There's all these extra roles that make the role far more difficult now than it used to be.

AM: *Do you think you have to work harder now?*

MG: Yes. I wouldn't actually tolerate this headship now with children at home. I couldn't. (*Whereas you did in Essex?*) Yes. I know the boys were teenagers then, but I could cope then. But looking back, it could be because I was in a very middle-class school, without the behavioural problems. We had no building problems. I didn't have to attend a child abuse case in all the time I was there, there wasn't the involvement with social services, I didn't worry about whether the school would be vandalized or broken into at night. In the ten years I was there we had one pane of glass accidentally broken by a child. So it's difficult for me to say. Although, when I did supply work in the north-east, I taught in the middle of Middlesbrough which was a terribly deprived area at the time. The children were coming to school wearing ladies' shoes with the heels cut off for the boys, it was real poverty, and we're talking about the 1960s, but it was real poverty, and yet those children did not exhibit the behavioural problems that we are dealing with today. And yet that poverty in many respects was worse than any poverty we have here. So one of the things I am beginning to feel is that society itself is making education more difficult.

AM: *Certainly things like drug abuse are more widespread than 20 years ago?*

MG: It used to be unheard of in primary schools. One of the social themes you could identify here, although it's in a deprived area, is the number of children who have a television in their bedroom, and their way of life is watching unsupervised television in their bedroom. There's no one to share their fears and anxieties when they're watching these programmes late at night. And this does affect children. They are seeing things they ought not to be seeing. That's why children were more innocent in those days. There are all sorts of other pressures. And I think you'll find talking to other heads that the message concerning education in the press and from the government is so negative that parents are no longer in awe of schools and education. I'm not saying being in awe is a good thing, but what we're getting now is a backlash, in which parents in many areas feel they have rights which don't take the school and its community into consideration.

AM: *Could you give me an example?*

MG: As a recent executive member of the NAHT, heads would ring me up and report accusations that have been made about teachers or things that have happened in school. Parents now seem to have an attitude that their child is always right, they're never in the wrong, therefore it's always the school that's in the wrong, and I think a lot of this has come from the message the government has launched. Heads and teachers are experiencing accusations by pupils against staff. Even in primary schools, children will say 'You can't touch me, I'll have the police on you.' I might just be somebody going to pick a child up off the floor. Now I don't ever remember this 20 years ago, and this is becoming quite a major problem. And they're going to have to make some amendment to it. (*What's this, the Children Act?*) Yes. For instance, if a child makes an accusation against any member of staff of a sexual nature, then automatically that member of staff has to be suspended from school, and it can take up to a year for that case to be dealt with. There have been cases recently where they have been cleared, but this doesn't mean anything, because they can no longer remain at that school, their careers have been tarnished, so there's always this feeling of apprehension now about how you deal with children. I still, if a child is distressed, put my arm around that child to comfort it, and the minute I can't do that as a person, then I will give up this headship. I shouldn't do it I suppose, but if I see a child in distress, a 5 or 6 year old . . . now these are the extra pressures that are put on people. I tell members of staff now never be in the room alone with certain children. These are all the extra pressures that make you work harder, because you're having to look at strategies, make sure your policies and procedures are in order and that at no minute during the day can you lapse.

AM: *What's your vision for the school, and how have you tried to achieve this?*

MG: Creating the best working atmosphere I can for the children and offering them values where they will appreciate other people, recognize the contributions they can make both within the school and hopefully as they get older, within the community.

AM: *How do you try to do that?*

MG: I suppose first of all by example, but at the very bottom is to treat the children with respect to start with, and from that I have encouraged both teaching and non-teaching staff to react in the same way. There's so many different aspects, like fairness for instance, and I suppose you have to put into place values, and once you've got your values in place where everybody is equally important within the establishment and treated fairly, you then look at how you can develop within the school other attributes. One of the ways we have succeeded in this school is valuing children's work and the display and the feel of the place. We try to make it a welcoming place. Why are we making it welcoming? Because we want parents to come and enjoy being in the school. We want children in the school to feel good about it, safe and secure, so they have the opportunity to develop their qualities, and then in an informal way you start putting procedures and strategies into place. There are so many aspects to it, I could go on for hours. It's how you work with your management team and how you work with your staff and other people to develop the ethos of the school.

AM: *That's the next question really. How do you manage people?*

MG: Talking about shared values sounds quite glib, but if you come into a school as a head, those are the things you have to establish. On a simple thing to start with and then develop further as you become a more collegiate staff. You don't start off being collegiate. When I first started here they weren't used to staff meetings, so the idea of anyone making a contribution was not the norm. I had to put strategies into place and I suppose that's why I said I can be quite Machiavellian, because I would deliberately, in the nicest sort of way, ask somebody for their comments by referring back to something that they were doing in their classroom. I would say you were doing this, would you like to share your ideas with us? It is manipulative perhaps. But once they have gained that confidence then they become committed, and they want to contribute. But you have to set up the strategy in the first place, so that people feel valued, feel they are listened to and that their contribution is as important as the head's.

AM: *Where did you start from with your values? If you say to a group of teachers I would like all the children to be treated equally, then most teachers would agree with you, but in fact in their practice or in the way the school is organized there may be things that deny that aspiration.*

MG: Occasionally maybe I'll notice that a member of staff is making too many comments about one particular child, and his or her lack of success. Obviously then, at some stage or other, I will intervene. Depending on the circumstances you can intervene in a careful way that makes them think perhaps they have gone overboard a bit too much. But every situation is different, which is why I say you have to be perceptive, you have to choose the moment and it's got to be a time when you don't belittle them in front of other people in the process. Maybe at the end of the day they will think just a little differently about the way they are treating that child. For example, if they are always complaining about a child, I'll say well, why is that child acting like that? What are the problems she is experiencing to make her behave in such a way? I think with 99.9 per cent of the children we are dealing with, if we look at them sympathetically and try to find out what the problem is, we can help them.

AM: *So you don't feel you've had major problems with particular staff? I don't want you to be specific about a clash of values, where people have rejected your values.*

MG: Some people I have had to work harder with. For example, one of the teachers didn't value art, she was very much the academic, intensive with words and writing, but in terms of children being creative, she was creative with music but couldn't be with art, and I think that's because she had a particular blockage about art herself. Over a period of time working with her, any time that she put up a particular artistic work I would make a point of praising it in front of the children, in front of her and eventually she changed completely. One of the things she said when she went for her deputy headship was how much her views in that period of two years had changed in terms of valuing children's work and putting it up on display, and that took me two years to work through with her. You find it's not so much clashes with heads, because staff don't operate that way; but at times if one teacher feels aggrieved he or she will get other staff alongside them in a supportive role. I've always found that I'll wait and see how things develop and then decide how I'm going to intervene.

For example, on one occasion a teacher had a particular view on some issue and she was trying behind the scenes to build up people's support of her. After a period of time I spoke to her directly and said that, although I appreciated what she was saying, I had to consider the benefit to the school as a whole and I appreciated her feelings but on this occasion I had to make a decision that everyone would benefit from, not just her. So I would do that in a quiet sort of way with the person involved, but I would also then explain the decisions to the staff as a whole. I suppose my way of dealing with any conflict problems would be to deal directly with the member of staff, but also explain to all staff what has happened and why it was happening, because in a way that stops misguided support.

AM: *How do you manage resources?*

MG: It depends where you are within your current establishment as to how you're going to spend them. In terms of management of money I've always believed in telling people and sharing with them budget implications, so they understand there are certain parts of budgeting and resourcing that I have no control over. Again, it's the collegiate approach. You can't change the cost of the staff unless someone leaves or someone's made redundant. I can't make many changes in terms of running costs. I'll ask everyone to help with saving the heating and electricity but it doesn't have much effect. The remaining resources which I feel we will be able to redirect into areas we've identified, we would manage as a whole staff. I would say to people, this is how much we've got left, this is the funding we had in these particular areas last year, what are the priorities for this year which we have identified in our school development plan, how are we going to share them? One aspect of resource management that I find doesn't work is when they are organized on the basis of each individual member of staff being given an allowance of money, that to me is the most ineffective way. (*Have you tried that yourself?*) I've been in establishments where that was the practice, as it was when I came here.

AM: *So you give the money to curriculum leaders?*

MG: Curriculum co-ordinators, yes. But curriculum co-ordinators have to consult with staff as to what staff needs are in that particular curriculum area. I think that works successfully. Whereas previously staff argued that the infants have got this amount, so the juniors must have this amount, we now look at the school as a whole and ask which is the priority area; or is there a class which is short of specific items, especially in a growing school? And the staff now are less selfish. I've managed to get cupboards emptied to become part of central resources and that helped tremendously to start with. And we've now got this resource room here and the spin-off from that has been super, not only do we have the resource room here but often in conversations I hear people say 'Have you seen this' or 'Would you like to use this', or if somebody comes across a useful piece of resource they will reproduce it for somebody else so you're losing that selfishness which I think is quite prevalent in a lot of schools.

AM: *What about basic classroom resources like pencils and paper; how are they distributed?*

MG: They're ordered for the school as a whole. Everybody states their requirements for the year, and then they're given to those classes for the year. But things like the art equipment that we order will go into the art stock cupboard and people will help themselves when they need it. The exercise books and the sorts of pencils that teachers want which are specific to your needs within that classroom, come out as a global amount. We do very carefully identify our priorities in terms of extra expenditure.

AM: *Presumably there's a baseline that's fairly constant from year to year, number of books, etc?*

MG: Yes, but we've spent quite a lot of money on history, so in fact our history resources are such that this year people have said that, in comparison to other areas, don't let's spend money there, let's put it into other areas where the need is greater.

AM: *What part do you play in enabling more effective teaching and learning?*

MG: When I first came here there was a lack of procedures, strategies, accountability, I had to put into place policies and procedures so that staff knew what was expected of them. We've arrived at a situation where I've now developed a culture where staff with curriculum responsibilities are beginning to feel more confident and take on the responsibility for their curriculum areas and work with other staff in ensuring the policies and schemes of work that should be being worked are in place. At the same time I'm now introducing a system where I go into each class each week and concentrate on that specific class. I see the children's work, I see every child in the class at work at a specific task, whatever the teacher's chosen and at the same time I'm using that non-threatening opportunity to go round talking to children, looking back on work seeing how they have progressed and so on. Instinctively I pick up how that class is operating, the sort of levels of concentration within the class, even where the teacher is talking about the children; the use of helpers; the displays on the walls, and then I give feedback to that member of staff at lunchtimes, I do it on a Monday, so I spend part of Monday lunchtime giving them feedback. I haven't got to the stage yet which I had in my other school where I do a written feedback.

AM: *So, it's one class a week you're going to do over the term?*

MG: Yes.

AM: *Do the teachers find that comfortable?*

MG: They were very worried to begin with, because it was a school that had a culture of closed doors, now the doors are open. I'm getting positive feed-back from it now.

AM: *How long have you been doing it?*

MG: It must be a year now. I'm starting my third round of visits this term. I was surprised at the fear of formal observation because I would wander round the school and go into classes on an ad hoc basis.

AM: *And this is quite independent of any observation that's done as part of appraisal?*

MG: Yes. Absolutely. It's completely independent. And the spin-off that has been very appreciated by the teachers is that the children love it, and now they're used to me coming in and they've started to look back on their work so that when I do come in they will say 'I have improved' – so it's a lovely spin-off. I'm toying with the idea that from next September I may have more of a formal feedback, something for them to keep, which I had previously always done in my other headship. But again, it's being per-ceptive enough to know what's right, what can provide a structure to build on, rather than have negative vibes about the process.

AM: *Do you look at people's schemes of work?*

MG: Yes. We have detailed teacher planning and recording books – in those there's the whole termly planning, the weekly planning and then the assess-ment as well. (*Assessment of what they've done?*) Yes, there's all sorts of things in there. The staff hand it in either Monday or Tuesday, I read it and pass it back. That gives you a better indication of all the different things that they actually respond to. The reading records, the school topic calendar which is a two-year topic plan for the whole school. The termly topic plans, which are individual to the class teacher, curriculum planning, English for the disciplines for English, Maths and Science, they are in great detail. That's the National Curriculum. I find that I work on a framework, then offer it to staff for suggestion, improvement and changes. I find that because of the pressures we're working under, if I waited for working parties to work together to produce it in the first place before going to staff, the time delay would be too great. But I'm hoping that perhaps next year other people are going to come forward more, which was my original concept. They are now coming forward with new ideas, but in a way I'm always pushing, all the time. I found that our records before this weren't sufficiently rigorous. Now I can see straight away where there is a gap or a problem, and I made a joke about that in yesterday's staff meeting when we were discussing it, saying how much clearer it is now to identify.

I hope they are finding the same thing, areas which they are perhaps not covering in as much depth as they should. All the areas that require weekly planning and curriculum co-ordinators' action are now identified in the new sheet in which they state what they have been doing in terms of their job. New National Curriculum annotation sheets have come from staff in terms of the SATs developing, the easiest way of recording the levels that children are working at in an assessment, if one class seems to have a specific special needs problem more than another and so on. These black books are this year's invention and I feel they are a great improvement on what we previously had, but previously there was nothing, so we're moving forward the whole time. Teachers didn't record in any formal way when I first came. I'm positive that the quality and the variety of the material being offered to the children is greater. But it needs a formal structure for this to happen.

AM: *So really that depends on them filling out the forms but are you able to monitor and assess fairly quickly?*

MG: Over a period of time you become thoroughly practised in noticing things. And to be fair I would say that staff operate on different levels. I've had a chat with one member of staff and said 'Look you're not being specific enough. You're giving a sort of contents page, but if an outsider read it they would not have an understanding of the level at which you are asking the children to operate.' Now I would pick up on those points and I can say in the nicest sort of way that I would expect to see an improvement the next week.

AM: *People would expect feedback, do you ever write comments or say anything to them?*

MG: I found in the red book I wrote more comments than I do in this particular format. But for instance, if they're doing class assembly or something like that I would give positive reinforcement and say how good it was. If it's something of a sensitive nature where I would want more detail filling in on the book I'm not sure I would want that permanently on record at this moment.

AM: *Can I ask how you manage external relations?*

MG: My philosophy is that any contact with external agencies ought to be of a positive nature. The school is part of the greater community and therefore I want support but also I would expect the school to give something back. Really the schools should be saying to the LEAs this is what the schools need. On the other side of the coin there are certain aspects of personnel and law and things of that nature where the LEA ought to be guiding the schools. We try to involve the press as much as possible in the nicest way possible. For these particular children it's always good to be seen in the press. We've only had one case where we were involved with the press because a parent made a complaint but the complaint wasn't upheld. The press are very keen on anything like that but you just have to handle things as sensitively as you can. The greater community, well we welcome people into the school.

We have a policy, again it's values isn't it, that if people help us we always make sure that we thank those people.

For example, we were planting trees last week. The mums did an incredible job with the extra ones that were left over on the following day. They came in and dug all day, they were absolutely brilliant, so we bought them a little plant each. They cost about £2 each to give to all those mums, but those mums were so appreciative of them. They must have been digging for six hours non-stop. (*So they dug all the holes for the trees did they?*) The children planted the rest the day before but we had mums helping then, some students came as well. We had Avon Wildlife Trust help us. It's a feeling that everyone is trying to make their environment better, and anybody who's willing to help is welcome. Another example: at my other school, you wouldn't allow a pushchair in the building, under Health and Safety Regulations, pushchairs just had to stay outside, but here I've given up completely because I've realized that if the pushchair doesn't come in, mum doesn't come in, so Health and Safety have gone by the board. In the mornings it's a matter of who gets in first, the mums or the children, but if the school appeared too threatening we would never have those mums coming in, and we desperately need them to come in and feel supportive of the school and not fearful of it, because some people have had a bad experience of school themselves.

AM: *Who manages you and to whom are you accountable?*

MG: I'm accountable to the governing body, I'm accountable to the staff and to the children in a way and the parents, and the LEA, but the LEA has less power now and formal accountability is to the governors, but I don't feel that, I feel there are other aspects of accountability.

AM: *How do you enable others within the school to lead?*

MG: I found that one of the most difficult tasks when I first became a head, was delegating responsibility, and then perhaps finding that the way they were delivering was not quite the way I would have delivered. I found that hard to come to terms with. I think I've learnt through practice to compromise on that, to try and ensure that enough discussion takes place before things are delegated whether to the Senior Management Team or to the staff as a whole, depending on what the outcome is, so that the person who's doing it feels sufficiently secure in producing the best they can. I think I'm also quite clever in that if somebody hasn't yet learnt the skills of presentation, say in a written form, it may look scruffy and poorly presented. Before it goes to the office we'll talk it through, I give them some suggestions, e.g. how we can format it, so that when they present it to staff nobody's aware of my influence or help, so that the member of staff who presents the document gets all the praise and the appreciation.

AM: *Do you check up on people informally?*

MG: I think we've gone beyond that stage. I think we work so much as a team that if anyone's experiencing difficulty they will actually come and ask for help. And also we have the strategy of setting date-lines. I try to make sure that if I've got a date-line, I keep to it, so I set the example that if we have deadlines we do actually fulfil them. This comes from thinking in terms of structures, for instance the termly planner has got everything indicated on there to be worked at. If we have to make changes then we discuss it as a whole group, so that things are not allowed to drift too much.

AM: *If I was working on a new English course which I was going to present to the staff, say at an INSET day in the summer, would we set a date when I would discuss my first draft with you?*

MG: Yes, and it would perhaps be brought back to the SMT on a specific date. For instance on Thursday of this week departmental meetings are planned for next term. We've now got into a situation where departmental meetings are minuted and dates set and those minutes are put up for all the staff to see. It's having strategies in place. Everybody knows now the next staff meetings that are taking place. We've got Jane next week, who's introducing history resources, then Simon is leading a science meeting which will be looking at attainment target 1, so it's all set out. It's a big enough school definitely to warrant it. Everybody for instance has the agenda for the staff meeting in advance. It takes stress off staff but it also keeps us on target. For instance, yesterday, I mentioned to all staff that it would be beneficial to be looking at their SDP targets that they established last September, which will be reviewed early next term, so I have already pre-warned them, despite the fact that the review date is not until May or June.

AM: *Is there any part of your work that you find particularly difficult or you don't like?*

MG: I suppose certain parts of the role where you have to make decisions that disappoint people, for example interviews, letting candidates know they haven't been successful. You try to be official about it, but because you care about people I find it's difficult when I have to reject somebody.

When I see some of the parents and the way especially the girls have been dressed up to look like young ladies to attract the males, things like this upset me. What does upset me, and it is upset rather than difficult, is case conferences and child abuse and it's all those extra emotional things that I have no control over. I can't stop them happening. All I can do is perhaps help the situation in the care that we show for the children at school.

AM: *What aspects of your work do you most enjoy?*

MG: I think seeing the children, parents, governors and the staff feeling a sense of achievement themselves, feeling that they have moved forward and applied in what they're doing, but also they haven't got complacent in thinking they have achieved everything. In a way I do drive that, this has been a great success, so where do we go next, there's always that question to ask. OK, we've achieved this, what's the next step?

AM: *You must have tons of energy, do you find it very tiring?*

MG: Draining, yes. There's been a high price to pay.

AM: *You could say, I'm a very experienced head, this school's working very well, why not give yourself a bit of a break and coast along for a bit?*

MG: I couldn't do that, I'd rather give it up. I have a volatile establishment here, a minefield. The minute I coast the school will either remain static or start going backwards. There are so many different incentives for the school not to carry forward the minute I'm satisfied that everything's all right. It sounds egocentric, it isn't actually.

AM: *You don't seem to be short of ideas about where to go, which is another aspect of it.*

MG: I have difficulty in thinking of where we are going to be in five years' time, I feel that you plan for a year, and from what you've achieved in that year, you plan the next stage forward. I think a five-year plan is too far in the future because you're not dealing with an innate plant, you're dealing with people the whole time, and the whole emphasis can change. What will we be required to do in five years' time? Will we be all be wired up to computers or what? You can see visions, but you can't plan in detail for those, you've got to actually go through the staff and make sure the goals and targets you set are achievable ones.

The most awful part of the job when I first came was the children. They didn't smile and they looked suspiciously at any visitor coming in. If you tried to come in the door, you'd be knocked down by anyone coming out or in the corridor, and things like this. When I now go around with visitors, the children smile at visitors, in fact we've had to warn them about opening the door and letting visitors in now.

AM: *Is the term headteacher still an accurate description of what you expect of yourselves and others expect of you? Is it time we joined the rest of the world and called our school leaders principals?*

MG: I'm not sure about that distinction to be honest.

AM: *You called yourself the managing director.*

MG: Yes, I know, but having worked in the States and seen. . . .

AM: *You didn't tell me you'd worked in the States.*

MG: Yes, I was Visiting Principal in Salt Lake City, Utah, I did an exchange for a term. I was already a head then. . . .

AM: *Were you in Essex?*

MG: Yes, I was in Essex then. The principal I worked with was fascinating, because she definitely was an administrator, there was no doubt about that at all. And there also wasn't the commitment to the establishment because they could be moved at any time to a different school and they were only on three-yearly contracts and they had to be re-hired as well. I felt they never became really attached to the school in the same way as we do in England.

AM: *You were saying that the actual job of being a headteacher has changed a lot since you entered into it and it's expanded, what has been retained?*

MG: Yes. I don't do supply cover any more, where I would have perhaps previously done in my first headship, but this is because of the nature of this school. I don't have a set timetable to teach so this aspect of it has changed. But I take things like assemblies, I can still go in a class and cover if there's a meeting and things like that, but it's not on the timetable in the way it was before. And now I think we're going to find as well that there are a number of good practitioners who will now never become heads because they won't be able to cope with the administrative part of the job.

There's definitely a group of deputies who have seen the reality of being heads and have decided not to take on the headship role. And there's also the feeling amongst heads of departments that they already have enough pressure. What is taking me away from being a classroom teacher, is parents – parents expect the head to be a social worker, they're not coping with their children so they're wanting advice. Social services and case conferences, external meetings which actually keep you up-to-date, and then, as we are a flourishing institution, we have students and all the implications of having students. Another change is governors, because although it's now supposedly the governors who run the schools, in fact the extra work that has been created for the heads – the duplication of work – is tremendous.

AM: *What do you mean by duplication, getting things ready for them?*

MG: Yes. In fact you do all the work. The governors are completely happy about the decisions you make, but you have to go through the formal procedure of holding a meeting, calling all those people on sub-committees together to go through and explain in detail a decision that you would have just taken alone – I suppose it's accountability again isn't it?

AM: *Have you faced any particular problems in your career because you are a woman?*

MG: I always felt that in order to succeed I had to prove that I was better than my male colleagues, particularly as I was a married woman with children. I have never used my family as an excuse for not being able to do something but have worked hard so that my home life doesn't suffer.

CHAPTER 3

Rosemary Whinn-Sladden

In conversation with Viv Garrett

VG: *Can I ask you first of all to reflect on your own education. Has this experience influenced what you have tried to achieve as a teacher, and a headteacher?*

RWS: I think it would be fair to say that it's influenced more the way I see myself as a teacher than a headteacher. That's mainly because I can't remember any contact with the headteacher at all in the infant school, although I can remember the headteacher at the junior school. I can picture what he looked like but can't remember anything he ever did.

Some of the things that have stuck in my mind are individual incidents. It wasn't until I was in third year juniors that I can remember the very first teacher who said 'If you don't understand something, come out and ask.' I am amazed it took until then for anybody to say you were allowed to do that: to leave your seat and speak without being spoken to.

Another thing is that I have a love of stories and an appreciation of literature which I also developed about the third or fourth year juniors when we were introduced to classics by this one teacher who was very keen and her enthusiasm came across. I was taught to read by my grandmother before I went to school. When I was about 3 or 4 I caught every childhood ailment that there was so I didn't really go to school until I was about 6. When I got there I could read fluently and this was not approved of. I did not fit in and got into trouble several times for answering questions; for example, I can remember once having to stand in the corner and face the wall because we were supposed to be identifying initial letters and I had read the whole word. That memory has always remained with me and I knew I would never do that but I would always treat children as individuals and let them do the best they could whatever it may be.

The other thing was that I got measles and developed a squint and was given the incorrect glasses and for years and years I couldn't see the blackboard so I used to guess what it said and make it up. Fortunately I was reasonably bright but until I was 9 I didn't know what it really said. I am now very fussy over where the children are sitting and whether they can see and hear properly. We have so many children who can't hear in one ear and I notice the teachers say 'Oh yes, oh yes, we'll let him sit here', and then they don't. They just carry on and forget all about it. I've always tried to make the children feel confident about what they are doing and I think if they don't, if they can't see or they can't hear then that's a problem.

VG: *What other experiences can you remember?*

RWS: We had one primary school teacher who took us on school visits and even now all I know about farming is based on the one visit that I made to a dairy. She made it exciting and she made it fun and whenever she did anything like that or history or geography activities we enjoyed it. I do feel very strongly that children should be allowed to enjoy their education and be allowed to laugh. Children have a distinct sense of humour and they need to be able to develop that.

As far as secondary school is concerned I had some good and some bad experiences. The good ones were the subjects that I enjoyed. They tended to be taught by the good teachers; I am convinced that I enjoyed the subjects because the teaching was good. The bad experience was that for a couple of years while I was at secondary school I had a very bad time at home and I went from being in the top two or three in every subject to being practically the bottom in every subject. Even now I am resentful of the fact that nobody ever asked me why, nobody ever seemed to worry about the fact that I had gone from being in what should have been the high flying group to being at the bottom. I have always said that children can't learn unless they are happy and everything is sorted and if they have a problem you've got to sort the problem out. That's another thing that I bear in mind now in dealing with children and having some sort of respect for them.

VG: *So when did you decide to become a teacher?*

RWS: I always wanted to be a teacher except for a couple of years when I had this deep desire to be a ship's engineer! My father was an engineer and I spent a lot of time with him on the docks going round the boats from a very early age and I loved it, but it was made very clear to me that that was not an acceptable way forward for a girl and so I gave up the idea. I think I would have made a very good ship's engineer and whether I would have made as good an engineer as I am a headteacher, I don't know but I was forced out of that one rather than giving it up voluntarily.

Then I went to secondary school and decided that I very definitely would teach. I wanted to teach PE, Games and French because they were the subjects I was good at. I never doubted I wanted to become a teacher until several people who had been away to college came back to teach at my grammar school and I panicked. I suddenly had a vision of my life of never setting foot outside the one school, going away for three years or however long it was and coming back and doing and knowing nothing else, so I gave up the college place. The school was not happy, my family weren't very pleased but said it was up to me. So I went to the careers guidance teacher who had nothing to offer because in those days you either went to university or teacher training college, or you didn't exist! Then I applied to the Civil Service because I couldn't think of anything else to do and I worked there for four years. However, after about two years, I realized that it wasn't what I wanted to do and I did want to teach and it took me another two years to get into teacher training college. I was fortunate enough to go to a college for mature students which was brilliant. I don't know how well I would have coped at that time if I had been sitting in with 18 year olds, because the difference is so great once you have left home and started work. By this time I was married anyway, so I did the three years at teacher training college and I chose primary because I had also decided by that time that I did not want to work with older children. The junior age range seemed to be what was particularly wanted, and that's what I did.

When I left college I was lucky that it was still in the days when you got a job straight away. I got my first job in a school with a very interesting staff. They had a very rigid way of working, very formal. The kindest thing the headteacher ever said to me was that I stuck out like a sore thumb. They did not like any deviation from the work cards that were set for every subject in the curriculum. My habit of taking children out of the classroom to do different things was not actually approved of. I didn't think he was a good head and, if anything, the one thing I learned from him was what not to do. I can't remember anything he did that I thought about and said 'I'll do it that way', but it was an interesting grounding. He seemed to specialize in making his staff unhappy and playing off one member of staff against another and I have always gone out of my way not to do that. I don't think it is the head's job to do that – I think the head's job is the opposite.

VG: *How many schools did you work in before you became a headteacher?*

RWS: I stayed at my first school and got a scale 2. They were given out . . . I'd like to think I got it on merit . . . I did deserve it but I didn't get it because I deserved it, I got it because I had been there next longest and all scaled posts were given out in order of seniority. There was one scale point going in May and that went to the girl who started in September and there was one going in June and I had started in January so that became mine. I got it for environmental studies and language development, but in fact I did PE and Science. I have no idea why they gave it me for one thing when I did another but that was how it worked. I then took a sideways move to another school in a very deprived area of Doncaster working for a head who everyone called 'Mad Keith'. He was brilliant – he didn't want to know anything about what happened in the classroom, didn't want anything to do with the children, didn't want anything to do with the parents, but it was a very happy school to work in. It was a mixed staff with a lot of men which is something I wasn't used to. This was a first to middle school and I taught reception and was Head of Science at the same time. Whenever I went to liaison meetings with the other primaries at the secondary school, they couldn't cope with the fact that I taught reception and Sci-

ence. I worked there for two years and then there were six deputy headships advertised and I applied for all six.

At that time the local authority said you couldn't visit a school before
you applied for a job; you could only go and look round the school if you
were short-listed and then invited. I was short-listed for a group 2, (3.5
teachers), school. I rang up to see if I could look round and was told that
we were all to go at 4 o'clock, not a minute before. I parked outside until
4 o'clock came round and went in and was informed that they had been
waiting for me because everybody else had arrived early! So that set the
scene. I went to look round the school with the head and thought it was
the worst school I had ever seen in my life! I decided as I looked round that
I couldn't possibly work with this headteacher. His views were so unlike
mine that I really didn't want the job, but I didn't expect to get it because
I felt the system was that you got on the rota and had so many interviews.
Eventually if you were lucky enough it was your turn to get the job. What
upset me was that a woman, who I did not rate too highly, was also up for
interview and I desperately didn't want her to get the job, even though I
didn't want it. I was very upset about it all and wished I hadn't applied but
it was too late and I felt really ill the following day. I had been awake all
night worrying about it but I knew I had to have a good interview and I
did. There were sixteen governors there – it was a church school – and the
head and the adviser. I didn't understand half the questions the head and
the adviser asked me and said so. They appointed me because they thought
I could stick up for myself. And so I got the job.

I went to see the headteacher afterwards to talk about what my responsibilities would be and first of all was told that I would have 38 first and
second year children – this would be reception and Y1s together. The other
full-time teacher would have 24 children and he would have 18. But however it worked out I had 38, she had 24 and he had 18. He said I wasn't
to worry about curriculum areas or responsibilities as a deputy because he
didn't really want me, he didn't need a deputy. If I just looked after the
children in my classroom and didn't cause any problems, after two years
he would give me a good reference and I could go and work somewhere
else! That was before I had even started.

VG: *Who appointed you to that school, the LEA?*

RWS: The governors. It was a church school with only one rep. from the LEA
and so all the governors turned up and they made the appointment. The
head had been there twelve years, having been a deputy in a middle school
before that. The deputy I replaced had been there 24 years. The other full-
timer had been there 18 years and the part-timer had been there 11 years.
The full-timer had responsibility for girls' games and playing the piano for
the infants, that was all she did; the part-timer didn't have any responsibilities because she was part-time; and the head didn't have any
responsibilities because he was the head, so I got the rest of it!

VG: *So how many years were you there?*

RWS: Four. For the third year he had a lot of time off because his wife was very ill and then he retired on medical grounds, so I had a spell of acting head for the third year which was very useful, except that he was still in post and came in for part of most days so in fact I couldn't do anything because he was always there. But I did learn how to walk on cracked eggs and I learned diplomacy because it was extremely difficult; so, although I hated it and did not enjoy working there at all, I learned a lot. I learned a lot of skills that have been useful to me.

VG: *Did you then move to a headship?*

RWS: Yes. I had one last year at that school when the headship was advertised and I didn't get it. Then I applied for the only job I have wanted in my life which was in a very deprived area. At the time I was working in the Youth Service and I had worked in this particular area, which was a dockland area with a lot of problems.

VG: *You were working in the Youth Service as well?*

RWS: Yes, mainly because I got divorced and needed the money. So I did several nights a week working in the Youth Service and that was very helpful. I applied for this job as a head and got it. That was in 1986, so it was at the time when heads were still doing what they were supposed to be doing which was managing the curriculum and managing the education of children.

VG: *Did you feel that your experience as a deputy head, albeit in a none too easy situation, was good preparation?*

RWS: Yes I am sure it was. It not only taught me things I didn't want to do, but I learned to curb my tongue which I am not naturally talented at. I learned to persuade people to do things that I wanted them to do in different ways. It wasn't a school where you could sit in the staffroom and say this would be best for the children because that wasn't a criteria, so you had to find other ways of persuading people to do what you thought was right. And I also had the most militant NUPE caretaker I ever met and I learned a lot from him. We ended up very good friends but, during that first year, how I avoided 15 or 16 complaints procedures about the water or clay work I don't know! But again it was good experience for dealing with people.

VG: *So you started your first headship in September 1986. How long did you stay?*

RWS: I stayed for three years. I originally had in mind that I would stay there for six or seven years, working on the principle that HMI said you were at your most effective between four and seven years. It was certainly a school that needed turning round. It was a first school with about 170–180 children, plus a 39-place nursery. I had an additional community teacher and a community nursery nurse which was helpful, although they weren't actually being used when I got there, and we had to develop the roles. But it was a good school to go to in that you couldn't go far wrong. There was a lot of scope. But I had never come across a school where the staff themselves felt so undervalued and inferior and yet they were wonderful, but they really needed the chance to believe in themselves. I was fortunate in that I had the chance to appoint my own deputy. That was tremendous because I knew the person I wanted and I rang this woman up. I had worked with her years before. She was not a close friend of mine and it was at least a couple of years since I had spoken to her. I just rang up and said 'I want you to come and look at this job.' She came and had a look and agreed with everything that I said about the school. We went round on a Saturday when there was nobody about and she applied for and got the job. I knew she was the right person and I wanted her for her ability to be a good deputy. A good deputy has to be able to fit between the head and the staff and wear both hats with ease and I knew she could do it. I knew she could support people and I knew she was one of the best teachers I had ever worked with. I needed a good teacher to raise everybody else's expectations and that's what really made it for me. You can say what you like about the qualities of a headteacher and I have read an awful lot about the value of good leaders but you do need a good deputy. If you have a bad one you really are up against it but if you have a good one they are doing half the work for you. It makes such a difference.

VG: *So, after three years, what happened then?*

RWS: The local authority decided to re-organize from first, middle, secondary to infant, junior or primary schools and one secondary school. I found that out after I had been in post for a month. 'Hello, welcome, we are going to close your school' was roughly how it was worded! My school was on the list of those that were not going to be re-opened and it was very much into the melting pot. Now about this time I had also taken over as the area NUT secretary, simply because nobody else would do it and I have always been a mug for things that nobody else would do. This put me onto the teachers' panel which was negotiating the agreements for the re-organization and that was wonderful. That gave me the opportunity to take part in formal negotiations on a level that I had not been used to and that raised my view of myself, it raised my standing in the area and it certainly broadened my view of education. I had always felt that I had a fairly national view. I had always read a lot; in fact I was the only person who ever took the *Times Ed.* home! This really gave me the chance to operate on a different level and I found that I was not afraid of dealing with the 'authorities' and was quite happy to deal with people.

But one thing I did learn from that experience was that I found that local authority officers frequently had difficulty dealing with women and particularly women in positions of authority. I was not only a headteacher but I was sitting on a negotiating panel with clout, because you have a lot of clout when you have that membership behind you. It was then that I first began to notice how differently I could be treated on some days sitting round a table. I would say that 'I think we should this, this and this' and they would talk it over for ten minutes and then a man would say 'I think we should do this and this, I think we should take that up', and they would all agree. Eventually I learned to say 'Excuse me, but that's exactly what I said here ten minutes ago.' They didn't like being told, but I did notice it more and more, especially when you were often not allowed to finish your point. If a man interrupted they would stop and listen but I had to get in almost physically. I have since learned a number of actions in order to be able to put my point forward. This was something that I realized then and I have noticed it frequently since, as a woman headteacher.

VG: *But you were able to influence what happened. Did the school eventually close?*

RWS: Yes it did, but I was able to influence how teachers were treated, how the jobs were allocated. I think that I did a lot to ensure that teachers were treated with respect throughout the re-organization and that they were treated fairly and knew exactly what was happening and why it was happening. I think everything has to be fair and it has to be seen to be fair and I think that's probably been my biggest concern in education. I like things to be right, and then nobody can argue about it.

So after the three years I didn't apply for my old job because I thought the new school was going to be a primary school. Although they were moving premises, it was still going to be a Group 4 which was what it had been when I started with 249 children. Had it been 250 children it would have been a Group 5! I was resentful of this because I thought it was a device on the part of the local authority to pay the head less and I felt that with all the problems at this particular school it merited additional pay for the head. It really was the hardest place I have ever worked in but I loved it. I thought it was absolutely wonderful there but it was hard work. If I had decided to stay at the new school for five to seven years, I would then have been in the same place for rather a long time. I didn't really want to work at any of the other schools in the area but I opted for the biggest split site school with lots of potential. It was a Group 5 to start with but ready to be a Group 6. It is a Group 6 now.

The first year was a transitional year so I spent one year at the first school with only three of the existing staff and five temps who had never taught primary before. For a year that was horrendous because I was also given one member of staff specifically because he was failing where he was and they wanted me to look at his competence. I had already, in my first headship, had one teacher who was failing and had started disciplinary procedures for incompetence and this was going to be my second. Well I did start it but he was moved on after a term, for which I was extremely grateful. It is not something I would recommend to anybody. So I had this one year with all these new people with whom I worked very hard and then they all left except one and I got a completely new staff apart from this one. And I got the primary school which was the first school building . . . and the middle school building . . . and all these new people . . . and most of the same children . . . and a 39-place nursery which was new! I have been there now . . . this is my fifth year . . . which worries me. It worries me dreadfully because I am supposed to be at my most effective now! I really am beginning to get into a state of panic because I am not sure that if HMI came to look at what I was doing they would think I was at my most effective.

VG: *Let's talk about that now. What do you mean by effective?*

RWS: What I would really like to provide is quality teaching and I put quality teaching before quality learning because you can't get the quality learning without the quality teaching. I see the way to get quality education as being a dramatic improvement in the quality of the teaching in the school. I want the children's education to be good. It's the only chance they get and I want it to be really memorable. I want them to be able to do their best. I don't want any child coming out of school and looking back on it and thinking 'If only . . . ' 'If they had let me do this . . .' 'If they had pushed me a bit harder at that . . .' 'If they had understood . . .'. I realize it's a very high standard to set. I have an assigned adviser – we all have an assigned adviser in my local authority – who frequently tells me that my standards are too high. I don't think they are too high. You have to know where you are going. I know how far away some days I am from it but I do think that children deserve the best and I think that's what I get paid for. I also think that's what teachers get paid for and sometimes they forget it.

VG: *How do you ensure that your staff have the same philosophy?*

RWS: Mainly by drawing their attention to it. I spend a lot of time saying 'Of course we do this, don't we?' rather than 'You are not doing that, are you? I want it done.' There have been times when I have had to say to people 'I don't want to see that child sitting here.' I can remember hating it if I was ever picked on for something good or bad – I can remember how badly I felt about being isolated or identified as having a problem with my work. Teachers are very good at picking on certain children and as a head if I see the same child twice I notice, if I see them three times I notice more, and if I see them a fourth time I want to know exactly why because I can't see that there is any need for it. You should be solving the problem, not simply picking on them. I have a lot of old-fashioned teachers at my school who were brought up in the days where you always made children stand out rather than deal with the problem.

VG: *So how do you go about trying to achieve effectiveness?*

RWS: Well I do it differently now than I did in my first headship and I am not sure whether it's been a change for the better or whether it's simply circumstances that have created it. In my first headship I seemed to have a lot more time. I talked a lot more and I listened a lot more. I used to spend far more time wandering from class to class. I'd get to the end of some days and not feel I'd done anything but I could see the difference the following day when something altered. With it being now such a big school (I have 15 classes at the moment), it is virtually impossible to get round everybody and I miss that terribly. I miss trying to make the time to talk to teachers about their teaching and about their children and about what they are doing. I feel that I can influence them because they do listen to what I say because I am the Head. They listen because you have status and they know

I can do it and often they can't talk to each other in the same sort of way. I think some teachers lack confidence and they need the confidence to try things and to know that you are not going to come round and say 'Why are you doing that?'

Time is one of the big problems and at the moment I tend to do a lot more talking to groups: there's a lot more influence through staff meetings and meetings with groups of teachers. I find I can be very effective if I am working with a smaller group, say one of the wings (we have these two buildings: Key Stage 1 in one building and Key Stage 2 in the other). Or what's best is a group of like-minded teachers but it is taking me longer and it's harder work than it was. I also think there has been so much change since we re-organized because a lot of the teachers had never taught primary. I have, for example, two domestic science teachers who had never taught more than 12 in a class and had never taught anything other than domestic science unless they were covering for somebody and they were given the book! And to suddenly get 30 children and ten subjects of the National Curriculum was a big difference! The fact that they can now teach ten subjects plus all the rest of it is quite an achievement and yet I am still looking at the quality. If we are inspected, OFSTED are not going to say 'Oh well I see you have got two domestic science teachers who have only been doing this for four years.'

I think the amount of work that I have to do that takes me away from managing the curriculum is to the detriment of education. I think that's what has happened to a lot of heads. A lot of heads try and do more teaching because that's their way, but I don't see myself as achieving progress through more teaching. If I am demonstrating or working with a teacher looking at a particular area, and that has an effect, then all well and good, but it's in my management of their work that I think I can make a difference.

VG: *So what sort of leader would you say you are? What are your key values? You've already mentioned respect.*

RWS: There are two things: fairness is the first thing and I think fairness as far as children are concerned and fairness as far as staff are concerned. Staff do not react well to thinking that there are a favoured few on the staff. We have to always be seen to treat everybody fairly. I think I am quite an understanding person in that I feel, just as I feel if the children have a problem, that if a member of staff has a problem they have enough on their plate without me adding to it. There have been a lot of occasions when staff have had serious difficulties and I feel it is my job to help them through it and I think that is very important.

I think respect is important and so is equality. I have a big staff and they are mostly all brilliant and some of my best staff are non-teaching staff. Some of my teachers used to teach in schools where non-teaching staff were not allowed in staffrooms. They were not considered to be an equal part of the school and yet you cannot move a school forward without everybody pulling together. This view of everybody going in the same direction and planning the future together is so important. When we have meetings, everybody comes: the governors come, the non-teaching staff come, it doesn't matter whether they are non-teaching assistants, teachers' aides, nursery nurses, whatever, they are all there. They can all be listened to and they all have a contribution to make. That has always been my view and it's taken some getting there. It's the same with parents. We have a lot of parents working in school. You've got to listen when they have got something to say because otherwise they go away and you've lost them. Everyone has to know where we are going. This has meant that everybody has worked on the school development plan, for example. We have done a lot of working together as a whole site with the governors, etc., but we have also done a lot of breaking down into smaller groups. This means everybody, so every group has a cross-section of the school population in it working on different aspects and then bringing it back to talk to everybody else and that has worked extremely well.

VG: *So everyone feels some ownership?*

RWS: Yes, and it has to be everybody. What I think we need to look at next is more of a contribution from the children because at the moment we are only getting that from small defined areas, safe areas where criticism will not come through. We could get beyond this. We can say 'Let's look at how it is and let's see what we can do to make it better.'

VG: *Do you think it is harder now to be an effective leader than it used to be?*

RWS: Very much so. The workload is phenomenal. Whatever they say about devolving more and more of the budget into schools they are devolving more and more work and I object to the fact that a lot of it is work the local authority already do. I'll give you an example. I get a lot of paperwork which I don't deal with. I am not the most efficient paperwork person, particularly if I don't fancy doing it or I don't think it is important. I thought it was daft doing salary assessments because they have got all this information on forms at the office and I thought they should do it. So I kept putting it off and putting it off and they kept ringing up and I kept saying it's getting closer, it's on my desk at the moment, or whatever. Eventually they sent me the assessments, two years worth at once. Now my argument is that there is a chap sitting somewhere, who rang me up, and who has now done the job for me. He's probably done it in 20 minutes at the most. Why didn't he do that in the first place? Why did they ask me to do it? Why aren't they doing that for all schools? Why are they giving stuff like that to headteachers? That's not my job. Yes, the governors have to approve salary assessments but all I want to know is where there's a problem. I get very upset that they are palming off paperwork where they have all the information and they can look it up on computer. So why give it to me to do? I am supposed to be managing the teaching and learning, the efficiency, the management and everything on the OFSTED list. I am paid to do that so why do I have to fill in forms for somebody?

VG: *How can you ensure that you continue to be an effective leader in spite of these difficulties? What sort of strategies do you use?*

RWS: One of the things that I am doing at the moment is 'Investors in People'. This is staff-development based so it fits in beautifully with my view of how things should be and how to move things forward, because I do feel so strongly that you move a school forward through the staff, children and parents. You have to ensure you include everybody, as it's fatal to forget. The emphasis on staff development and quality, in order to progress the school's aims and objectives, gave us opportunities. It has given us the opportunity to look at how far we have come since we opened, to look very carefully at where we are now, where we are going, and how exactly we are going to get there by improving ourselves, each other and the input that the children are getting from different sources. It also gave us a chance to reaffirm the fact that everybody is involved.

We started off by having the whole school together including mid-day supervisors, the lollipop lady, caretaker, the governors, everybody . . . in fact, if anybody was walking past, they were just about drawn in! We worked together as a large group but kept breaking down into smaller groups which included everybody. I put people in charge of each group in turn and the first thing they had to ensure was everybody had the opportunity to put an opinion forward and that everybody's opinion was written down. Therefore if one of the mid-day supervisors suddenly got a bee in their bonnet about something you made it important. Now I mention mid-day supervisors for two reasons: one is that they feel under-valued, they feel they are on very different levels from the rest of us and they also have this vision of teachers being in some way superior. Now there is this problem about teachers feeling superior; the majority of teachers feel they are genuinely better than everybody else on the staff, including nursery nurses who have probably spent as much time in college as they have and are better at certain areas than they are. I could never run a nursery unless I had a damn good nursery nurse there. Mid-day supervisors might not have had the same opportunities to go to college. So the process was good in that the teachers had to make the effort to include people that they perhaps didn't feel ought to be in that group, and allow them to make decisions about important things like the curriculum. They not only have the right, but they have a lot to offer. So that was the starting point for it. It's been brilliant because of the willingness of other staff to contribute and a recognition of the fact that we are all in it together. If one area fails we all fail, and that is quite an interesting view.

VG: *How long have you been involved in 'Investors in People'?*

RWS: We signed the paper before the summer holidays 1994 and we are aiming to complete by the end of 1995. We are taking it fairly steadily. I have learned over the years to decide how long I think something is going to take and double it, because I am extremely impatient and you can't rush these things.

VG: *How much is it costing you as a school?*

RWS: We are hoping for a grant from the TEC which will cover the £500 that we have to pay. We have been allocated a certain amount of time by our consultant who happens to be our school-assigned adviser. Now that's very interesting in that a lot of schools don't want their assigned advisers who are closely involved in what they are doing, because they think it better that they don't know everything that is happening. I am painfully honest about things at times. I see no point in hiding where we are or what we are doing because I work on the fact that she is there to help. If she ever proved disloyal to the school then I would certainly take exception to that but I have to say she has been extremely supportive in working with us and I think that's how it should be. She does not have an extensive background in primary education but she is very good at staff development. That is where her skills lie and from that starting point she has developed her expertise by working with us and vice versa. In fact it has been a learning process for the school and for her and she has been very helpful.

I would also like to say something about GNVQs. We are looking at training our staff properly as far as 'Investors in People' is concerned and we have ten non-teaching staff: mid-day supervisors, non-teaching assistants and teachers aides, who are working on GNVQs related to the work that they do. We have managed to get funding to pay for it and a member of staff, who is a trained assessor, is assessing five staff and somebody is coming from outside to assess the other five. We are becoming more and more responsible for developing our own staff, and parents and voluntary helpers as well. We are also offering placements to other people too. Again it's back to the people, if you make the most of the people you get the best of the children.

VG: *What about teacher development?*

RWS: We have a very good but different appraisal system. The local authority appraisal system is set down and we follow the guidelines broadly but our staff do not keep all the information to themselves. They decided that they would all be appraised together, not in bits and pieces. There would be equality of suffering (!) and they all selected areas of classroom management to look at. They might be different subject areas perhaps, or different points of view, but they all chose an aspect of classroom management with a view to them coming back to the rest of the staff with what they had learned from it. Anything good that came out of it they would bring back. In fact that has been wonderful because they are a very open staff now. They talk to each other about their strengths and their weaknesses, and they know where to go to get help and that's been very positive. The authority are not entirely happy with the system because they have this thing about confidentiality, and also they can't get used to the idea of a whole staff working on an appraisal together. It somehow doesn't have the ring of the authority's guidelines but we are fulfilling the criteria in that it is seen in the light of that teacher's personal development but it is also of benefit to everybody.

We also have a deputy head responsible for staff development and he is able to not only look at staff development in terms of the school's objectives but in terms of a teacher's own potential and where they need to be in the future. We also try and identify certain people who are interested in promotion. At the same time we try and identify those people who are not, but who want to be a good classroom teacher. If you are not careful the emphasis on promotion can be crushing; people are pushed into it when they don't want it and then fail, or the ordinary classroom teacher feels devalued because they are not interested. We certainly, as a governing body and as a staff, don't agree in paying people extra for excellent classroom practice; but what we do pay for is when people do things over and above the call of duty relating to their classroom practice which benefits the school and benefits them.

VG: *Do you think a lot of these things that you have been able to do, like IIP and GNVQ, work because you are a bigger school?*

RWS: Yes it works because we are a bigger school and it works because I am quite a brave person. If I think it is worth having a go, the staff have confidence that they can go ahead and do it. You can do anything if you put your mind to it. Now there is one argument that says I shouldn't be spending my time doing all this; I should spend more time doing what I say I am supposed to be doing, which is looking at what the children are doing. But I think it all benefits the children. I think if you improve the quality of adults around them and improve what's there for them and make them feel genuinely valued, and their parents valued, then in fact children make more progress.

VG: *Can I move on now to external relations? How do you manage those?*

RWS: We have a thriving 'Education Business Partnership' link. We have just set up a group in the area for looking at 'Education Business Partnership', funded by the TEC, and there are a number of heads and teachers on that now with a number of local firms. We have made a lot of progress in looking at primary schools and how they develop their business links because we feel very strongly that by the time children get to secondary school it is too late. They already have decided what they can and can't do, what they want to do and what they don't want to do, so we have to get in early, and we have developed a lot of links with the primary sector. We have a member of staff with responsibility for the partnership and I am on the steering group anyway, and it has a lot of spin-offs for us as far as the curriculum is concerned.

We have good links with most areas of the community, including all the churches which we rotate because we don't want to be seen as looking to one church in particular. We have good links with other schools but I think that is due to the re-organization. We set up a heads and deputies group when we re-organized and we have stuck together. We have a 'do' at the end of every year and we try to support each other. We are trying to get away from the view of competition that a lot of schools have. It's a small area and there will be competition but we have got to get on. Often it has been very helpful in our relationship with the local authority because we stand together. We are known as the 'Goole Mafia'!

VG: *What aspect of your role do you most enjoy?*

RWS: I like being in charge. I'm sure this is one of the seven deadly sins . . . I love being the head. I absolutely love being the head. I love being able to do things and see something happen. I have always been a lousy Indian and I have always known I was going to be a head. I have never, even when I went to college, doubted that I was going to be a headteacher. I simply knew I was going to be a headteacher and I enjoy it. I love walking round the school when it's full and when it's empty. I look round and I think, 'Look at that, I did that.' All right, I might not personally have done it, but I got it done. I look at the improvements in the way staff are working and I think, 'I did that.' All right, not single handed and not without everybody working together, but where else can you have a job where, whatever you do, a little wave just gets bigger. I love it when the kids come up with things. I have an open-door policy with children which means they can come and see me any time they want to for anything. It's amazing the odd problems that crop up that you didn't know about until a child tells you. Children find it easy to accept that they can walk straight in. I do keep the door open – it's very rarely closed – but if it's closed it means that I am there with somebody. That is lovely because they trust me to do it and I think that's good. I just enjoy it very much.

VG: *Who do you feel you are responsible to?*

RWS: That's a really interesting question. If you had asked me when I started as a head I would have said the local authority first and that I work in part-nership with my governing body and the parents and the rest of it. Now I do not think that I am responsible to the local authority at all. My governing body are my employers. They are the people who are responsible for everything I do. More and more I am coming round to the fact that there are very few aspects of the local authority that I personally need as a head or as a school. I never thought I would get to this point but I do feel that anything I want I can buy in. This has come to a head recently because we are possibly changing local authorities because of the restruc-turing of Humberside. Now if we change authorities we will be losing certain things. It is likely if we go into a small unitary authority we are going to end up all being grant maintained because there isn't a way for-ward otherwise. This may be heresy or it was until Tony Blair sent his child to a grant maintained school. However, I would miss the area finance officer because you can ask her a question and she goes whizzing through the machine and out pops the answer. But I suppose I could buy that in from somewhere, plus the fact that my secretary is doing an accounts degree at the moment. That was part of the staff development in the school objectives.

VG: *Are you paying for that or is she?*

RWS: No, we pay for everything if it's for the benefit of the school. I don't allow staff to fund their own development if it is in any way going to benefit the school and I give her the time off to do it. I have several nursery nurses who are doing the advanced course; I give them time off to compensate for the fact that they are working in the evening because I think it is too much otherwise. They do have all the extra work to do. The same applies to the secretary.

VG: *Let's go back to the question of responsibility.*

RWS: I feel most responsibility to the governors. They in turn are taking on more and more responsibility because I am working with them both as individual governors and in groups on different aspects of the school and school development with a view to increasing their understanding of what we are doing and where we are going. They have got to be involved in those decisions and not just ratify something that I say, because that would be too easy.

VG: *You've spoken about formal responsibility but from a lot of other things you have been saying I would say that you have a very strong personal accountability to the children, about making a difference to their lives.*

RWS: Yes, and that is supported by the governors. If you asked them what we were there for they would all instantly say 'the children'. There would be no doubt about that. They have been known to give me a hard time over certain things but that is fair because I give them a hard time over things. We do work together, very much so, and that's good.

VG: *Do you think 'headteacher' is still the correct term? Do you wish to use a different name?*

RWS: I think 'principal' is quite a good term in that it doesn't imply that I am simply a senior teacher and I am not anymore. I can teach but I can turn my hand to anything. The headteacher is a 'jack of all trades' and that includes fixing the toilet when it overflows. I am not being facetious. I have never met a head yet who hasn't fixed the ballcock when it's required, but head of the teachers I am not. When you look at our school I am the head of the people there and the children and the whole school community which is completely different. I think 'principal' has a ring about it that implies that you are head of everything, that's it's all your responsibility and you are in charge of it. You don't have to say 'Well actually, that's not my bit – it's all your bit.'

CHAPTER 4

Keith Bovair

In conversation with Steve Rayner

SR: *Please describe Durants, your present school.*

KB: Durants School is an all-age school for children aged 5–19 and a Group size 2 – what was an old 3S with 120 pupils in the school. It provides for a variety of need but in the main for moderate learning difficulty (MLD). There's about a 15 per cent ratio of emotional and behavioural difficulty but that is a secondary aged related problem and is actually part of the learning difficulty the children are experiencing.

SR: *What is your vision for the school?*

KB: It's an all-age school. I see it changing focus to becoming a Secondary Centre – changing the title from Special School for MLD – and changing into a mind-set about it being a school that works intensively with individual needs. People come to us through the admissions procedure which describes the type of individuals we can work with in this setting and it's always the professionals who are trying to get placements. They therefore should know how to approach us through the admissions policy without 'approaching' the label of the school. I think that's one thing, the other, is also to make it [the school] more proactive in contributing to the greater good of the local community. It has to be more than just a school centre and I see elements of research, development, initial teacher training, training of probationers, induction courses, and post to post exchange with other teachers, offering opportunity to develop skills, working intensively with individual children. I see it working for student placements, at a variety of levels, to give them that experience. I see this development possibly linking into adult literacy projects and programmes which with materials developed in the centre could actually extend these programmes.

SR: *That sounds exciting, how do you go about achieving it?*

KB: Well what I've been doing is starting dialogues with schools in the area, taking a look at what their perceived needs are, and having a dialogue with officers in decision-making positions for handling the minimal finances available, to show that this could actually maximize those minimal resources. I'm having this sort of dialogue with them, looking at how we can have inclusive education which will involve the whole community. There are elements of the school as it stands which can be based within mainstream, to achieve greater access. We can reduce or avoid any later stage of labelling, and provide a secondary type of setting where the placements need to be transitional so that we can make that provision more effective – or – in other words moving children through appropriate provision more flexibly.

The approach is not simply about physical resources or a traditional outreach arrangement. I think more in terms of dialogues with other heads of primary schools and that we all see it as joint ownership, that there would exist certain lines, there would be a line management arrangement but also a sense of trading at some point, of expertise from the centre, to assist all the people involved, and not just the specialist teachers who are in the mainstream schools but also other teachers in the school setting. That's part of the dialogue; the individual headteachers and other staff have site management of it. The headteachers deal with the personnel issues and all of that; but they also share in looking at the dialogue and agree to identify that there are not units on the school grounds and that they would move classes around if they needed to draw up new provision, say portacabins, or the timetable or anything else. They would move school provision around and put the classes for children who would be coming, say, from this place, into the mainstream building, so that they are not isolated.

SR: *What does that mean for the management of the place, in terms of what you seem to be describing as a change in the nature and identity of Durants School? You mentioned in conversation the words 'mind-set'. Is that a crucial part of it? It seems to me that there's a lot wrapped up in that package, especially in terms of change. There's going to be a great deal of fundamental change!*

KB: Yes! It is! There will! It's full of change. And again, that's part of the challenge of the job right now because they've had this change that has been going to happen here for the last five years and nothing has happened! I think I'm accelerating it happening. People have been hanging in there with that type of change to come, not knowing what shape it was going to take. It's definitely a process of change and, together with the mind-set changes, it's about recognizing how the school has been viewed in the community. It's very historic with the whole negative labelling thing there for the school.

It is like having a kind of re-launch, even just for the physical premises, buildings, trying to change a piece of that, bit by bit. I think it will revitalize the place and the community because we are not only just getting involved with the schools. We're involved with industry links for example and are looking to see how we can fit into the schemes around . . . they have a regeneration budget in that we're situated on the side of town where the money is coming into and we are busy seeing what role we can play. I think this kind of development is enabling for those involved and is about enriching provision.

SR: *This describes a far more open provision, one which is flexible, that is, I'm thinking about the school shifting to some sort of centre as an institution. I guess that would be threatening for staff and people accustomed to working in school with its recognizable features, the school day, the timetable, there would be organizational difficulties, classes, the curriculum and so on. How do you see all of that developing?*

KB: Well. Again – the staff – there are staff who are anxious. There are some staff who see this as a challenge and the thing is it does create difficulties in management right now because of the fear of change. But it's tackled through educating; team-work; working through projects involving collaboration which through this activity extend their own personal experiences.

I organized an outreach recently, where teachers now for the first time are team-teaching in primary school and they've come back alive. It's actually now happening! Our first integration project was in France. We began with some of the kids cleaning up Enfield Lock – now – they're cleaning up an ancient monastery in the South of France. Finding this old pond became the source of a major archaeological find. We've been there now for two years in a row and when I first moved here – they knew that I'd written something on the teaching of French – and they said, 'I suppose you're going to have the kids learning French.' I said, 'Yes but in my own way.' Well – the kids are learning French and they're really going somewhere as they learn – learning and travelling to France. We are now as a school taking on initiatives. We have travelled too as we moved into mainstream so that we can bring back the experience into the special settings – which means extending this provision further and thereby letting the staff realize they can operate beyond the boundaries of the school.

We have team enterprise where staff and pupils have set up a business, run the business and then they – believe it or not – *close* it. Very British that! To have to close it! I think to myself so very very British! I don't want to really emphasize that do I? Well in that project, we're setting up a product to sell, and the kids are going to take it to Enfield Market. The Enfield Market experience is the test-bed. They also actually set up a market in France, for a whole week, working with a French school, with the French Chamber of Commerce and the Enfield Chamber of Commerce. It's a contact which we have built up. There have been other similar small projects which we've built up, extending opportunities for other children and we've done that through a variety of art projects too. These are just small things but they are also the opportunities that give individuals confidence so that they can get out there and grow.

SR: *Does this help the staff to share the vision you've been describing?*

KB: I think gradually . . . yes . . . I think so . . . the school's been historically . . . it's not a criticism of the staff and that . . . but it's been . . . and surprisingly so at this stage . . . unchanged. A special school is meant to meet the challenge of the National Curriculum but for quite a few the school has remained the old model of insular but caring, a deficiency-based curriculum, with a very protective ethos. The idea is to move towards a broadening of that curriculum? Broadening is the key word. It is . . . like . . . spreading the message . . . like Pablo Cassell's quote that children should be dignified by their learning and this gives the basis on which to move forward. I think this is perhaps one of the key features of my vision? I picked it up from Lambert Bignell, he's ex-HMI, he uses that in a quote. I always hang on to it.

SR: *I'd like to switch the focus a little now, away from the school and just focus on yourself. How would you describe your own education and to what extent has that experience influenced you as a teacher and headteacher?*

KB: First I never thought I would be a teacher. When I started into my career I started in Psychology, but going back beyond, before that, I got into trouble in high school. I got thrown out of a Catholic high school. I got put into what we call a public school – a state school here – and they put me in the remedial department because I got thrown out for hitting a priest. It's a true story. It was over an issue of religion – but I won't trivialize it and go into all of that – but I had that incident hanging over me which meant I came with this record that really was not true. It was just one of those things and as a result they put me in a remedial department for my last two years of high school. They put me on a work experience for most times in the afternoon.

SR: *The incident seems quite serious?*

KB: Well, it was a privileged boys' school I was thrown out of and they gave me this sort of lecture on learning. They wanted me to stay for the fee but – you know – on their terms. They lectured that there'd be Jewish people, Lutherans out there, different religions, and there would also be girls – you know – that's what clinched it! No. No. No. I got out of there and I actually fell in with a couple of good teachers. They – you know – the typical thing. They influenced me, got me interested in things. I found I'd got a bit more to me than I thought and while working in the afternoon I got into jobs, drove a truck, worked in a warehouse and ended up getting drafted into the Air Force for four years. I did a lot of time and a lot of thinking – you can when you are in that position.

SR: *This is in the States Keith?*

KB: This is in the States. Yeah. This is the time of Vietnam. And I did not want to go in the Army because I already had had two friends who didn't return. You could go into the military with a choice, Air Force, Army, you had a choice . . . your choice would be two years in the Army or four years in any other military, Navy or Air Force, and you got the chance to learn a trade. I thought I'd learn draughtsmanship – so – somewhat typically, I actually ended up as an Administrative Specialist.

I think that was a time during which I did a lot of growing up. I got interested in Psychology. I took night courses and I got the grades – found I had the ability. I'd never gone to university because of the service and if it wasn't for the GI Bill, well I'd have missed out. I went to the University of

Michigan because my grades, while I was in the Air Force, night school at Boise State College were good. I talked my way into the University of Michigan, which was interesting, you know, because they said Boise was a State College. It was not a university that the good grades came from – and all I said was – look I've just come out of the service and I got drafted because of this Vietnam thing and I'm coming over to talk to you. They thought I was going to arrive with bandoleers and guns blazing or something. I got out there, they had the application forms all ready for me.

SR: *They were expecting a 'first blood encounter'?*

KB: Yes, yes that's it – they were expecting mayhem. No seriously, let's not get into that, still it worked well for me. I got into the University. I started studying Psychology and my mentors were Fritz Redl and Bill Morris. American Bill Morris. I talked to them. Well I talked to Bill Morris and he encouraged me. He said the field of emotional impairment would be of interest. Okay, now how's that influenced me. I mean there's Morris's story. I did that work. I went into a programme of integration. I had 110 children where I had pastoral oversight. A group of students with emotional impairment – you know – in a high school of 2500. We managed that quite well. It was my project. It was interesting. And it really worked because we had all the resources to make it work. I got it all going and we received a Community Mental Health Award for the work. That's it up there on the wall and that's how that came about.

This took place in the very inner city in Detroit. They've got inner and outer schools in Detroit. They've got little cities within cities and Ferndale was inner city. Ferndale, Detroit, Michigan, a very mixed school, high incidence of racial incidents – you know – drugs were around but it was a good school and part of the job was to deal with all these problems. It was about helping teachers on one side and being a crisis teacher on the other side. Again it was about the value of the individual, and that, finding ways kids can create, getting their energy right so you can go from there. I then came over here. I think as I went along I felt – you know – giving people a good chance and buying time.

SR: *You get a buzz from that?*

KB: I got a buzz from it because I know from myself that one or two people along the way gave me a chance – like I said.

SR: *And do you see that same sort of experience influencing the headteacher period of your life?*

KB: Oh yes, I see it as a key thing in that and I think my favourite story in lecturing is about taking this kid that no one would take to go anywhere because he was very aggressive, very large, speech impediment, hearing impediment, and disciplined rough at home. This takes us back to Newcastle upon Tyne. The Royal Shakespeare. I took five children to see the Royal Shakespeare Company. I worked up differentiating the curriculum but I didn't know how to spell that then.

In my own mind, I took Paddy because I wanted to give him a chance, because, well no one would take him anywhere and everybody thought I was crazy doing that, taking him to see Shakespeare. It was 3½ hours long. I'd worked with him before that in class. I'd worked with Paddy on Kings and Queens of England and stage presence, and words, how the Tudors would understand the words. He sat there for 3½ hours until the ending scene where Richard was fighting one of his assailants and Paddy was quiet through the whole experience, he'd never before been to a theatre. At the end, where Richard was defending himself, Paddy jumps up and yells 'Get the Bastard!'

The actor, Howard, I'm not quite sure now who, smiled and looked up, and Paddy apologised and sat down. Now, now that for Paddy was what anybody else would have done in Shakespeare's time and that's how theatre used to be . . . yeah . . . and he got that, all of it in that experience. After that, from then on, I was able to build something more with Paddy, and that's a starting point, one of the key moments, giving a kid a chance. In a sense what I'm saying is that working with individuals is a key feature of this approach and the vision that we were talking about before. You can't get removed from the individual in any of this if you are going to be true to it. Another one of my pet sayings is that anything that you're true to, it sounds a bit heart-on-the-sleeve stuff, if you have the child at the end of your hand you can't go wrong – if you're doing it for that reason – you can challenge any officer on policy or practice.

SR: *In terms of your experience, let's focus on the headteacher bit. Could you track through your experience as a headteacher?*

KB: The experience began with Washington Hall School in Durham, a residential school for children with emotional and behavioural difficulties, a first headship. 1980 to 1984. Then I moved down to Cambridge and took up Lady Adrian School. It was an MLD School and that was from 1984 – and then I went to Birmingham University to lecture in special education in 1991.

The time in Cambridge, a period of around six or seven years, was when things really buzzed for a while – extending opportunity for kids at a school about the same size as Durants School, approximately 110, 120 on roll. We averaged, at our golden time, 50 children per week out in the mainstream setting. They were there at different times for their timetable but still based with me, which allowed us to extend their education, and the curriculum opportunity available, and then the National Curriculum came along.

SR: *The curriculum has been an interest for you throughout your career?*

KB: That's the heart of it, I believe, some people argue, I know, especially in the EBD field that if you can get the curriculum right in the sense of valuing individuals, their self-worth, self-esteem – you know – you've got there.

SR: *What of the old debate on care and education, particularly with EBD youngsters in mind? The need for therapy as against or in contrast to the need to teach – how do you see this?*

KB: I perceive that the curriculum can be the therapy. You can have therapeutic ways of handling educational material. It is not more appropriate, for example, in a special school for children with emotional and behavioural difficulties to run a specific therapeutic approach – say psychodynamic – instead of an educational approach. The psychodynamic stuff has its place given a training in psychology but I think a lot of times it is one of these things that you can get into a structure. I think that the children need a little more of a framework than only that of an openness of exploring feelings. We're here to teach.

SR: *Yes – that used to be one of my favourite sayings.*

KB: We are here to teach . . . we're not into social services and that stuff but that's not negating any of that because in my own writing I have supported the development of counselling skills and the personal approach. I think it must be stressed that it is a key and that's part of it. It's not the main part of it. It would be easy to be into an approach which is more about psychodynamic relationships anyway because you don't have to assess – you don't have to move on and learn. I can see the attraction of the more care-orientated approach. It can be more convenient – easier perhaps for those involved. Although taking a therapeutic approach properly is never really easy. But it takes the focus away from the challenge of educational development.

I think personally one of the things about therapy and everything else is really that the training base of individuals has been very low in this country, whereas, I'm not saying it's better in the States where I was trained but it is more pronounced there. I did my background. Psychology. I worked as a locum, like a doctor, in several psychiatric hospitals. You realized a depth of psychology and that gave you your framework. That's a base thing you got then, to understand children, to understand their behaviour, so that the 'normal behaviour' was part of your reference. I mean in my lectures on behaviour I always ask the question 'Whose behaviour?' – so that's what you're talking about when you get into dealing directly with behaviour.

SR: *I was interested in what you were saying about your first experiences of headship – let me ask you the question how and why did you first become a headteacher? I guess we're thinking back to Washington Hall School. How and why did you go for headship?*

KB: I felt people were working for the children and I felt there was a structure. I was there as a deputy and I saw that they were operating what I thought was a deficiency-based curriculum. It was reinforcing what the kids knew about themselves – what they couldn't do. The curriculum on offer was Maths, Art, PE and Art disguised as project work, that type of thing. It was whatever the teacher happened to know, or had an interest in, at that time. So you could have one teacher teaching German and in the Maths class too, that's right, until the teacher leaves and it would carry on year after year, you know, that was the difficulty with it. It wasn't planned. It wasn't organized, kids were drifting and again I felt that the behaviours they were showing were often because they weren't being stretched.

SR: *Now these youngsters would have already been identified as EBD?*

KB: Yes. They came from about ten authorities. It was a private school. Before

Washington I was in a state school in Sheffield. The reason I went into a private at that time was because there weren't that many jobs in EBD. The Sheffield provision was not a special school. The Sheffield 'school' was a project. I arrived over here on the boat with one suitcase and at that time it was one of the few jobs in town. It was IT [Intermediate Treatment].

I started by setting up IT in those days. Yeah. It was all about coming over to this country and social services and education – it was providing education in the project for IT and the idea was to get IT working in the community. The thing is – the only base they had was out in the Peak District – it was a hunting lodge. Yeah – intermediate treatment – it was wonderful. I had another colleague – we were both teachers in charge. We both worked through a community home in Sheffield. We worked with kids at risk and we both believed we had to do more for the kids than just sit around and talk. Kids at risk because of their involvement in crime, drugs, disturbing or disturbed behaviour, abuse. Everything a body could get or give – we had 12 children every 90 days. And we turned them around on a programme. We worked to re-establish relationships with the schools they came from to get them back after a fixed period of time.

SR: *I can see the progression with EBD work leading you, somewhat ironically, given your nationality, up to Washington, Co. Durham. Is that right?*

KB: My background training was emotional impairment in the States, that was my interest, the psychology of children. I saw the job as deputy at Washington developing the whole package, or that's what I thought I saw at the time but I got in there and found out that the Director was an entrepreneur. I left before he declared bankruptcy and returned to the state sector. I left to get out of the private sector and because we had got up to inspection standard. I had put a curriculum into the place, this was part of the previous question, you know, you were asking me if we needed the curriculum, I was giving it needed structure.

I provided a structure and it gave credibility to the school for those inspecting it – they knew where I was at with the curriculum. This was important to the Director who had to ensure registration with the DES through an HMI inspection. We were inspected several times. I left when the final report came through that accepted the school was efficient. I eventually left after I had looked up one morning and saw a stranger sizing up the car park. The future was looking uncertain and I thought it was time to think about a move.

SR: *So it wasn't dissatisfaction with day-to-day business?*

KB: No, no. The school was getting there. It was the motives which lay behind the operation, like the owner, he had it all planned as a profit-making business operation.

SR: *However, moving on from there down to Cambridge, linking it together, still the desire to be a headteacher, to see a school develop?*

KB: Yes – to take things forward – to shape the dynamics for children to learn.

SR: *Have you always felt as the head you had the power to do that, to shape the dynamic?*

KB: I basically had a belief. I always have had a strong enough belief for that to happen. I think possibly being American in some ways gave me a different edge in leading and influencing this kind of development because I was not being placed in certain roles as easily, you know, so I used it to create change.

I do not mean any disrespect, but, you know, protocol, tradition, all of that in the baggage. I have also had the experience of having something integrated – truly – so I had the confidence to say no I've been there, have you? It is perhaps that type of thing. And I keep going that way, without being bullish, without being entrenched on anything, without looking as though it's them and us. I am actually trying to be collaborative and co-operative.

In Cambridge it was easy. It was collegial. It really was and it worked. We had 19 schools which had really developed into a healthy relationship, and as part of that relationship, because we had a healthy one, anyone who started tampering with us – I didn't have to say anything – I had the secondary heads and the primary heads saying something. This involved the schools cluster called Heads North of the River – then we changed it. We called it Schools North of the River. Then we got into formal clustering and all of that and it worked very well.

SR: *Were you there when Cambridge brought in LFM and did that shake the collaborative nature of the cluster?*

KB: I was there in the early days. The group was very strong because it still worked on a collegiate basis, trying to share in non-competitive ways, maybe towards the end, now we're talking 1987, 1988, 1989, they started becoming formal, trying to work out collegiate Codes of Conduct. People were going grant maintained but they still tried to work out Codes of Conduct and they still wanted to keep it together based on co-operation. There was a strong sense of belonging.

SR: *What of the effects of recent legislation and reform? Do you think it's harder now to be an effective school leader than it used to be – I use the word 'leader' advisedly?*

KB: Oh yes. I think so because I feel you have so many other people to be accountable to and I'm not saying it's a bad thing. It's trying to work that relationship out because sometimes they want you to be managers of the setting and at other times they want other people to be empowered in the management of the setting. Perhaps there's an ambiguity that could develop in that but there's also the sort of thing that involves officers or other agencies who are being re-organized. They're often feeling threatened in their positions and the whole thing can be about empire building. You end up being over-managed yourself and responding to things that aren't actually moving the school along but instead actually justifying or keeping people in their positions.

SR: *Do you find it easy to discern between the two?*

KB: Yes but I usually talk to colleagues about that because I think you've got to be sympathetic to them. Just like you would for anyone undergoing stress, say, they're giving us a hard time, but they're just trying to justify their position and you've got to try and take that into account, just try to understand and it's easier to manage.

SR: *You mention accountability as being important. Are there any other aspects of leading a school today which, in comparison to Cambridge ten years ago, there's a big difference?*

KB: I think I'm seeing parents who are starting to feel more ownership of the setting, rather than being dragged into the setting. I think that's very good. Yeah, I'm a great believer in involving parents, because you're dealing, especially in the special school, with people who are trying to come to terms with their child's difficulties and the relationship and you need to remain very aware of the impact that has on individuals. It can be the case that when the professional gets involved parents get to feel totally de-skilled, overwhelmed by the experts and the procedures and the process.

I mean, for example, when you have them sitting down and more involved in the school, talking about what they want, their aspirations for a child, for their child, and they can begin to realize that they are actually being heard, that they're part of that dialogue, it empowers them that much more and the child moves on that much more quickly in their development. In that sense, the children feel the support of their parents, and the relationship is positive, and it helps the child in school. In a sense too we're much closer to parents than is customary in mainstream. Part of the reason for this is that it is a time thing, the time we've built in to allow for it. The thing is we've got that in place, it is accepted, and if there's anything that's special here, it's just that, if you're going to declare anything that is special, it's creating time for a closer and more involved relationship.

SR: *We've talked around the curriculum reforms and my impression is that you think they've not been a bad thing for special education but in terms of LMS and other reform, the business aspects of schooling, has it made a major difference?*

KB: Yeah – I'm running a site now, and I've got to consider the walls and maybe how we affect the neighbours. In the past, I would have just picked up the phone, but now I have to consider how we can sort the thing out, and how we can budget for it. I do the budgeting with the help of my two deputies and the school secretary. One of my deputies is skilled in finance and adopts a role of School Bursar. I also would say that the best thing about my time in service was my experience within accounting and finance. It actually gave me administrative skills. I was an administrative specialist for those years and it was good training. We're not actually sitting up at night doing the budget – not the day-to-day invoicing – but we shape the policy and planning and take it to the governing body.

We're so well caught up with computers and everything else, it doesn't take a tremendous amount of effort, you don't have to keep pushing pounds around. You have to start making judgements – we're lucky – this year we have a £23,000 carry forward. There's winners and losers in all of that – but when I first came here we found that the LEA owed us £40,000 and I got it back. It helped put me in a good position with my governors because we got it back and it was rightly carried over. There is a tendency to think parochially but I think individual schools can only look to themselves for a certain period of time. The thing is, again, like any institution, you can become too insular and you start to get right back to it, you back up on ideas, attitudes, dynamics and results.

SR: *There's a bit of distance, isn't there, between that as a reality now, and your vision, which seems to be very collaborative, very sharing, in its essence?*

KB: Well, what it is not is simply theoretical. It's about being, trying to realize a concept of affiliation with the community. We're affiliated to the secondary schools in this area and so we almost create ourselves as a branch or a subsidiary of it. We maybe need to create the financial models for the future as part of this organization. You are involved but retain your identity within their context, and it helps to maintain your viability because you're coming up with better provision. In this way you're not just using your staff but involving other staff and resources. I see it as collaboration, with people coming here and using us as a resource, for meetings, classes, a base or an outreach.

     Alternatively, there's institutional survival in this in some ways. It pulls on you, something like being attached to nine tails, nine cats, and you don't have to say anything. That's what we had in Cambridge. It was that kind of relationship. We were so inter-related. We ended up supporting 200 children in primary at Cambridge and, what do you call it, we had movement skills, which was part of the work we did at that time. We worked with disaffected pupils, helping pupils in other schools, helping our pupils, helping children with severe learning difficulties, our pupils working with primary children, disaffected pupils working with them and everything else. We put together this whole network, sixth formers coming in to our place. We upped the community tolerance for everyone and worked at any one time with over 200 people and I only had one member of staff for it. But then they started messing around with that, and they weren't really messing around with it to improve it, they were looking for financial things, but people still saw there was more value in that than there was to be gained in false economy.

SR: *In a sense too, is part of your vision for special education a definite notion of community and the idea, if you like, that this notion of inclusivity is one of the aims of special education, that is, to educate the community in a response to special needs?*

KB: Yes, that's right. It is about how to build up tolerance levels and alleviate prejudices and I think it can, as if say you're a Catholic standing outside a synagogue and you're wondering what's going on in there and you're trying to pass someone who says it's a school, the message is stay out, it's not for you, and that's why I think I'd like to lose the name special school, or the label special educator. I might call it a centre for learning difficulties.

SR: *But what happens to the nature of the school as it is turned into a centre? It's by definition something different – it means something different.*

KB: Again – its who you want to be in that, I think, who's it for and if you're serving the individuals and they're being educated within that and you're actually enhancing their opportunity – what's in a name? I mean, I do, I play around with it all the time. We are not special educators, but we are educators who work in special education. We've got to get that emphasis on education back. I remember a small bit of research by Christine O'Hanlon on this area of professional status. It showed that special educators are as marginalized as the children they work with in much the same way. There is a real problem of stigma, which special education has been wrestling with for a long time. We've got to move from that towards the inclusive idea. I'm an educator first. I've worked mainstream but I also have worked special and my interest is in special education.

I want to shift that thinking forward. When this starts to happen we begin picking up feelings of people in the community. In the same way, we work with parents and help parents' groups to work better, like the other night, we were identifying that if a child is having difficulties with special needs in the school and other parents are protesting that the child is too great a problem, how to handle the issue. I would get together with parents to talk that through as a group. To begin creating networks which offer support, create dialogue and inform further development.

SR: *You mentioned accountability as a big change just a moment ago, who manages you?*

KB: Who manages me? That's a good question. And again I could say the governors – they're getting more into a management position.

SR: *Who do you say manages you – specifically – does anyone?*

KB: Not really – you know what I mean. There are officers I respond to but I feel we're all working together in that area of management. There are certain things that go to the Director of Education, that they're responsible for, the authority's ethos for education. I feel somewhat of a free agent except for the need for keeping the chair of governors informed and making sure the governors are aware of my vision. I don't feel too structured. That was part of the job when I took it on here because I was asked because of my background in lecturing. They asked me, would I feel constricted, and I replied are you going to constrict me? If you are I don't want the job. I'm not the person for you. What you want is to make change happen here. In that case you've got to create the room to allow me to take it as far as I can – but – informing all the way. I see that as my responsibility – to inform everyone along the way. I do think I have a considerable amount of freedom but in a more general sense, I guess I am accountable to the officer of special education.

The education officer is one line manager, then you've got the assistant director, the area officer for special needs, but at the same time because we are in a new culture, I see them more working for me. Right now we're going through the shift. Mainstream schools have gone through this same process and now – they're autonomous – I feel because we, as a special school, have to work within the LEA mandatory requirements we still have that kind of half-way house scenario facing us.

I'm accountable to the governing body and they're the ones I do keep informed. I don't go ahead with anything until I've informed and let them know. I've got a very good relationship with the governing body, and the thing is, they see it's not just a theoretical vision. It's actually happening. The children are coming up trumps. It is like an acid test, and it's surely one of the most important measures we can use in school. If I use the term 'client' in discussion with staff, it helps their response in clearly seeing it.

SR: *In that sense – you mentioned the term 'vision' – I think you're talking principles, your educational values. What are the two or three basic principles which guide your thinking?*

KB: I use Maslow's list of assumptions, that is, everyone wants to be a part of it, everybody. I agree with the humanistic psychology which explains human motivation and so I think that's part of it, everyone wants to be valued in what you're doing and that you have to make sure you do that, not do anything at the exclusiveness of anyone. I'm a great believer in people's potential and that's what we're moving towards more here, now, empowering children and encouraging them to be in control of their environment and what's happening to them. I believe in this way, and taking that further, that I need to empower my own staff. They need to make their own decisions. The difficulty is that they in turn have genuine difficulty with that because I've given them opportunity and this sometimes hasn't worked. When I came here what I did in the first years was give them balls to run with, then I saw who carried them, who dropped them, who dropped them and picked them up, who never picked them up at all – you know – see who did what with it.

SR: *And then what happens Keith?*

KB: Well then you start getting down to tackling the difficulties in that, and me making an assessment about it and some people are historical – not historical, I can't phrase it. It is that they are at such a point in their career that you may not be able to move them to a new way of working, so, you've got to see what their strengths are and use that as a base strength so that you're not putting them under any extra stress. When they're not with you is the problem. To that extent I guess I am looking at strengths and weaknesses and working to the strengths while hoping to strengthen the weaknesses. The way to do this is to go with those strengths. It's like the Children Act. I always say to the staff we know the children's weaknesses. We have enough reports about them. The hard job is to go about finding the strengths, and so it's, it's orchestrating, orchestrating strengths.

SR: *That's an evocative word, orchestrating; paints a clear picture of working through other professionals. Now with all of that in mind, I mean, leading and managing people's performance – to sum up – what sort of leader are you?*

KB: A non-coercive manager! I don't try to manipulate people. I try to give them experiences that'll take them along, yeah. It could be seen that as you give experience it's manipulation but at the same time you're trying to give them a taste of the vision you have, trying to give them opportunity to share in that, including more realistic things, you know, that are in the short term with them being in control. I've got someone now who's doing team teaching out in mainstream in a six-week block – and the whole deal is that they won't have to do it again – but what they've done is come back saying it's really great and that'll encourage someone, lead on to it. I don't know . . . yeah . . . I think . . . it is the truth about management skills. Yeah, I do consult with people, but I do also feel that consultation does not mean you have to make a decision in line with that consultation, you know, I've heard everyone but this is how I feel and this is what we've got to do about it.

SR: *What kind of headteacher is Keith Bovair? What would the staff say?*

KB: I think they would say – we're not sure. They're still waiting for this change to happen and they're not sure about it. They're not really aware yet of that idea about the primary phase in school going out there. I keep them informed on the way but taking the primary out of school. I don't discuss that because it's not certain and is still with the Authority. I don't want to raise the anxiety level if it's not going to happen. I can manage the anxieties that will come with it if it is happening but if not, we're going to take them down the road again like they were for five years here before I came; it's got to be really happening.

SR: *Why do that?*

KB: Why do that indeed – so – they see me making decisions and not making decisions and that's because I know, I don't want to expend energy that maybe we're going to have to expend again in the future.

SR: *That's a general response but more specifically, on a day-to-day basis, forgetting the future for a moment, how would they regard you in the here and now?*

KB: Well. I don't know. I think they would see me as fair. I think they would have difficulty understanding my involvement in a lot of meetings and they would feel I'm out a lot and again that's the changing role of heads today. They might see some of this in a relatively negative light because they see the day-to-day stuff needing to be done. They see the figurehead there and that's the security blanket for them. Well, that's part of the cultural change in school management and I've got to live with that as they do. I know it's there. I think they would say I'm very fair. I do have an open door policy. The thing is, they say they see people use it, but some people use the door more than others, and some people don't use it at all. One way I find out what staff were thinking was to set up my appraisal. I set it up so they were interviewed about this new re-organization.

SR: *Did you find that helpful?*

KB: I put myself into it. I felt the reason I did it was to have the process demonstrated, to show that I'm open, open to the whole process. I used it deliberately to make a point. It was just to say, look we've got to be true to this idea of open working. I've put myself up front here and I will want you to do the same.

SR: *Just to round off on the kind of leader you see yourself as – I pick up from the last few moments this sense of you, a part of you, stepped back two or three paces, that's always looking for an angle, in management terms, a strategy, a way to move things forward, if you like, is that accurate?*

KB: Oh yes I think I'm a strategist but I think I am always trying to be a strategist in the most positive way but not a manipulative manager. I try to always remain positive. It's like anything. It's like my humour. My humour is never at the expense of anybody else. I don't favour the put down. I think it is important to have humour in the classroom but you don't use sarcasm. It's the same thing working with staff, it's that we're all doing these things, you know, I'm out there . . . too.

SR: *How important is the humour in everything you do?*

KB: One hundred per cent. Yeah. In a sense nothing's flippant but I feel. . . . Well, you've got to keep levity in these situations. It's a way of keeping balance, drawing perspective, maybe even drawing a breath? It also helps in communicating and understanding. I like to use analogies, it's like using sound bites. Maximum attention, impact and take the people with you. You have to be a person of many parts. You've got to hold people's attention and create active listening and participation, just like in the classroom. Sometimes it gets busy like recently we've got budget situations and we've got this re-organization and trying to get these ideas in place and you know when you haven't tended to those things you really need to get to, to reach and realize. It's the same with staff.

SR: *Do you ever get tired, do you ever sit in the chair at seven o'clock at night and put your head in your hands?*

KB: Oh yeah . . . I think everybody does.

SR: *You have your moments?*

KB: Oh gosh yes, yes – I had one the other night – it was after a meeting that everyone felt, well it's what I call the February meeting where everyone felt flat and tired. We have people off sick and ill. Everybody's been sick. Everybody's been covering for each other and everyone's a little bit nippy with each other about right now. It's what after ten years of headship I call the February Meeting. Everybody vented at me. All the angst. This is not working, that's not working, one deputy's out all the time, you know, the whole thing came out and that, what a meeting. I then had to go to a meeting and be proactive about the school. And I had to get the energy back. And then I . . . had to go home. I was tired. By the time I got home – you know living at Cambridge – it was 12 o'clock and I woke up in the morning my shoes were still warm – you know – because I had to get up at six. I came to work feeling a bit tired but everybody here was happy as can be because they needed that meeting. I think they felt that they could do that at the meeting.

SR: *Do you still enjoy being headteacher?*

KB: Yeah. I enjoy it. Yeah. I think . . . I think you've got to keep yourself together as an adult. It's sometimes hard to service yourself. Sometimes you want to respond emotionally. Or on occasion just try to make your own space.

I do feel it's this traditional thing about the old patriarchal position of the headteacher. It is the security blanket for staff, you know, you go out and the building starts to shake and the staff immediately see rainy break-times and restless kids reacting to an absent headteacher. It can't afford to be like that now and it's trying to get people up to that and give them a bit more power to take decisions. It's difficult though because a lot of people who worked the old model, they don't like that, they're afraid of that, so you know, I feel I want to be an adult again.

SR: *How do you perceive headship in mainstream compared to headship in special education? Are there differences? And if there are, what are they?*

KB: I think the differences are the extent of the curriculum organization and the access to certification to recognized qualifications. But still, if you're doing it properly, especially in a learning difficulty area, then you should be well aware of all the new developments NVQ, GNVQ, the National Curriculum itself. I feel that I am. This is what I've written about over the last few years. I'm now tackling the GNVQ in the same way as the National Curriculum and finding access to foundation courses. I don't know how other colleagues would be with that but when I left the States, I had had experience of acting deputy of a high school. I had that experience under my belt and I had a subject background in teaching English, so that's there, and yeah, I feel I could manage a large site. There might be a major difference for some colleagues because they have not easily gone down the National Curriculum route, and then they might find it difficult keeping several sections on the go, and the delegation might be a difficulty for them.

SR: *Are the roles really different, are they two different jobs then, being head of a special school and being head of a small comprehensive school?*

KB: In a small secondary school? I think . . . you get to know all the children in a small school whereas you'd have to recognize in a small secondary school that you might know pupils in time, but you'd have to accept the fact that you'd be more distant from individual children until they cropped up as concerns, or whatever, in the routine of the day. I think in the secondary school they are more sort of involved in the administration of education whereas small special school headteachers are like primary headteachers. That's a difficulty for special and primary. I mean that primary headteachers were traditionally also classroom teachers and they had management duties in addition to this 'primary' role but now they are managers – that's where there is pressure – that's why a lot of colleagues in primary are in difficulty – so – in the secondary school there's not the same tradition of role conflict or difficulty in management.

SR: *So in terms of a career development would you see the two routes still being parallel or separate? The idea of transfer between the two is not really possible or desirable?*

KB: I think there are limitations there if people allow themselves to travel too far down a certain avenue, and they haven't extended themselves in their thinking or practice.

SR: *So there is something special still about special. It is different?*

KB: Yes . . . it's the problem with special.

SR: *What would you regard as the special needs of a headteacher in special education? I'm assuming that there's something special still about the job.*

KB: I think . . . it's the depth of understanding of the dynamics individuals find themselves in when they're dealing with children who are having difficulties. Their own personal difficulties are a priority, I would say, parents, partners, or whatever and also to understand the complexities of the wider brief, the different systems we're operating in, because it's not just one single thing, it's not just about the individual child. Its about how you handle the situation. If you just handle the individual then you're not really going to move the child on and especially when they're no longer in an educational setting because it's an either/or situation. It's a contract. I think what you've got to do is work with both and that's the thing, it is about working relationships with parents.

Colleagues in mainstream are tackling the same issues but do not always have the same intention? A lot depends on the time element and the majority of contact I've seen in secondary school would be in parents' evening for a ten-minute slot and then you have the social events of the year which are again, short, superficial opportunities. I think Records of Achievements, and things of that nature where they sit down with individuals and talk about their role, and review it, give opportunities to have more depth for the individual child in secondary schools now and actually putting people in that position and I don't know whether that will be coming in more for the parent. I think the parent is more distant but not intentionally distant but it is nevertheless a distance, much more than you would have in a special setting. . . .

SR: *What differences did you experience in the transition from teacher to management?*

KB: I think, because of my past experience as administrative specialist and running an office at 20 something with 50 individuals, civilian and military, aged 21 or 22, I didn't have any difficulty with the idea of administration or the move from teacher to administrator. I also have my own work ethic because the approach in the educational profession in the States is that you recognize your route from teaching to administration. You are recognized as an administrator when you move into the higher positions, you are trained further for that kind of movement. There was no formal educational training. Preparation for headship was an accumulation of various experiences and maybe, to a large extent, my military service. I was lucky, although I didn't appreciate it at the time, having to get involved with the military. It was then that training was happening for me in an indirect way. I was running an office, having to work with budgets. I was in accounting and finance. That was a good grounding. I think all teachers should have some sort of experience outside an educational setting.

SR: *Would you opt for formal training for those who aspire headship or take on headship?*

KB: I think it should be more than a single element in educational training. Maybe it could take the form of something like the HEADLAMP initiative. An arrangement for induction and training. If you want to go to administration you train for administration and because I think it breaks away from this pull which headteachers have to resist that they should remain teachers. It creates a great deal of stress in the field. It's shifting now but I also think it gives recognition and acknowledgement for anyone else that you are an administrator. You know, you're not the symbolic teacher, the headteacher. The difficulty of that is that you have to also cross with that new role and teaching so that you still have a base, a knowledge of teaching, which helps you to make decisions around the educational table. I think you've got to have a good grounding. It's like an artist before they go abstract. They've got to have a good grounding in the use of colour and form before they actually go off . . . yeah . . . I think that's the thing.

I think the rationale for management training must be it will be applicable to what we're about, that is, team-building. And then what the future is going to be about. Vision – finding. What the school is going to be like, what you want for this institution, and then what we need to support people responsible for these positions. It is in a sense a form of frameworking. When you sit there and say right those are the skills you'll need, and I would give that to everyone and so they feel there's a purpose behind it. It is about drawing people together and as part of that to make sense of the purpose of education.

SR: *What kind of leader are you?*

KB: Positive. I think I'm a positive leader. An optimist. I've been described as dynamic by other people. I mean it sounds funny to describe yourself that way but yes, I am dynamic. I am a talker. I believe I can take people with me when I talk. I think that's the way I manage people? Taking them with me.

SR: *What happens when they don't see it your way or travel in your direction?*

KB: That's the trouble. That's one you always like to crack. You want to take everyone with you but sometimes you can't for a variety of reasons. It's not your agenda and they have other agendas for themselves. You recognize that and allow for that . . . that's a hard one!

SR: *Changing tack, could you describe how you manage resources and external relations?*

KB: I think . . . I get . . . try to get as much resources in place as I can. I try to enhance the resource, increase resources, like things you've seen as you walk around the school. The task is to enhance resources, to give teachers the best to work with, not to allow them to work with mediocre materials, and now all of that within the budget – sometimes you can do that. I manage external relations in the same way. I've got a good working relationship with officers, that is, because I'm positive. I offer what skills I have to enhance what they're about. It's like the person coming in today. They were looking for me to help get their INSET off the ground. It's got to be two-ways. That's the whole thing, my relationship with schools and getting this project off the ground is definitely two-ways! I'm very open, if people here need to use the resources and I feel it's part of the community – it's state education and I want them to have 'ownership'.

SR: *With all of that in mind – what would you say is the key priority facing yourself and colleagues sitting in the same position in special education? What's the key task?*

KB: How to operate the re-organization of special education – not how to operate it – how to handle it, how to deal with it, how to shape it, how to become engaged in it. The need for re-organization comes into play for a number of reasons. It's very much a consequence of Audit Commission Reports identifying that special education is expensive. We need to develop ways to measure the value of what you're doing. You need to make sure that what you're offering is of value. That's the challenge. It's to make us more proactive rather than more inward looking and segregated. It is the biggest problem we face because you're also working with limited resources.

The problem is with things being cut more and more, you feel yourself being exposed and you feel, before you can move into place concepts which will maximize resources, you might find that they have to cut back yet again and then they do not exist at all. While it might be fair to say this issue is about survival I would say that it's not the survival of the actual building itself but ensuring that resources and skills are there to meet the needs of individual pupils. In the re-organization, or in the dissipation of resources, it is important to maintain this effectiveness or better still, improve through change. Or we may see the closure of institutions have a negative effect, and it is important that the resource to meet the needs of individuals isn't dissipated because it has no focus. I want to save special education as part of that picture. I think there is a need for a sort of brokerage base to encourage good practice and to remind people that all individuals have a right of access.

SR: *Given all of that it seems fair to say we're in the centre of a complex flux – increasingly so – but if we focus on you for the moment, is there anything in the role you play you find especially difficult or thankless or even simply tedious?*

KB: I don't know, perhaps day-to-day decisions about where a plug should go, should we have new shower curtains and what colour should they be, dealing with things like that, for example, sanitary napkins and how to dispose of them, yes, things like that, and I'd sit there thinking I'd rather be doing other things. There are times when the job can seem tedious. I haven't felt uncomfortable very often, the problem really is just how to manage it. Yeah, how to handle it. I've had difficult staff. I've faced situations where I've had to make a decision whether to suspend a member of staff or not. To do that without demoralizing the individual, you know, because there's an allegation made, that type of thing. I mean how to handle that without losing that person amongst that, that's a little difficult, because you have procedures which dictate what you do but you also have an instinct about the dynamics and what's fair for everyone. Fortunately the decision, how I managed it, worked out well for everyone. It was a problem-solving challenge but I don't think, feel . . . there's anything I can't handle. I don't feel . . . it sounds silly . . . there's anything daunting in it for me. It's a problem to solve, a challenge to meet, not a threat to fear.

SR: *With that in mind – I'd like to ask what particular aspect of the job do you most enjoy?*

KB: It's when the kids come around and say they really like what's happening in the school. They come back from something they were unsure about and say – 'That was fantastic.' The kid coming into school who stops at the doorway, takes in a breath, and slips his shoes off because he sees new carpet on the floor. It is moments like this, behaviour which says they value where they're at, that's it, when the kids start valuing where they're at.

The hard thing would be when I hear a kid coming in not happy with where they're at. I feel I've got to see what I can do. There are moments when you feel a sense of failing if that happens, a sense of frustration? I'd put it down more to frustration and saying what do we need to do to re-organize things for this individual child, to make it better if they're unhappy, to ask why are they unhappy, it's frustration with finding time to 'unpack' it all.

SR: *Is the headteacher still an accurate description of your role and what others expect of you?*

KB: I think headteacher should be replaced by the term 'principal' as we use in the States. I think principal rather than 'head'. I think a principal is the key figure but I think it's an administrative role not the teaching role.

SR: *Is that what you're touching upon – the idea that the headteacher is the 'best' teacher but that this does not automatically translate into effective manager or administrator? There are different skills at work?*

KB: You should have good grounding to come to the position of headteacher. You should have demonstrated it but once you get there it doesn't have to be an expectation that you carry on with that because you've got to be out there more, wheeling and dealing, you've got to try and bring resources into school any way you can. In that sense it is like something I said earlier when I think you asked if I was a 'wheeler dealer'. I think it's part of my personality and maybe my style of management. I make people feel what they'll be involved in will be worthwhile, is of value, will be valued. There will be recognition of it with the children. There'll be a nice feeling from it because staff will see something from it.

SR: *Carries them with you as well!*

KB: Yeah . . . carries them . . . yeah . . . they'll be involved. Of course it's a two-way thing . . . I'm never just going to take.

CHAPTER 5

Roy Blatchford

In conversation with Peter Earley

PE: *How do you remember your own education and to what extent has that experience influenced what you've tried to achieve as a teacher and headteacher?*

RB: My own education had been following my father around. He'd been a headteacher of a primary and a middle school in his time and I went to three primaries, and a couple of secondaries, both of which were grammar schools. I don't think they were particularly strong grammar schools, but the thing that they gave me was the extra-curricular emphasis on, particularly, theatre and sport. So, in terms of formal education it's the extra-curricular I remember, in the sense this has always lived with me as a teacher. The other thing I would say, of my own early education, was that my father was a much stronger influence on me than any teacher I came across. He said whatever you do, don't go into teaching! . . . When you look at Damon Hill and his father's profession . . . you know how influential that can be. My brother's an accountant so he did follow the advice!

PE: *How and why did you become a teacher and headteacher?*

RB: When I left university I had always been very keen to follow my father's advice and not teach, so I went into publishing.

PE: *Which university did you go to?*

RB: I went to Reading University and did a degree in Linguistics.

PE: *Where was your father and family based at the time?*

RB: At that time they were based at Southampton.

PE: *So, it wasn't too far away, but far enough not to live at home?*

RB: I originally went for an interview in the French Department and I was not at all impressed by the calibre of the people who were interviewing me. Their spoken French was not as good as mine. I felt very despondent about that. I remember going back to my dad and saying 'I can't do that', so I ended up doing Linguistics, partly because I didn't know what it was and partly because of my interest in language, which I very much inherited from my father. The degree was very interesting, but as with so many things I did in my formative years – through 17–25 years – it was only later that I realized the richness of the experience. It's a case of university being wasted on the young! So I went into publishing: I was a theatre critic on *Time Out*; I translated for an international magazine, *Adam*; I worked for Haymarket Publishing. What I didn't like about publishing was being behind a desk five days a week. So I started truanting, taking long week-ends (as one discovers some teachers do before they leave teaching), and then I started doing some voluntary work in Brixton Prison. I walked in there one day interested in adult literacy and they took me on. Then I decided to go down to the local comprehensive in Brixton and started sup-ply teaching. And stayed!

PE: *You were able to teach without having a teaching qualification or PGCE?*

RB: I went in as an untrained graduate and quickly realized if I was going to make a career out of it, then I needed to do something. I followed an aca-demic diploma, part-time at the Institute of Education, and then an MA. I worked long hours in adult education and youth education at the week-ends and evenings, and really threw myself into education in all aspects. I kept the publishing and free-lance work going . . . that had always inter-ested me.

PE: *What sort of things were you writing about in your free-lance work?*

RB: Theatre reviews, book reviews – you may remember the old ILEA *Contact* magazine – I used to keep them going! So mainly book reviews and theatre reviews, and the occasional article about the politics of the ILEA, to which I was very drawn in my mid-20s. I just think the richness of what the ILEA offered – whether music centres for youngsters, or the English Centre for teachers (I was involved in probationary in-service with Cam-den and Westminster) – there was always something to do if you wanted to be the extended professional. I think that there was a great richness in those days, which I guess is no longer to be found.

PE: *Well certainly not in the same way, those kind of centres have largely gone. So, at what stage did you think about headship? Was it something that sort of crept up on you or did you have a distinct career plan in mind, once you'd gone into education as such, and you'd become qualified and had worked in several schools in London?*

RB: I was a Deputy Head of House in Stockwell Manor, then a Head of Year at Pimlico School, which had about 1600 children, multi-racial, multi-everything.

PE: *Who was the Head around that time?*

RB: Kathleen Mitchell, who had a strong vision about education and person-al/social education. This was in the mid-1970s. If I look back on my career I was never happier than when I was a Head of Year at Pimlico. I'd always interpreted that post as being head of their academic as well as their pas-toral lives. I was always resisting being labelled as a pastoral person or an academic person. The fact that I taught English and wrote of its practice, at least my self-perception was I had kept both the pastoral and the acad-emic going. That was a marvellous job, simply because of the range of children's ability at a genuinely comprehensive school. I was there for five years and I thought well, perhaps in order to be a head, I'll have to be a deputy head and I think it was that way round. So I looked for the experience – and I had some good guidance – to go to a different kind of school, having worked in two Group 12, mixed comprehensives in central London. In the end I went to William Ellis school, which was all boys aged 11–16, on the same campus as Parliament Hill, which is 11–16 girls, and a wonderful joint sixth form provision. It was a grammar school going comprehensive, even as late as the early 1980s.

PE: *Was it a deliberate decision to get a different experience to round out your c.v. if you like?*

RB: Yes, it was. Also at that time – 1982 – I remember thinking I should try outside London and did indeed apply for some deputy headships, but realized that both professionally and personally, I wasn't ready to move out of London. So I went to a very different sort of school and part of its attraction was the voluntary aided nature of it – there were very few like William Ellis which was the old direct grant school which had then gone comprehensive. Peter Newsam was on the governing body at that time, having persuaded the governors of the merits of comprehensive education! So I did a deputy head's job there, very much as a change agent. After four terms the head left to join HMI and so I had a period of acting headship.

PE: *Were you the only deputy?*

RB: No, there was one other.

PE: *You were given the nod, as it were, for being the acting head?*

RB: Well I think in the old style voluntary aided you were appointed as first deputy, and so I was appointed by the governors as first in line.

PE: *As first deputy, did you have both curricular and pastoral responsibilities?*

RB: The responsibilities were anything and everything! I've always said the role of the deputy head is what you make it. Even thinking back ten years, I don't think people were as clear about job descriptions then as perhaps they are now. As a former grammar school we had a deputy head (boys' discipline) and senior master (examinations). When I went there it was an opportunity to start trying to carve out new roles. In essence I had the 11–16 responsibility and my colleague 16–19, and we each deliberately had cross-academic and pastoral responsibility. As in all effective schools, there emerged team management, so we had experience of everything.

PE: *How did you prepare yourself for becoming a headteacher?*

RB: It was the range of schools that I'd taught in that was important, because within those there were all manner of issues: dealing with parents, staff, governors, community, politicians, councillors. At the same time you have to fit yourself to the particular school, you can't just say you want a different experience . . . I remember going to an interview thinking 'This is not for me.' In terms of preparing for headship, it is also about the extended professional role and I pursued a range of things, e.g. chaired the National Association for Pastoral Care Education in London, and was an external examiner for an ACCESS course at North London Polytechnic; I did a range of lecturing at Roehampton. I was deliberately trying to give myself some experience outside London, just to see what was going on outside the capital. I deliberately chose a couple of national courses to go on, outside the ILEA. I went to one at Bulmershe and an HMI COSMOS course.

When I had the acting head role at William Ellis, there was a great advantage for a term in being a head in a school you already knew. I'd already been there four terms, so I think an element of trust had come from other staff. They also knew I was only going to be a term in post and I didn't apply for the headship. It was keeping a well-oiled machine going. The staff were right behind me as long as they knew there were no new initiatives! In terms of bringing me into contact with governors for the first time, that was a really useful experience, particularly in a voluntary-aided school. It was there also that I first had to deal with a disciplinary case with a member of staff. I think that is the most difficult thing heads often have to deal with and it was very good to have gained experience of that. The voluntary-aided status again was valuable. I thought in the light of the William Ellis experience, that this local autonomy was the way ahead for schools and when I moved elsewhere I would play it accordingly; that is, the governors were the people who one is accountable/responsible to in the first instance, the local authority is second. That was certainly true of course in the voluntary-aided sector. In a way it anticipated much of what was to come with Local Management of Schools. I felt I was able to draw on that voluntary-aided experience immeasurably. If I had to say anything about training heads, if possible give them a period of acting headship. There's a serious point there for senior management teams: that point when you're alone to take the more difficult decision.

PE: *You didn't apply for the headship. Did you give that any serious thought?*

RB: No not at all, I thought this wasn't right for me. I had already begun to think that I wanted to move outside the ILEA because I knew that there was more to education than the ILEA offered, albeit it had provided tremendous in-service opportunities and support for me.

PE: *How well prepared were you for your first experience of headship? You mentioned the sort of opportunities you'd had outside of ILEA, in terms of staff development, INSET. Had you taken full advantage of what was offered to you in preparing for deputy headship, for headship and so on?*

RB: Yes, there had been some courses run by Doug Caldwell (Senior Inspector). You were almost head-hunted – there were groups of people identified. One year, about 15 of us worked on one of the Open University modules. We had to write assignments and we came together for some in-service – probably two or three days a term – meetings with other people from across the ILEA. That kind of provision, I think, was excellent, an early forerunner of HEADLAMP perhaps?

PE: *That was, if you like, selecting or inviting people . . .*

RB: Yes, you were kind of spotted . . . in a way that the ILEA had to be seen to be doing it in an equal opportunity way, but it was on recommendation from your headteacher or divisional inspector. Within the ILEA, there were opportunities to take you out of your own school environment – my work with new teachers meant you found out what probationers were doing across the division. That opportunity was marvellous. I guess that as that has fallen away then there is more the need for such initiatives as the HEADLAMP programme. It's about being a self-starter and looking for those opportunities. If you're lucky also you'll have a head who is keen to help. I hope I've learnt to carry that on with my own deputies.

PE: *Did you find that was the case with the heads that you had at William Ellis and Pimlico and other schools that you worked at? How much did you learn what to do, or perhaps what not to do? Were there significant role models or significant influences on your own professional/managerial development?*

RB: I have worked with seven headteachers, and you do learn. I remember one of them saying to me 'Well, you'll watch me, you'll watch me make mistakes and you'll go elsewhere and you won't make these same mistakes but remember you'll make your own!' I always remember that! And I can think of people that I've worked with from whom I learned a great deal about what to do and what not to do, in the certain knowledge that you're going to make your own mistakes. I can think of working with Katherine Mitchell at Pimlico whose vision about education in an inner city context in the mid-1970s was inspirational. Even though her own way of running the school would not be mine, the ethos which emanated throughout the school from her sense of excitement and educational vision was tremendous.

I can think of someone else I worked with whose values in education were very explicit in all he did and again I think that rubbed off on me. Another head I worked with believed very much in (I used to call it 'fudge' when I was being critical) 'phyletic' development. It was really like one of those great spider plants that goes in all sorts of directions, in other words whichever way the school grows that's the way we're going! I could see even in that particular context: don't go in to a new school with a fixed way of doing things. I can think of another head whose attention to administrative detail was second to none. And the way he prepared staff for an HMI Inspection was a seminal experience in my career. I learnt a lot from him. I think the one thing I really learned is that you need amongst your senior management team someone who is good with people and someone who is good with paper. And unlikely to be the same person!

PE: *So, those experiences were obviously important. When you decided to go for headship, had you at that stage decided you were going to work outside of London, and can you tell us a little bit about the first applications that you put in and your first successful post.*

RB: I did actually apply for a couple of posts in inner London and got down to the final three and it's fair to say that in one of the cases I would've liked the job and in another case I talked myself out of it. I think it was after the second experience that I thought I do want a change. It was partly wanting to have a different perspective on school and education, allied to the fact that I felt increasingly frustrated with the separate empires of 5–19 education, adult provision and youth provision, even though it was in Peter Newsam's notion of education for the whole community. I had worked in all of those sectors and wanted to come to a different environment, where community education – 'the cradle to grave' – was found. I felt very strongly about trying to develop community education and therefore did look at Cambridgeshire and Leicestershire. Then some posts came up in Oxfordshire and I applied for three headships which all came up together. Partly, I was persuaded by the Brighouse rhetoric about community education. I liked his educational values and I'd also heard – and since found it to be true – that it's a very hands-off local authority. As I now say, if every school in Oxfordshire opted out no one would really notice.

PE: *What kind of leader do you see yourself as?*

RB: That's a notoriously difficult question favoured by interviewing bodies. I think those I've worked with ought to be asked that question. Our OFSTED report said the school is 'purposefully led, by a committed and energetic headteacher who is supported by an able senior management team of three'. Now my deputies said it should have read 'who is restrained by the senior management team of three!' Of course, you never know with an OFSTED report whether 'committed and energetic' are damning with faint praise. I hope the school is purposeful. Paraphrasing Tom Peters, who talks about 'hands on, value driven', I've always thought of my style, whether I've been an English teacher or head of year or headteacher, as 'hands on, values driven'. I'm convinced about what children require from school in terms of basic discipline, structure and expectations. I have a conviction about what children require from education. I also believe strongly that the best teachers remain children at heart. My style of leadership is constantly to recognize that. I shall continue a headteacher as long as I choose at lunchtimes to watch children rehearsing for a pantomime or 'Blind Date' rather than sitting in the office looking at the latest budget cuts. If I ever felt that my inclination was taking me that way, I would realize that I would've lost the heart of what I believe in.

PE: *It probably would be better for me to ask other people that question, but if I were to go down the staffroom and interview a cross-section of staff . . . what kind of leader do you think they'd see you as? If I could use the terms: facilitative, transformative, would they be the sorts of ways that they would describe your leadership style or you as a person? Or would I get different views from different people?*

RB: No, I think you'd probably get similar views from most staff who would probably say that it's quite 'hands-on' but not in an interfering way. Possibly, some might say interventionist. What I did learn from my father was that what people most value is your time. I think that's how people would see it, but there again, I remember once saying, you could take two headteachers, equally good and one never leaves her room and one who is never in her room. So I don't think I would say there are obvious ways of doing it but I would say in my case they're less likely to find me in this room. It's the 'hands-on' aspect, whether that's on the corridors or in the classroom, that I love each day.

PE:　*Does that mean you're on site most of the time? What time would you normally get into work and go home if there wasn't a governors' meeting in the evening?*

RB:　Well I normally get in at quarter past seven and open the post, which is always a good time to get rid of the admin by 8 a.m. I live about 20 minutes away.

PE:　*Your secretary doesn't filter any of that for you . . . you get the dross as well?*

RB:　No, I like to know what's going on . . . I'm also in free-lance publishing remember . . . so yes, I do that from scratch. It's very quiet then and I don't answer the phone before 8 o'clock. From 8 a.m. to 8.30 a.m. before we start I'm either around the corridors or meeting with staff.

PE:　*And at the end of the day?*

RB:　We finish school at 3.45 p.m. I would say most evenings, other than Friday, there are meetings perhaps that would go on until 5.30 p.m. If there are governor committee meetings or PTA meetings and so on, then I would probably be here most evenings until 7 p.m. and many evenings through until 9.30 p.m. That's a choice I make because I like spending the time here.

PE:　*So, the findings from the workload survey that the School Teachers Review Body recently did – which said secondary heads do 60 to 62 hours a week on average – that would sound like a slight underestimation?*

RB:　Yes but I think if you're in the profession . . . I usually come in on Saturday mornings unless I'm at a conference or something like that, I come in and watch the rugby and the football. I do a disco, one Friday a month here, and just do a couple of hours on the door, those sorts of things, take students to the theatre . . . as a professional those are the hours you do.

PE:　*Certainly your staff wouldn't question your commitment to the school, in terms of the amount of time you were putting in . . .*

RB:　Yes, they would see me as someone who puts in the time. I think that's because that's the way that I can best do it . . . I've worked with headteachers who didn't need to put in that level of time to get the same level of respect from staff.

PE:　*That's the way you choose to operate. One could talk of a more effective use of your time.*

RB:　I'm not saying that if you're here for 80 hours a week that every minute of those 80 hours is effective.

PE:　*That's the way you choose to operate, it's part of your leadership style. Is it harder to be an effective school leader than it used to be and if so in what way and why?*

RB:　If we're comparing it with 1986 when I started being a head, or 1983 when I had been an acting head for three or four terms . . . then I don't think it's actually changed in terms of 'Is it more or less difficult?' over that period . . . I think it's just different. And as I said earlier looking back on the heads that I've worked with, they were all effective or less effective in different ways. Some did give an enormous number of hours to the school . . . others were good thinkers, good with their paperwork or good with people or whatever it might be. I don't think it's any more or less difficult to be effective now if you believe in what you do. It goes back really to the values. The moment you feel you're not happy with those values then . . .

I'd like to give you a couple of quotations that I've used for a review and development plan. One is from Robert Frost, the second from a naval magazine. The poem from Robert Frost reads:

> . . . why abandon a belief
> Merely because it ceases to be true.
> Cling to it long enough, and not a doubt
> It will turn true again, for so it goes.
> Most of the change we think we see in life
> Is due to truths being in and out of favour.
> As I sit here, and often times, I wish
> I could be monarch of a desert land
> I could devote and dedicate forever
> To the truths we keep coming back and back to.

And the second:

> Two battleship assigned to the training squadron had been at sea on manoeuvres in heavy weather for several days. I was serving on the lead battleship and was on watch on the bridge as night fell. The visibility was poor with patchy fog, so the captain remained on the bridge keeping an eye on all activities.
>
> Shortly after dark, the lookout on the wing of the bridge reported, 'Light, bearing on the starboard bow.'
>
> 'Is it steady or moving astern?' the captain called out.
>
> Lookout replied, 'Steady, captain,' which meant we were on a dangerous collision course with that ship.
>
> The captain then called to the signalman, 'Signal that ship: We are on a collision course, advise you change course 20 degrees.'
>
> Back came a signal, 'Advisable for you to change course 20 degrees.'
>
> The captain said, 'Send, I'm a captain, change course 20 degrees.'
>
> 'I'm a seaman second class,' came the reply. 'You had better change course 20 degrees.'
>
> By that time, the captain was furious. He spat out, 'Send, I'm a battleship. Change course 20 degrees.'
>
> Back came the flashing light, 'I'm a lighthouse.'
>
> We changed course.

Essentially the point of these quotations is that there are, on the one hand, truths that keep coming back and back, which you hold on to if you want to be an effective head. But equally there are some things, like in the story, which sometimes really challenge your assumptions and that you've got to be careful they don't really deflect you away from what is your core mission. I think the great thing in headship over the past seven or eight years that I've been doing it, is that it has been endlessly refreshing. When I came here from a voluntary-aided school, we were just beginning to think of greater autonomy for schools; we've had LMS, delegated budgets, appraisal and National Curriculum issues and it has been endlessly refreshing. As Goethe wryly observed: 'Everything has been thought of before. The problem is to think of it again.'

PE: *The NFER headship project I'm involved in has asked our cohort of heads, whether or not they feel they have sort of 'plateaued out'. The response in the main has been similar to what you've just said, that there have been so many fresh challenges or whatever, that they simply haven't had time to sit back on their laurels and take things easy.*

RB: Yes and this school itself has been gradually increasing in size, so it's not been a difficult issue in terms of managing contraction, the budget is looking reasonable and so on. The future promises to be a little more difficult.

PE: *What is your vision for your school and how do you try to achieve this?*

RB: Perhaps I can use a quotation from the 'Three Wise Men' report and though aimed obviously at primary schools, I often use this when I'm working with colleagues, particularly with primary heads but also secondary heads of department. It says: 'The headteacher should lead by example. They may not have timetabled teaching commitments, but all teachers should teach. Actions speak louder than words and the headteacher's teaching, can and must exemplify their vision of what the school might become.'

I can see how that phrase was aimed at people in primary school. What I've tried to say about it for secondary heads is, what word can you substitute for the word 'teaching' in that quotation? I would probably go back to my rather 'hands-on' approach. The teaching for me is personally quite important. And how I try to achieve a vision is also by making sure I am in and amongst the children and teaching them.

Can I just say that I feel my vision about community education has always been a little stifled by local education authority structures and strictures – I think it is still quite difficult genuinely to realize the 5–19 or 'cradle to grave' continuum because of separate empires that operate in local education authorities. It isn't a green field site. I certainly have a vision for the children and the families that are here, the staff, the buildings and resources. And I have a vision of where those should be developed. I do believe in the local democracy that comes through local authorities of some kind, but I find some of its strictures quite inhibiting. I believe that secondary schools would raise standards in all sorts of ways, if they were independent of LEA control. I certainly have a vision for raising children's self-expectations – my core vision if you like – and I think implicit in that are teachers' expectations of pupils. And I'm particularly interested in the vision that there is a wider world beyond your own classroom or town. I guess wherever you work a teacher should be about widening those horizons for young people. I hope we do that through assemblies and all sorts of initiatives. Clearly, any vision for a school is about raising achievement and it goes back to the values about how you define achievement in the broadest sense.

It's interesting to think of Howard Gardner's forms of creativity and intelligence and how we champion these in schools. How do I do it? I would say: 'hands-on', and putting in the time. Also, you appoint the right people and you achieve your values through them. If those values have not been celebrated I can only blame myself. One thing I would mention is the importance of self-criticism. It was interesting that when we had the OFSTED inspection, one of the action points was 'to introduce more formal procedures at all levels for monitoring, evaluating and reviewing the school's values statements, in order to test their implementation and to test their strengths and weaknesses more effectively'. OFSTED appreciated we had high values but they questioned whether I was testing them in a systematic way. For example, if you say you are a family school, what does that mean for the Head of History; if you say you are a learning school what does that mean for the Head of Year 8? As a result I picked that issue up as part of my own appraisal this time around. It was very useful to have the OFSTED inspection say 'You have these high values, you have a clear vision, are you sure they always communicate to everybody in the building'. Looking through the Investors in People documentation also highlighted that.

PE: *Yes . . . to what extent the staff are aware of the vision, as expressed in your mission statement or whatever . . .*

RB: Remember when OFSTED arrived and said 'Do you have an equal opportunities policy statements?' I said 'No, we don't but equal opportunities I hope, permeates all that we do.' I was really heartened to read in the final OFSTED inspection report the phrase 'equal opportunities permeates the school' and I would like to feel that those values and vision do permeate, but I suspect that the reality is that they don't all the time.

PE: *I'm interested in the fact that you teach for a third of your time. Clearly that does reflect the way that you enact headship, you see yourself leading from the front. But conversely people might argue 'What are we doing employing a highly paid principal for a third of his time to teach kids, when we could get any half-competent teacher in.' Your job as principal really is to motivate the staff rather than motivating the children. I think from what you're saying you'd want to do both and you achieve both through the staff, but how would you respond to that, to what is quite a high proportion of your time, a third isn't it?*

RB: Maybe I'm not using resources most effectively. I'd agree that's a very fair question. I'm always interested when I'm talking to someone like yourself, or inspectors, to have such questions raised. Also I worked it into my appraisal last time around. The conclusion that we came to then was about time management. I think you have to ask yourself what would you be doing with that time. Some headteachers might spend that time doing paperwork in their office which I might do at another time.

PE: *That's the thing that I've noticed from your comments . . . a third of your time is a third of your timetable not a third of your time . . .*

RB: It has to be said that I have been told by the senior staff that I mustn't teach more than that. Often it's a pragmatic issue on the timetable about having an extra French set here, for example. I've always wanted to teach a GCSE examination group so that I know that when it comes to discussions about workload and marking, I know what it actually means. We have a whole-school PSE programme that I feel it's important that everybody teaches because that's again part of the values that everybody's involved in. But I wouldn't deny that a headteacher I greatly respect in Oxfordshire doesn't teach at all and says that's how he best manages and I'd go along with that.

PE: *What sort of timetable teaching commitment would your deputies have and say your middle managers, heads of large departments or faculties?*

RB: The deputy heads would just have under a half timetable and the HoDs would have something like 24 lessons out of 30. Average teacher contact time is 0.78 which is a lowish average, and I think with potential educational cuts ahead that might have to be raised. It is a very fair question and it remains an open question for me. About two years ago I decided to do less teaching in order to look particularly at differentiation. I did a bit more supply teaching as some heads do and I did some systematic work on Year 9 differentiation and lesson observation.

PE: *How do you manage people? How do you manage resources?*

RB: I'd like to raise something here that you brought up earlier and it refers to the role of the senior staff team. When I was first appointed here I did have a senior staff. There were four of us who sat round the same table, although I think it would stretch definition to say it was a team! It was a group of people, professionals but we didn't necessarily hit it off as a team in the way the present team does and that has been in operation for about four years.

PE: *They were all appointed by you?*

RB: Yes, two externally and one internal. I think the great thing about that team is that we are privately very critical of each other and publicly loyal. I would say in response to the questions 'How do you manage people?' and 'How do you manage resources?' that we do that together and I could not separate out my management from the team's. For example, when we had a meal last week and I sat alongside my secretary, the deputies and the bursar, the six of us were talking, reviewing the term, the financial accounts and so on, and it was 'writ large' there for me how many things go on in the school that I don't have the same touch on as others in the management team do.

In terms of how we manage resources and people, we have done that significantly through appraisal and mutual observation. There's a lot of give and take in managing people . . . we use postcards to each other rather than memos! There are lots of different ways, but again it's about time. I've described myself as quite hands-on. I think that's also true in people terms. You have to learn by doing and I was much less confident with people in 1987 than I hope I am now. Although I said we are 'hands-on' we do run a system here of devolving resources to the various cost centres. I'm very 'hands-off' with that, because I do believe that if you've appointed the right people, then they're being paid a reasonable salary to manage a team of people.

PE: *And if we look at the delegation to the middle managers, do you think that they manage people and resources in the way that you would want?*

RB: I'm sure in any school that the heads of department and heads of year are as consistent and inconsistent as the senior staff team are. I think at our best we're good and at our worst, we're average. I don't think we're below average. I think people respond well to delegation; there are clearly some individuals who handle that less well and need a lot of pressure and support.

PE: *You made a statement a moment ago that you are able to manage some people better than others and you put this down to a combination of factors . . .*

RB: I think what I'm trying to say is that I recognize . . . that I naturally get on with some people and others you have to work hard at. I think that's where the strength of the senior team is. It was very interesting when we were looking at appraisal, although we have this system of negative preference here nobody said they did not want to be appraised by the person suggested. As a senior staff team we clearly linked ourselves with people with whom we would best get on and get the best out of. Over a period of years I've had, on occasions, to say some sharp things to several members of staff . . . we've made a judgement in relation to appraisal it was thought better if somebody else appraised them. Appraisal has worked well here.

PE: *In terms of your own appraisal, and appraisal of other members of the SMT, was there mutual observation of teaching or did the appraisal focus more on management issues?*

RB: I think it was a requirement – whether it was our internal requirement or based on the DFE ones I can't recall – but we did say that even at head and senior teacher level, we would look at teaching because we feel that's very important to all of us.

PE: *What part do you play in enabling more effective teaching and learning?*

RB: I'd like to make a couple of references in relation to this question. I've been involved in writing some material on the effective teacher. I'm particularly interested in looking at how classrooms are managed (see p. 31 of *Effective Teaching* published by the National Primary Centre, 2nd edition). I'm very interested in looking at the teacher as provider, entertainer, actor/actress, learner, listener, language user. At the back of the book there is a checklist for the effective teacher and that material was worked up based on observations in classrooms. I do feel very strongly about trying to bridge that primary/secondary gap. How do you enable more effective teaching and learning? I think you do this by making this a core focus in whatever you're doing in a school by way of reviewing. I've noted down class size (which is the key resource), setting by ability, in-service, mutual observation, primary/secondary interface. In relation to all of those I like to feel that you allow teachers to decide the best modes of working, in languages or science or whatever, but that you lift the carpet regularly on that practice. And you intervene if you feel that quality teaching and learning are not being delivered.

PE: *How do you manage external relations?*

RB: The more you see, the more you perceive you aren't doing what you should be doing! As far as external relations go, I'm good on those who come to see me, but I'm less good on those who I need to go and see and be more proactive about. I know many heads who are and do that very well, and maybe it is a weakness of myself and the management team. We're good on the campus but perhaps we don't go out enough to see local employers and journalists.

PE: *Do you have much contact with other heads? Do you attend meetings of Oxfordshire heads?*

RB: I'm very committed to the Bicester District and the primary/secondary partnership. I feel very at home here because I do feel it has a distinct identity. I also like it because it's gender mixed. I do not like the male clubability of any secondary head gathering. Because I have a very good senior staff team, and I also have a fairly good network of educational contacts, I personally don't feel the need as an individual headteacher to go and sit in a row with other heads and talk about the state of the nation. I feel very strongly that any organization that would only allow the head to attend and won't allow the deputy head to attend is mistaken. It's crucial that deputies can attend although there are other heads who will argue against that. They will state 'No, it's the head who must go because she/he has the final say.' Well, I've never been to a meeting and made a final decision at that time. I've come back to the school and discussed it and by definition I really think the senior staff should be able to do the same thing. I feel quite strongly about that in terms of the professionalization of our work.

PE: *In terms of insularity, you mentioned it's more a matter of people coming here than you going out, but because of the contacts you have and the other work you're involved in, would I be right in assuming that you wouldn't regard yours as an insular institution?*

RB: Definitely not. Because we make an effort to work with researchers, publishers, the media and so on, and particularly the various Departments of Teacher Education. We have a lot of visitors here – ask the children! – and I think that's absolutely essential.

PE: *Who manages you and to whom are you accountable? I suppose in strict line-management terms, you would be accountable to the Chair of Governors and the Director of Education?*

RB: In thinking about this question I was reminded the other day by one of the governors – I think I was being pretty critical of a decision by the Chief Education Officer – and I said 'Well, you know in the end she employs me'; and the governor said 'Remember always I employ you.' He was speaking as a county councillor. As far as accountability and the Chair of Governors is concerned, I like referring to when Graham Taylor was manager of Watford Football Club and Elton John was chairman. Graham Taylor said 'We have this understanding, Elton and me, he tells me nothing about football, and I tell him nothing about music.' Correspondingly, a chief executive of a large company was asked what he wanted from the chairman. He said 'I like the chairman to have an extremely demanding and full-time job. Somewhere else and a long way away from me!' So, to that extent, yes I think I am accountable to our chair of governors here.

In truth, I am managed by and accountable to the usual list that you'd come up with – governors, parents, councillors, the auditor. I'm managed by the secretary, the bursar, the senior staff team, the classes I teach, and, in a sense, by the last parent I've met and who has put me in my place! For example, I've got a letter here from a complaining customer received earlier this term. I'm a great believer that you should see your institution as your complaining customer does. The letter reads 'Dear Mr Blanchford (sic) . . . I was both amazed and annoyed on reading Robert's timetable for this year when I read that the poor child has to do more cooking. He's already done two years and nearly everything he's cooked has gone in the bin because my wife and I consider his offerings inedible. As he hates the subject we will not be sending him to school with any ingredients.' It continues 'Now, as Robert, (and going on the school leavers currently being employed in my factory I'm sure he's not alone), cannot form a sentence, his spelling is generally appalling, surely would it not be more practical to employ another special needs teacher, hopefully at the expense of an HE teacher, to improve these basic skills? I'm sure cookery is not taught at schools like Eton. Also there are literally thousands of cookbooks if one is so inclined.'

And my answer was to invite the author of the letter to the technology department to show him round.

Returning to the question about who manages you, I think those sorts of critical letters and phone calls are about day-to-day accountability. In terms of an annual account, this is done through the auditing, and through the governing body more formally. I would have to say that these days one doesn't have a great sense of being accountable to the local education authority (who or what is the LEA?) but to the collegiality of Oxfordshire, to teachers in Oxfordshire. I think one's accountable to them, particularly in relation to, say, something like employment practices and equal opportunities to make sure you're doing things fairly.

PE: *It's interesting that in your comments above you haven't mentioned OFSTED, especially as you're a school that has been OFSTEDed. Would you include OFSTED as a body to whom you are accountable?*

RB: No, I wouldn't. But I think from the conversation we've had this afternoon I've mentioned OFSTED several times, so it may be an omission on my part, but I wouldn't mention it explicitly. But I would see that now as an important part of the system which has helped move this institution forward in the 12 months or so since we began the preparation. I have respect for much of the operation.

PE: *How do you enable others within the school to lead?*

RB: I remember when I was at William Ellis, we asked at a HoD's meeting, how do you extend the able child, and the head of Classics said, 'Oh, well you teach them Greek.' And I could say, as glibly probably, that the best way I enabled others in this school to lead, was that I went on a one-term sabbatical and gave the senior deputy an opportunity to do the acting headship. The other thing I would say in response to this question, and we haven't touched on it before, is the size of school and the length of headship. They are I feel key determinants and I'm not sure that I would necessarily be as effective a head of a school of say twice this size, with 2000 students rather than 1000. I would probably find myself – and I have talked about this to another headteacher as part of his appraisal – as missing out on some of that 'hands-on'. So I think the question about how you enable others in the school to lead, is very much about size but also about the length of headship.

I would say that getting the pressure/support equation right in your early days is much more difficult. You have to be alert to when people are outgrowing their roles and, where possible, either 'kick good staff out' or look within the institution where you can move them around in some way.

PE: *Is that proving to be more difficult now than say when you started in 1986?*

RB: Possibly. In my first three or four years here we had almost a complete turnaround of staff. Since then there has been relatively little movement. Last year only two staff left. I think one of the challenges here, that came up in my appraisal, is (a) How do you keep yourself fresh? and (b) How do you keep staff who are in the system, and haven't experienced another school, keep them fresh, and not tired. It's important to be alert when they've outgrown their roles and want to move on. Again, I'm deeply dependent on the senior staff team to pick that up for me as well as my being aware of it. It's also important to appoint some staff who you know are ambitious and likely to move on after a few years. Stability must never mean stagnation.

PE: *More and more of what we're saying does remind us of the importance of having effective deputies working with you and that the notion of leadership is very much a kind of collective leadership.*

RB: Very much so; I'm not sure how true that is in other walks of life, but I know it to be true from experience in school management.

PE: *You often hear and read a lot about the collegiality that exists in schools. Your role as an educational leader certainly seems to have been facilitated by the fact that you have a good team of people around you?*

RB: It's important to assert that they are not a group of clones. You have to be brave in interview and make sure you are going to appoint people who are going to challenge your views and be different and have different strengths.

PE: *Of not having a poodle but someone who says 'Hang on, do you really think that . . .'*

RB: I think that is part of it. I would say gender balance is important, crucially, I think that is my number one criterion. But I think also I would try and make sure you've got a combination of those who've been in the school a long time – who can say we've been there, done that, why should we try it again – and a mixture of people coming from the outside. But equally important I would recognize, particularly where I sit at the moment, that it's important for me to move that senior team on and not let us become complacent. Two of those people should move on to headships for their own sake and probably for the school's sake.

PE: *Has any member of the SMT over your time here gone to headship?*

RB: Yes, and I think two of them will soon go on to headships. It's important I move them on.

PE: *It's all so important isn't it to have that sort of turnover of staff?*

RB: It is but it's difficult for the head, who feels well protected by the excellency in the team!

PE: *What kind of a leader are you?*

RB: This seems to be very similar to an earlier question! Is this a psychometric test where you ask the same question in a different kind of way to check on a person's response? Am I going to be tested here on my response?!

PE: *Have you ever undertaken any of these psychometric, or competence-based assessment tests? In Oxford, as you know they've got the education assessment centre. Have you ever been involved in these?*

RB: Yes, the ones that we've done here at school have been as a senior staff team, where we've done them as an aspect of in-service. We thought we would do it as an exercise.

PE: *You have actually used the SHA materials?*

RB: Yes. My deputy and I – again this is part of keeping yourself fresh – had been running 'Preparing for Deputy Headship' courses for other Oxfordshire middle managers, and as part of those, we used psychometric tests, just to see how we would do as teams of people. Basically we were encouraging them to go back to their schools and use them in teams. And we've used them here with Year Tutor teams. I think we were using them really to ask 'Are we making sure that we are questioning each other's values?' Were we staying fresh and not just reinforcing each other's prejudices?

PE: *Is there any part of your role which you find especially difficult and/ or do not like?*

RB: I've said it before but 'You don't know what you don't know' and I honestly can't think of more than one or two things that I find especially difficult. Would it be worth asking one other person, say a senior staff member, to write some notes about what I find difficult? It would be quite interesting, particularly in the collegiality of a senior staff team.

I used to find disciplining teachers difficult. It's particularly hard in your first year, when who are you to say, but at the same time one knows if you don't get that done early on . . . I've found people saying if you don't 'weed out' early on you don't do it later. I actually haven't found that. But it's never easy; essential, yes.

The only thing I really don't like is Sunday night's marking! Yesterday, I spent a whole day marking which had its good points because I was looking forward very much to giving the work back, but in terms of the time commitment, which I can only do at home, I find that hard. English and French both involve a fair bit of marking.

PE: *What aspects of your role do you most enjoy?*

RB: Writing governors' reports I really like. I like being with children in classrooms, the corridors, and extra-curricular. I like assemblies, and that I think comes back to my values. Sometimes you can hear a pin drop in the hall and I know the children are thinking. I like sharing our values as an institution and our successes outside school. The great thing about being a head here is the independence to be involved in a range of activities beyond the school. It's a matter of not being insular – that's what I really enjoy as well. The work for SCAA, with primary colleagues, conference addresses or whatever. That's not to say I still don't find if I'm out for a day something hasn't happened that requires headteacher intervention. You can probably believe you're indispensable even if you aren't!

PR: *Is the term 'headteacher' still an accurate description for what you expect of yourself and others expect of you? Is it time we joined the rest of the world and called our school leaders 'principals'?*

RB: I had to consult the dictionary on this! The term 'principal' in the Collins dictionary is defined as – 'first in importance, rank, value – chief'. If we're talking about the headteacher who is the principal who is first in importance, what does it actually mean? And rank? Value? I think it's an interesting one. Chief? Yes. It's interesting that the French have Monsieur le Directeur, who is not a teacher at all of course. In France, a friend of mine who's been teaching the same length of time as I have – he's been a classroom teacher for more than twenty years – this year he's on a one-year stage in Bordeaux, where he's visiting a range of schools with some in-service with other classroom teachers. Next year he will be assigned to be a Directeur somewhere in France, which if it isn't in his beloved Bordeaux region he's not going to go. He will move back to being a classroom teacher. Contrast that with the USA – where they have principals and vice-principals of large institutions – and maybe much hinges on the size of the institution.

PE: *You're principal of the community college aren't you?*

RB: On the letterhead I'm headteacher. Some audiences and some people use 'principal'. I tend to use them interchangeably outside school but internally and with governors it's the head. I guess it's what really suits the community. I thought there were two parts to this question because it says 'Is the term "headteacher" still an accurate description (a) for what you expect of yourself and (b) what others expect of you? I think maybe it's a case of both a Yes and a No because increasingly one is perhaps expected to be seen as the principal. Mainly I think by educationalists rather than parents, governors and pupils.

   I think to be a successful head you need to enjoy it, you need to stay fresh, you need to enjoy being with children. You've got to enjoy questioning the institution at all levels. And if you don't enjoy those things then I think you really ought to get out and make way for someone else. If you are doing all those things but still it is time to move, then someone in the institution needs to tell you that, because you may not be the best person to judge it.

PE: *You mentioned, when you were talking about France and North America, the fact that the term 'Principal' was used in the USA – as too is the term 'Administrator' which we don't tend to use – but is there a danger of a division developing between the administrators of the school or its management, and the faculty or teachers? If we were to move towards the notion of a principal or non-teaching headteacher would there be a greater tendency for that type of conflict or division?*

RB: My experience of a term in the States was very much in terms of size of school – even and especially in the elementary schools which were often 900 students plus – and there was that separation between the principal, certainly in the large 2000-plus secondary schools. I tended to meet with both principals and classroom teachers and each reinforced that division. I wouldn't feel happy with that here in the system as we currently know it.

PE: *The size of the school here allows you to maintain that 'hands-on' approach. I wanted to ask you what your future career plans were and whether you're looking towards another school, possibly a bigger school?*

RB: I'd be interested to know how other colleagues respond to this question, because my own view from where I sit now is that the larger the school the more difficult it is to play the headteacher role. Perhaps one becomes drawn more to the principal role. It's quite interesting that once you get to a certain size – maybe it's just self-aggrandizement – but people call themselves principals more readily than they do headteachers. It's an open question for me whether a school of a much greater size would attract me or not. I certainly feel having had the opportunity over the past two or three years to do a fair bit of work in places like the Department for Education and other outside bodies, that I know that I still very much want to work with institutions, broadly called schools, and probably be a headteacher. It goes back to my previous point about making sure that one stays fresh and also moves on at the right time for the institution.

PE: *Would higher education or university appeal?*

RB: Naturally you look at what other things are around. I sometimes think higher education, albeit in a great state of flux at the moment, might be quite challenging. Also I think working in a local/district education authority at a senior level could be quite interesting. But I'm not interested in some of the more administrative aspects; it's not as though I'm not interested in policy making, I am very much – I don't think my strengths are in meticulous bureaucracy. I'm motivated to set and sustain values.

PE: *One of the other avenues, although it wouldn't be a full-time position, would be to train as an OFSTED inspector. You could do that, say once a year, as a kind of staff development activity. Would that appeal?*

RB: Possibly, though not as enjoyable as being a good parent and spending time at home! Again it's a case of looking at your institution and what you can then take back. Also the way it frees up opportunities for others in the institution is important. I would also say, as a head, I very much enjoyed working with you on the NFER project, as did the governors. It was an opportunity for us to be reflective practitioners. For example, when you interviewed our chair of governors it opened up discussions between him and myself that we hadn't had; we were prompted into them.

Perhaps we could end almost with a question mark – whose responsibility is it to move the reasonably effective headteacher/principal on to her or his next post? Margaret Thatcher talked about passing on the torch when she felt someone else was ready to take it – events dictated otherwise! Maybe there'll be a Putsch here and Blatchford will be out! Or the auditor will decide it's time for me to go!

PE: *The key question is who actually discusses this with the head . . .*

RB: My secretary and I have this 'voluntary euthanasia' pact; we shall tell each other when it's time to go. We've worked together effectively for eight years – we'll be strong enough to tell each other when the time is right to call it a day.

CHAPTER 6

Bernard Clarke

In conversation with Lesley Anderson

LA: *I'd like to ask you about your views on leadership, what sort of leader you are and what made you adopt that style of leadership. Can we start by talking about your own education and to what extent those experiences influenced your work as a teacher and headteacher?*

BC: When I think back to my own education I think of two things. One is a hatred of primary school and fear of primary school teachers. The other is loving being at the local grammar school and almost worshipping various teachers. I absolutely loved that part of my schooling even though it did not teach me how to study. It was, in fact, devastating for me because I failed my 'A' levels. With hindsight, the experience of failing 'A' levels was a most significant learning time for me. I think it actually gave me an understanding of what happens to many people, and to young people in particular. I don't think many headteachers have that experience.

I always wanted to be a teacher, when I didn't want to be captain of England at cricket, or drive a railway train. But, of course, the result of failing 'A' levels was I couldn't train to teach because I couldn't get to university. However, it did mean that I gained experience of other types of work. I started in a bank although that only lasted for about three months. I thought I was dying. So I left and drove a lorry for a time and then, eventually, I went back to college to do 'A' levels again. But I still did not take them because I developed glandular fever. So I arrived at the age of about 20 with nothing and no sense of direction just like an increasing number of young people today. However, I was lucky because, by chance, I went on to work as a VSO teacher and so I gained teaching experience by the 'back door'. However, there was still a problem when I came back to Britain. In conventional educational terms, I was no further on because I still hadn't got any 'A' levels and I still had not got the entrée into higher education. So, for some reason or other, I found myself in residential social work working with delinquent boys and it happened to be in Bradford. I knew there was a university there so I went to the back door and asked for a place. I got one and I enrolled for one of the liberal 1960s general degrees in applied social studies. This was fascinating because I ended up not only getting a degree, but also professional training in social case work.

LA: *So that was without 'A' levels?*

BC: Yes, that was as a mature student with a little experience along the way. With hindsight, one of the most important parts of my training as a head-teacher was the training I received as a social worker. In those days the work was very much related to the dynamics of individual and interpersonal behaviour, understanding what happens in groups, and when people talk, trying to locate what their real feelings are underneath the words they use. I think that was a very valuable training to have, one which every teacher should experience. It ought to be part of teacher training. It seems crazy to me that teachers can find themselves in front of a class of 25 adolescents without having any real understanding of group dynamics. I found these earlier experiences very useful in my teaching.

LA: *You said when at school you'd always wanted to be a teacher. Where does that come from?*

BC: I've no idea. Neither of my parents were involved in education in any sense. Neither were educational successes. They went to elementary schools and left at the age of 15 for work. I had no relatives who were teachers and I didn't like primary school. I suspected that it grew out of a sort of adolescent hero-worship of some of the teachers I encountered at secondary school.

LA: *So it was probably established in secondary school?*

BC: Yes, that's right and I think it was literally about those people. There is very little I can remember of what I was taught, but I can remember those people. I suppose the other, in a sense, negative experience which has informed my educational ideas, was watching my two brothers at school. They went to public school and it was decreed by my parents that I should go as well at 13+. But I was so happy and settled at the local grammar school that I did the unheard of thing and refused to go. This caused a tremendous 'hoo-ha' in the family. Subsequently, I saw how unhappy my brothers were. I suppose I was a bit pious but, even at that early age, I had this moral objection to the notion of private education and I saw it didn't work for either of my brothers.

LA: *Was it a boarding school that your brothers attended?*

BC: Yes, it was a boarding school about 30 miles from home and I watched my elder brother gradually become more withdrawn and isolated and socially inept. Then my younger brother committed the cardinal sin of failing the 11+ and was sent to the same school rather than the local secondary modern. (What would the neighbours think of having a child at the secondary modern?) His rather fragile confidence had already been affected when he failed the 11+ but it was destroyed at this school and he ran away. I think I can trace the effects of that school experience throughout both my brothers' lives and as a result of all of this, I developed pretty strong views on education.

LA: *So when you graduated you went to train to teach?*

BC: I went to Bristol and did a PGCE. I'd been at Bradford for four years so by this time I was 25 or 26. It was also at this time that I got married. I'd heard about the Department of Education at Bristol. In those days, there were three very eminent professors of education there. William Taylor, a young William Taylor, a wonderful man called Ben Morris and a sage and guru called Roger Wilson. I'd heard about these people so I got a place and studied for a PGCE at Bristol.

LA: *It was a conscious decision because of the people working there?*

BC: Yes and it turned out to be an interesting year. However, as I said, we'd got married and so I decided it was time to stop training and get a job. I got one in Bristol. I was appointed to work at Filton School half-time as a youth leader and counsellor and half-time as a teacher. In those days there was some opportunity for this arrangement.

LA: *So that role enabled you to draw on your earlier experiences?*

BC: That's right. I did the job for five years and then decided to become a 'legitimate' teacher. I became head of lower school at Filton. This was a good formative experience although it was an environment in which I felt somewhat limited. The atmosphere at Filton was not one of experiment and trying new things. It was run as a tight ship, a very safe organization and after 11 years there I felt rather constrained.

LA: *You were there quite a long time?*

BC: I was there a long time, longer than I intended. I was looking for a promotion for about two years and I wrote for scores and scores of deputy headships. I think my chequered career and the rather whimsical direction it had taken meant that I didn't have a lot of success. I really got rather depressed and quite desperate to get a move and a promotion and I wasn't getting them. I had a number of bits of advice along the way about letters of application and so on and then, towards the end of the resignations deadline in 1980, I saw an advert for the post of Vice-Principal of Burleigh Community College in Loughborough. I sent for the details and when I read them they jumped off the page at me. They really did. They were quite unlike anything else I had read in the way of details about a post in a school. They were written in a particular style by a woman who turned out to be one of the formative influences upon me. She was called Joan Gregory and was the Principal of the College. She was quite outrageous, but her educational vision was absolutely wonderful. There were issues about her personnel management and she was strong meat. But, most importantly for me, there was a clear role for the deputy; to work as sort of lieutenant to her.

It was the most brilliant experience working with her and it was all the things I had been longing for. She was the sort of person who would throw 15 balls in the air, knowing that ten would crash to the ground and two would be picked up by somebody who would run in the wrong direction. But she knew that three would be taken on. If things did not work out, her approach was always to have another go. Her view on management was to let people get on with their job. If things went wrong, she would pick up the bits. In fact, you didn't dare make a mess of it.

She was constantly nipping at people's ankles, always restless in a professional way. She had little phrases some of which I've assumed as my own. At Peers, we don't use the word 'kids' but one of her expressions was 'What's in it for the kids?' What she meant was whatever we did in school the students' experience was the bottom line for all of us. Another of her phrases was 'School should be full of second chances.' I think that's brilliant. I just believe it's so true. She was a wonderful influence.

LA: *So had you decided before you went to Leicestershire that you wanted to be a head? You were obviously very influenced by Joan Gregory.*

BC: I think it's about readiness. I hadn't planned it through. When I was at Filton, I'd been there three weeks when a guy, the head of sixth, came up to me and asked what I was going to do next. I told him that I don't know, that I'd only just arrived. But I went on to ask him what he was going to do next. He told me that he was going to be an HMI. He'd got his career planned out in detail. Mine wasn't like that. But I knew the time when I had a sense of readiness for headship. I watched the people I worked with, my immediate colleagues, and there came a time when I thought 'I could do that.' It first happened at Filton. So there was the influence of working for five years with Joan Gregory. That helped me in my readiness. Then she retired and I was part of the process of appointing and seeing in a new principal. The College was a big place. There were 1700 students and the man appointed to replace Joan was the very highly regarded Keith Forman. Before he came to Burleigh, he'd already been a head for 17 years at a village college in Cambridgeshire. He'd been through grave personal illness and had been awarded the OBE for his work in Cambridgeshire. So working with Keith was an equally fascinating experience.

Jumping on, when I applied for this job at Peers and was interviewed, I was asked why I should be appointed. What made me the person for the post? I was able to say, without hesitation, that I'd had this apprenticeship and experience of working alongside these two remarkable, powerful people each with an entirely different style.

LA: *So you learned about headship from Joan Gregory and Keith Forman in Leicestershire and, indeed, from the head at Filton as well?*

BC: From Filton, yes. The head I worked with there has retired now but my time with him helped to clarify the sort of head I wasn't going to be. There was a sort of caution and a control in the place which I didn't feel comfortable with. I suppose the guiding principle was 'Don't rock the boat', whereas with Joan, particularly, it was, 'Yes, let's give it a whirl. Let's see what happens.' I believe you find out by trying.

LA: *Am I right in thinking you are talking about the contrast between Filton and that lucky break in finding such a person to work with as Joan Gregory?*

BC: Absolutely, and to his great credit, Mike Smith, the Head at Filton recognized the 'fit' and gave me strong support. I have always been grateful for this. I owe Joan a huge debt of gratitude.

　　She was, however, also infuriating. There were times when I thought 'What are you doing, Joan? You can't do that.' But she'd carry on. People could either follow her or want to leave; she was such strong meat. But it provided a context where there was a real job for me to do and enabled me to watch her in action. The apprenticeship taught me never to be complacent. I remember a time when a group of HMIs were in the College to look at one particular department. Their report was glowing and, at the debriefing, they were really effusive about the department. Afterwards, Joan saw the head of department and congratulated him but then she went on to advise him not to let the department's staff relax. She wanted them to be praised but also challenged further. She wanted to know 'What were they going to do next?' This was all part of her restlessness. She continually asked, 'How can we make it better?' Joan was into annual school improvement long before it became the general culture.

LA:　　*Is this is your first headship?*

BC:　　Yes.

LA:　　*How well prepared do you think you were for it?*

BC:　　I go back to readiness. I'd watched Joan very closely and, as I've said, it was a huge privilege to work with her, and then with Keith. Their style was such that they were grooming me, I knew they were. I looked and I reached a point where I found myself feeling that I could have a go at most of the things that Keith did, and that Joan had done. And I couldn't have done all those things when I arrived. I learned from working alongside them, and from the many conversations with each of them.

　　For example, when there was a need to have a tough conversation with a colleague, they would sometimes talk it through with me beforehand. As a deputy, it was a huge privilege to be a confidant to the head. Imagine, the boss tells you he or she is about to have an extremely difficult conversation and he or she does not know how to do it. Joan and Keith would rehearse it with me and then come back afterwards to talk it through again. I remember after one such conversation with a colleague who wasn't delivering the goods, Keith saying to me that the conversations are never as hard as you think they are going to be. He told me to 'always bite the bullet' because the member of staff generally knows it's coming. In this particular case, it was actually a relief for the member of staff to hear the boss say that things weren't right. So, whereas there is an inclination to avoid tackling the difficult conversation because you don't want to lose popularity or you don't want to be disliked, Keith's message was to act.

　　So there was a sense in which I felt ready, at least, to have a go at headship. But I think my experience as a deputy made me realize I wouldn't be happy in any school. I knew I had to look, and find, the right fit. As it happened, there was a very significant meeting that helped me find that right fit. This is an anecdote. Tim Brighouse visited Burleigh. I remember he came into my PSE lesson. I was teaching a group of year 11 students. I'd briefed them and told them that they were going to meet this guy who was a Chief Education Officer and a pretty remarkable man. I'd told them to talk to him and find out about him. The conversation went well; the students ran it. They asked Tim lots of questions about his work as a CEO and what had he done before that. Someone asked him what he wanted to do next and he replied that what he would really like to do was run a school like this. I remember making some sort of flip comment that I hope I was not on the same shortlist.

Later, I don't know how long, the advert for the Head of Peers appeared in the *Times Ed*. I remember thinking that it was an interesting post. I knew about Bob Moon and I had heard him talk. I wondered who would follow him. Then I put it to one side. The following Monday morning, the telephone rang and it was Joan. She asked me what I was going to do. I replied that I didn't know what she was talking about. She asked if I'd seen the *TES* and the Peers job? I told her that, as a family, we'd planned to go north next. She just said 'Apply' and that was the end of the conversation. When I was interviewed for the headship of Peers, Tim was still CEO in Oxfordshire. There were four other vice-principals from Leicestershire shortlisted, so, although I didn't know much about the school, I had a sense in which I felt it was broadly on the same wavelength as Burleigh. So it was about feeling ready and about there being a sense of fit.

LA: *What is your vision for the school? How do you go about trying to achieve it?*

BC: I think my experiences of academic failure, and my background in social work, have led me to be a bit of a sceptic as far as the curriculum is concerned. Obviously, I do think it matters. But I do really passionately believe that if young people are going to learn and be successful, the conditions for learning are the most important thing. So my vision of leadership, such as it is, because I've never set it out, is being responsible for creating the climate in which young people and adults can do their best. You will find headteachers who are the real curriculum thinkers in their school. I am not. You will find headteachers who know every last detail of their budget and timetable and I am not one of those. My view of headship is of somebody who tries to articulate a set of principles, persuades people of those principles, and then, puts them into practice.

The best way I can explain it is by example. Another of Joan's catchphrases was 'Do the words fit the music?' Now, Peers has always had a reputation of being on the liberal wing. Remarkable things have happened here. For example, the introduction of the modular curriculum in the 1980s. But when I came here, it seemed to me that there were occasional discrepancies between the rhetoric and the reality. The rhetoric was about relationships but was not always acted out in practice. So I wasn't sure that the words did always fit the music. Shortly after I'd started here I was walking around the campus and everything seemed fine. Suddenly, I heard a loud male voice and I looked across and some distance away there was this tall male verbally assaulting a small female who appeared, in my mind's eye, to be getting smaller. I, as a greenhorn, asked his area co-ordinator to have a word with him because his behaviour really wasn't good enough or necessary. It was very important to me. So I'd dealt with it and felt quite pleased with myself.

However, I was reminded of this incident a few weeks later. It was the first staff meeting and, in those days, there were 65 or 70. There was already an agenda in the school about leadership and management and the staff were still 'sussing' me out. We got through the business and onto AOB when, unannounced, a friend of the chap who had been shouting those weeks before, stood up and asked me if I had a policy on shouting. I told him that I didn't, but that I would say what I thought about it. I remember saying three things. One was that if we disagree, we don't scream and shout at each other. Second, I said I thought it very hard to ask young people not to raise their voices if adults were heard shouting and, finally, I believed it was impossible to say that the school did not tolerate bullying if big powerful males verbally assaulted small powerless females. I heaved a sigh of relief and the meeting was over. I remember reflecting as I was leaving on what the staff would have made of my response. But, more than that, it occurred to me that it was actually a trigger for me to say to everyone in the school that what was sauce for the goose should also be sauce for the gander.

I believe that one thing young people can spot at a thousand metres is 'bull . . .' and if we say we want them to be independent, autonomous, decision-making young adults, but tell them that they must do exactly as we say, then they know that we don't mean it. So, as a result of that initial conversation, I began a discussion with the Senior Management Team about what we, at Peers, ought to be able to expect of each other, whoever we are, in order to get on with our jobs at the school. From this, we drafted a document which, in those days, we called a Code of Conduct and we put it to the staff.

LA: *A Code for adults and children?*

BC: Everybody. We invited comments from the staff on the draft but there weren't many because it was like the abolition of sin. There wasn't much anyone could disagree with. The only exception was that some of the staff, and I would describe them as the more anxious people, were concerned about what they would do if the students didn't conform. My reply was that we'd got a disciplinary structure, we had strategies for dealing with people who break the rules. But I think the question should have been 'What do any of us do if any of the others don't?' Not us and them. What happens if any of us transgress?

Staff and student discussions were held and these were used to redraft the document once more. It then went to the parents and the other agencies on the premises, the library, the kitchen staff, the sports and arts centre and, finally, the governors ratified it. So, at the end of the day, we could hold it up and say we have all agreed the Code and, through it, we'd agreed what we stand for. We review and refine it each year. We have also moved away from the rather military title of Code of Conduct. We now call it 'Rights and Responsibilities'. The strength of it is rooted in the notion that the school is a place of work and it is everybody's right to get on with their work. But it is also about the expectation of everybody that they will get on with their work. It's couched in the assumption that we will do our best. The assumption of sets of rules is usually that if you don't control young people, they will break the rules and they will, therefore, need punishing. I don't agree with that. I think young people see through it immediately. But, if you assume the best of them, they will come up trumps.

Let me give you another example. When we have visitors I take them into the hall. At morning break there are two or three hundred students there with just one or two staff. When visitors see the way the students behave they generally ask where all the rough kids from Blackbird Leys are. In fact, I have virtually never had to deal with misbehaviour in the hall.

I believe it's about people adjusting to a context and doing as is expected of them. If you have the highest expectations in terms of work and behaviour, students endeavour to come up to these standards. Of course, they don't all the time but neither do any of us. So we hold up 'Rights and Responsibilities' to each other because all of us are frail. I might 'flip my lid' and raise my voice at somebody, and teachers, especially when they are under stress, might infringe 'Rights and Responsibilities'. Equally young people, who are growing up, don't get it right first time. But 'school should be full of second chances'. Five years ago, if we had visitors who wanted to look around the school we would decide which lessons I thought it would be okay for them to visit. Now, visitors go anywhere, literally, anywhere. The atmosphere in the school is purposeful and calm. Difficulties are dealt with quietly by discussion in a rational way, by confronting youngsters with the consequences of what they did. For example, I had a conversation yesterday with a student who had misbehaved. I told her that she could choose to behave in that way, that is her right and I was not going to prevent her. However, I explained that if she did behave in that way certain things would happen and she needed to know.

LA: *It seems that you are reiterating the example you gave before, where you were facing up to dealing with a difficult member of staff. It's about facing up to things, isn't it? It's about being explicit, sharing exactly what is happening and what you expect.*

BC: And avoiding manipulation by students, staff or yourself. Being honest. One of things I think is very common in schools is for the manipulative teacher to try and put the head or the senior management of the school in the position of having to support and justify what is ultimately unacceptable. So I think 'Rights and Responsibilities' gives us a basis on which to identify what is rational. So I had a discussion with a student on Friday who had been deliberately rude to a teacher. I asked him why it was necessary. He told me that, in his view, the teacher was useless. I said that he was entitled to his opinion but that being rude to the teacher was not a helpful way of dealing with the matter. I told him that it is his responsibility to say something to somebody if he did think a teacher was not delivering the goods because it is his right to get the best possible education. By being rude he had shifted the agenda so that I had to deal with his rudeness. He may feel this was unfair but, by the same token, I did not feel that his behaviour towards the teacher was fair. She was hurt and offended by what he'd said. I told him that I wanted to reach the situation where we all, the student, the teacher and me could sit down together so that he, the student, could tell the teacher what he thinks about her lessons and the teacher can tell him what it is like to have him in her class. We would then be in a position to try to move forward.

That seemed to be the rational way of dealing with the situation. That's how adults do their business, or ought to! There is a great tendency in institutions to regress and, this is the social worker bit in me, to an infantile attitude. Staffrooms are very interesting barometers of that. Staffrooms will occasionally take up the cudgel, rather like a family, on behalf of a beleaguered member. They do it for quite irrational reasons, to get at the angry or the oppressive dad or parent. There is, frequently, an interesting dynamic that goes on in staffrooms.

LA: *So what kind of leader do you see yourself as?*

BC: I want to say I'm all the nice words, like a democrat, benign and so on. I suppose I would aim towards those characteristics although not for sentimental reasons. I think there is something in all of us that wants to be liked. However, it seems to me, that as a headteacher you can't do much, you can only achieve with the people you have around you, working with you. Therefore, it is very important to involve people and for them to feel that they can participate, but not take every decision. I have worked in situations where we have tried to open up the decision-making process. Burleigh is an example of this. But I concluded, as a member of staff as well, that people don't want to be involved in every decision. They haven't got enough time apart from anything else and they may not be particularly interested. Part of the judgement of a leader is deciding which things to consult people about and engage them in and which things just to say, 'Okay folks, this is what we are going to do.' So I don't regard myself as a democrat. It seems to me that the buck does stop with me and there are times when I have to say to people, 'This is the way it has got to be.' But one hopes that it is said in a context where people feel aware of the importance of their role. I'm afraid I fail all the time on the importance of praise but I do endeavour to handle situations with sensitivity. We had some interviews here recently and, as it happens, the internal candidates were unsuccessful. I think sensitivity to those people was vital. I think the importance of having a word with them cannot be over-estimated.

My own view of myself, my own hang-up which I alluded to earlier, is that I am not very good on detail. I tend to be broadbrush. I tend to be as I remember Joan. I say things like, 'Why don't we give it a whirl?' So, for example, we have this link with a school in Tanzania and, in 1990 when Desmond Tutu came to Oxford, somebody in the staffroom suggested that it would be great if he came to visit Peers. So I wrote to him and he came and it was just a jewel in the lives of lots of people. Desmond Tutu came and talked to us. He greeted, hugged and shook hands with everybody. It was a golden moment. In one sense this is nothing to do with the job of headteacher, but, in another way, in terms of giving the place a lift, I think it is. I see my role in terms of finding ways to make the school better. I know it has improved but I want it to be even better next year and so I ask, 'What can we do?'

All the time, the bottom line for me is the motivation, the expectation and the achievements of the students. I ask how are we going to help these youngsters who are not the most advantaged educationally in this city of dreaming spires. How are we going to help them get themselves on the map and feel good about themselves and their education? I keep a picture in the middle of my notice board. It's a charcoal drawing of a girl. I keep it because the girl artist came into year 9 a few years ago. She had a rep-utation for being an impetuous, and occasionally aggressive girl. She was quite a struggle in years 9 and 10, but, by year 11, she'd calmed down. The head of art spotted her talent for the subject and so we persuaded her to stay on into the sixth form. This was much against the odds and very unlike-ly in her circumstances. She is now at Brookes University reading Anthropology and History of Art.

For me that is what it's about and it's good to keep stories like that one in mind. The other thing is, and this will sound pious, but I think there is something about being authentic and being at one with your beliefs and your principles. That's why I feel so angry about Tony Blair. I don't feel pious about it but I just rejoice that my own kids chose to come to Peers. Our second transferred from another city school into the sixth form and got such good 'A' levels. She got two As and two Bs. When she got the results, I asked her about her decision to move to the sixth form at Peers. She told me she wanted to prove that she could do as well at Peers as any-where. She was hacked off with the North Oxford attitudes to Blackbird Leys and the prejudice which exists. Two of our other children are at Peers as well. Tom is in the upper sixth and Jo is in year 10. I didn't persuade them to come, they chose it. To me there is a message for parents in the fact that our children come to Peers. 'If it is good enough for the head's kids, it good enough for mine.'

We now have ten members of staff, teaching and support staff, who have children in the school and they are doing well. So there is a sense in which there's an increased investment in the place and, in fact, the chap who I told you about earlier, who was shouting at the student now has a son here. The teacher admits his attitude has moved. He used to say things like

'They're kids, I'm the teacher. We know where we stand. I am not into all this student business.' Now he sees the benefit. So I think there is something about trying to be true to your principles because the leaders I have admired have all been people who you knew didn't say one thing and do another, so to try and do that is important to me.

LA: *You suggested that you are not good at the detail. What do you do about it?*

BC: Delegate . . . although I mustn't overplay it. It's very easy to be self-effacing or cavalier. I have to manage a certain amount of detail. I have to get a balance. But, actually, I get quite bored by the detail. The sort of buzz I get is from working with business people or setting up a study support centre or working with the university or going to see David Blunkett, like I am later today. It's all those things that I believe are important. I think being a head is the most privileged job there is and I get a daily buzz from it.

To me, you deal with the detail as a deputy. You saw one of my deputies earlier. That was Chris Dark. He's brilliant at the student affairs end of things and as a project manager. He'll produce a newspaper or a presentation in three weeks. Glynis, the other deputy, has a background in the pastoral care side of things. She took over from another deputy who was second to none. Glynis moved into the job and had a huge amount to learn. But she has got it and does the work brilliantly. I feel comfortable about her handling the timetable, the staffing and the curriculum. Chris handles student affairs and project management and Peter Walter, a former maths teacher, manages the budget. Peter is rather like Newman Noggs in Nicholas Nickleby. He's rather diffident and stands on the edge of things. He whittles away at the minute detail of the budget. But I only have to ask him what the five key points are and he can loosen up and give me them. It is comforting to know that he is poring over the details of the budget.

LA: *So it's about knowing how people tick and how you tick as well?*

BC: Yes, playing to people's strengths and looking for the gaps and seeing what we haven't got. Then asking if there is anybody who could do it. I am not ever so good at the formal structures, like the weekly senior management team meeting, and I think, maybe, that is an area I ought to sharpen on. But it seems to work, although it's easy for me to say that, but I hope the others feel that it does. We do have pretty ready access to each other. People come in and out and have a chat. My office is a corridor really! So, yes, that's how we handle it. We haven't been caught out yet on detail and there is a brilliant tradition at Peers of pulling the stops out if it's needed. So when we found three years ago, that we had the opportunity to apply for the Government's Technology Schools' Initiative, we got a group of people together around the table and we started to bang it out. We produced a brilliant submission and we got the grant.

LA: *What are your key educational and managerial values?*

BC: I think that the overriding values which guide the way I work are, firstly, the importance that I do things through my colleagues. Therefore, my greatest responsibility is to develop and encourage staff. Without that, nothing can be achieved. A second value is, and I hesitate to say this as a man to a woman interviewer, a deep commitment to equal opportunity and a sense that we are actually all in this together. As headteacher, I am no better than the youngest, most disadvantaged youngster in the school. Simply because I happen to have a few more years and a few more qualifications and a few more advantages does not make me any better. And if we can create an atmosphere in which there is a genuine sense that we are of equal value, I reckon adolescents can buy that. And teachers can buy it. Now that this philosophy has become fairly rooted in the school, I don't think that there are many teachers who would have it otherwise. I'm not sure if it's a value but another principle which I hold dear is the belief that we have a responsibility to ensure that every year is better than the last, in as many ways as possible. I suppose if by value one is talking about the role of the head, in addition to what I've already said, I think my role is to articulate the vision. I believe in holding up the vision and I know that another reason why my apprenticeship was so invaluable was because I had the opportunity to work with visionaries. I may not be quite clear about my vision all the time but I know I have a vision and I am working towards finding it.

LA: *Is it harder to be an effective school leader than it used to be?*

BC: Well, I've only been a school leader since 1988 which, in itself, is quite a significant date: Educational Reform Act and all of that. It is true that the job that I applied for is very different from the one I am doing. In some ways I'm sure it is more difficult. There are much greater pressures and demands on heads in terms of public accountability, the political context in which we operate, like league tables, open enrolment and the pressures of formula funding – both at the level of the inequities which are inherent in formula funding but, also, in the actual practical business of managing budgets. So I certainly wouldn't think headship is easier than it was before 1988. On the other hand, it is all I've known and I have to say that although it is difficult in the sense of hard work, it is hugely stimulating. Every day is a different challenge, and so 'easy' or 'difficult' don't actually fit my descriptions of the role. As I say it is hugely stimulating and, occasionally, it can be frustrating. I think it's a bit of a roller coaster.

LA: *It's changing for you as well as the climate generally?*

BC: Yes, that's right.

LA: *It's probably not possible to make comparisons?*

BC: I can't make a comparison. Occasionally, I talk to heads from other parts of the world, and they can't believe what is required of headteachers in this country. Being head of a school always seems to me to have been a big job, as much in symbolic terms and in terms of the role in relation to other people as in terms of the actual tasks that have to be performed. So I think it has always been 'big' in that sense, in terms of the public and student perception of the role you occupy. The British education system has a tradition of the head as both an academic and pastoral leader and that makes it big – bigger than a head of a French school, for instance. If you then lay on to that the business manager aspect of the role, and the marketer, and all the other things, then it becomes a huge job.

I remember a visit we had from the chief executive of a multi-million business. The visit was part of a Business in the Community initiative and was called 'Seeing is Believing'. We spent time work-shadowing each other and at the end of the time he spent with me, he commented on two aspects of my role. One was that my job is infinitely more demanding than his and secondly, it is more stimulating. He'd sat in my office for half the day and was surprised by the range of people and issues I dealt with. He remarked on the number of constituencies that I address, was available for and accountable to as the headteacher. In his own role, he knew exactly who he would be dealing with, just the employees, the board, and the share-holders.

LA: *The range is both demanding and stimulating?*

BC: That's right.

LA: *Who manages you and to whom are you accountable?*

BC: There's the technical answer, which is the governing body, which, in our case, is hugely supportive. I can't over-estimate the sense of confidence that provides. They are not a push-over, they want to know answers, they are rigorous at meetings, but they are solidly committed to the school and solid-ly committed to the view that I'm the manager and should get on with the task of managing the school. They want to be kept informed but they don't want to interfere and they don't want to take decisions at a day-to-day level. That's very good.

Personally, I think that there is no question that the most important check and balance in my professional life is my family. My wife is very sup-portive but, also, very acute in her perceptions. She's from a professional family herself and a nurse so she knows about many of the pastoral issues that we are dealing with. But she is also interested in the personnel mat-ters. The greatest support I get is when I discuss in-school personnel issues with her. She is able to put them into the context of her understanding of people and what makes them tick. Also, I've already said how useful I find it having children in the school.

LA: *I suppose you get a feedback from your children?*

BC: Endless feedback, and much of it not favourable either about me or the school. But, at a deep level, I know they are solidly committed and that is very important. They want to do well. They have a personal investment so they want the school to do well. I hope that's not too much of a burden for them.

LA: *Because it was their choice to come here?*

BC: Yes – all three of them. Lucy was the first of our children to come here in to the sixth form. It was about four or five years ago and the school was not what it is now in terms of its status and public perception. So I swallowed hard when she made her decision. In one sense I was pleased but there was a bit of me that was anxious as a parent that she would do okay. So I was hugely gratified that she did so well and enjoyed it so much. Tom came at the same time in year 9 and he has done well and is doing his 'A' levels now. Jo chose to come two years ago and she's now in year 10. I suppose there's been a bit of a family mission about the place because my children have been not insignificant in encouraging friends who might otherwise have gone elsewhere to come to Peers as well.

LA: *So is their feedback to you fair or do you feel that they are hard on you?*

BC: Oh I don't feel families are ever fair. They ought not to be fair. If kids can't sound off at their parents, they can't sound off to anybody. Although, actually, what they say is generally fair. They will challenge me if they think an injustice has been done. They will challenge me if they think there are weaknesses in teaching or resources in the school. They will say that I really ought to do something about this or that. Which is very good. They will tell me if something is rubbish. They won't hesitate, but they will say less about the good things. But, as they are settled and doing well, I conclude that they don't need to say much about the good things.

LA: *And they act out their support for you through the things they do?*

BC: That's right. And I feel that one of the other sources of comfort is the increasing number of staff with children at the school. I'm talking about both teaching, office staff and others. As I said before, I believe there is quite a good message in that fact.

LA: *Do you still enjoy being a headteacher?*

BC: I absolutely love it. Which is not to say that I would necessarily love it in any school and, as I've already said, I'm increasingly sure about the importance of fit. When we interview people for jobs here, we talk about the object of the exercise being to get the best fit. And it's not just a one way process. I don't think this school would be everybody's cup of tea, just as I'm quite sure that there are lots of schools that wouldn't suit me. But it gives me deep satisfaction to know that there are so few aspects of the school with which I feel out of kilter – I can't think of one, actually. I think there are always issues that need addressing in any school but at a level of any significance there isn't an aspect of the school with which I feel out of sympathy. I regard myself as very fortunate. And, of course, being in this position, I am well placed to ensure that this situation continues. So I play a significant role in guiding the direction of the school – one that I believe is appropriate. This is the vision and I try to encourage people along that same road.

LA: *You're drawing more people into that vision?*

BC: I think that's right, and so I do not feel complacent. I hear that there are people around who really rate Peers because it has doubled its higher grade GCSEs in four years without changing its key values. That's the most exciting thing – you can really say we still believe in equal opportunities, we still believe in the value of every student, we still believe in all those key principles and yet we've enabled youngsters, and their teachers, to raise their performance, and all being well, that will continue. So that's the buzz.

CHAPTER 7

Helen Hyde

In conversation with Peter Ribbins

PR: *Can I begin by asking you to reflect on your own education. Did this influence your views and values as an educator and manager?*

HH: I don't remember much about my early education. I am not sure that the primary school I went to had much of an influence on me. I remember having problems with my writing. During my primary years I was kept after school endlessly because they couldn't read my writing. I had to do writing practice – I hated that. My secondary school was very different. It was a girls' school. I loved it. I felt very comfortable at school. But I never, ever, said anything – I was far too shy. But in my last year I got so angry in a class debate that for the first time in my whole school career I put my hand up and spoke and won the debate. I was thrilled by that. I discovered I could talk and that others would listen. But I did not talk again for a very long time. I was still desperately shy. As I recall it, the school was traditional, with a strong emphasis on order and learning. It influenced me but not as much, perhaps, as my growing involvement with a Jewish youth movement. That had a much greater influence on me at the time than anything else. This has been a lasting influence.

While I was at school I found that the only way I could really learn was to go into our garage, and use an old table tennis-table and use chalk to teach myself. Partly because of this I suppose, my parents have told me they thought I was going to be a teacher. I was sure I never was going to be a teacher. I was going to be a perpetual student. At secondary school I loved learning. When I finished school in 1964 I had to decide what to do next. This was not a difficult decision. I was going to go to university. Everybody went to university. There was no real pressure on me, particularly from my family. I dreamt about being a pilot, but since I was terrible at Maths that idea flew straight out of the window.

Having a Belgian mother and a German father and being in the Jewish youth movement were important in shaping my interests. We spoke French and German and English at home. Our custom was to speak English for a week, French for a week and then German for a week. I now speak them all, none perfectly. At university I just knew I had to study French – then the love of my life came up – 'Biblical Studies' – Theology. I loved those three years even though I did not take much of a part in university life.

PR: *You studied Languages and Theology?*

HH: Yes, a double Bachelor of Arts degree. I was not naturally clever. I hope my mother never reads this, I get on very well with her, but she always said to me whenever I achieved anything, 'You did it and you don't even have brains!' To this day she says 'You're the headmistress of a school and you don't even have brains!' But I really did enjoy working which was fortunate because I had to work very hard to achieve mediocre grades at school. I worked exceptionally hard at university. I sacrificed a great deal for this, even friendships. This was and is probably a part of my compulsive nature. I have to work. I see studying as more important than anything else. I remember a conversation which I had with my husband when I agreed to marry him. I said 'You must not get in the way of my work.' That was the understanding we got married on, my work would carry on.

At university I met someone who was to have a lasting influence on me. He was the Professor of Biblical Studies, Professor Geyser. He was a high-powered academic who pushed and encouraged me. He was the most caring teacher I have ever had – he loved his subject and his job. All he did was designed to promote his department and his subject. He was absolutely wonderful.

PR: *If you were writing for the TES on this, would you describe him as your 'best teacher'?*

HH: Without any doubt. At the end of my three years I had a Bachelor of Arts degree and found myself having to decide what to do next. I decided to go to Transvaal Teachers' Training College to do a PGCE. I had a lovely year – very relaxing. It didn't have any relationship to reality but I did have lots of fun. Then I went straight back to university and got married in the same year. What really struck me in going back to university was that I was going back because I really loved studying and I loved the subject I was doing. I did a further year of Theology for an Honours degree.

I was still speaking French and English at home. I found myself reading a lot – reading is one of my ways of escaping. I read a good deal of rubbish and a good deal of fine literature. At first, I read fairly equally in English and in French fiction. But gradually all my leisure reading became French. The only things I read seriously in English are for my work or Theology. I suppose this is another example of my compulsive nature. My father is a person dedicated to all he undertakes – I have inherited this from him. I have to keep up my French. My husband calls it paranoia, but it's not – it gives me intense pleasure.

PR: *Your PGCE year sounds more like a pleasant marking of time rather than a serious preparation for being a teacher?*

HH: It was a very pleasant interlude but it helped me to think through how teaching needs to be organized. I am a very organized person – I get that from my mother. I came to understand that to be a good teacher you need to be clear about what you want the children to gain from each lesson. I think this was the only thing I gained from the PGCE course. I can't remember the tutors, nor anyone watching a lesson of mine. I'm sure they did. The education theory, the philosophy was a joke to me. It didn't seem to have relevance.

PR: *Why did you do a PGCE?*

HH: I didn't know what else to do. I really didn't think that I'd ever teach. I had to do something – everybody else had got their degrees and were going places and doing things. I didn't know what else to do other than to study.

PR: *You hadn't made up your mind to be a teacher?*

HH: Not at this stage, but I did not find the experience of teaching threatening. I had been a youth leader and was still a youth leader. I had moved up through the age groups starting with little ones and by the time I was doing my PGCE, working with the older ones. I had taken them on camps, living with the 'whole child' and this experience has affected me in anything I have done ever since.

PR: *Did you specialize in Theology for your PGCE?*

HH: I read Biblical Studies not Theology. My studies were not philosophical but essentially historical – a study of books of the Bible and associated material in a historical context. We examined the sources of theological evidence – historically and scientifically. My degree had no relationship to teaching Scripture. I've never taught Scripture or Religious Studies.

PR: *Biblical Studies remains a major interest?*

HH: It has been and is a major influence in my life – one of my main hobbies out of school.

PR: *Was your secondary school a girls' school?*

HH: Yes. It was a large school although not quite as big as my school. It was fairly formal, with a uniform, some stress on discipline . . .

PR: *White?*

HH: White – absolutely – in those days you wouldn't have a black child near the school. I don't want to give you the wrong impression. There was quite a lot fun involved. But everything in the curriculum was compulsory except for French or Latin and Biology or Physics. I dropped Physics as soon as I could.

PR: *It seems to have been a serious place?*

HH: It was a serious place. You knew you would move on from there to university. I felt comfortable there. I remember our school assemblies, the headmistress used to process slowly on to the stage. She was a huge lady and her dog would usually follow her – a fat long dachshund which came onto the stage with her. Once there she would say 'Right we'll sing hymn so and so.' I am Orthodox Jewish. I love singing and sang hymns from the bottom of my heart. But I cannot remember a single reading she ever read. Those were the only assemblies I ever went to because at none of the schools in which I taught did we have proper formal assemblies.

PR: *It sounds like your mother was the key family influence?*

HH: My father is as quiet and as serious minded as I am. He came out of Germany at 19. His family suffered terribly – but he was the quiet, silent type. Always reading, often away on business trips – totally dedicated to the task. Maybe that is where I get this aspect of my personality from. My mother was always around. She was a very outgoing lady, who didn't go to university, who barely finished secondary school. She was full of fun, always playing jokes on people in her school. But she didn't take her own education very seriously. Even so, she made me work very hard.

PR: *Was she trying to achieve through you, what she had not achieved herself?*

HH: She never put pressure on me to do anything important. I think the understanding was you studied until you got married. She did feel that I was either always away studying or wearing the youth movement uniform and she did not like that too much. Only later did I come to realize she was fairly domineering. It was easy for me because I was quiet – my sisters found her much more difficult. My mother is very, very proud of me but she always seems amazed at anything I might achieve. Also because I study Theology with such a passion, my mother thinks I am going to be a Rabbi. She never had a thought of going to university herself – she went to work straight after school. But had a lot of fun. She was an outstanding sportswoman – who swam, played hockey and tennis – that was her life. I suppose I get my passion for exercise from her. Looking back, my parents have had a lasting influence. I'm sure it is at the back of my mind to try to make them proud of me.

PR: *I can appreciate that. You left South Africa in 1970?*

HH: We set out upon what was intended as an extended tour. My husband, I think, wanted to get away from my parents – because they were so domineering. I also thought it would be good for us to go away and become independent. We spent three months in Paris where I continued to study French – but I kept on buying Theology books in French. We had a wonderful three months. Every art gallery in France was visited. Then we came to England. By that time we had run out of money. My husband is a doctor so he found a locum job straight away. I needed to work. I tried my hand at business – I can't remember what it was – I had to count up figures. I lasted about half an hour and then left. Then I got a job at the Michelin Tyre Co. writing out envelopes – for about three weeks. Then I thought, well the only thing that I can do, I am trained to do, is to teach.

Walking through the school where I was called for interview, I saw these absolutely colossal boys. I rejected the job before I got to the interview. I was terrified. Instead, I went to a school down the road – a co-ed school called Acland Burghley and stayed there for fourteen years. I started working four days a week while I was doing a Masters degree in Theology at Kings College, London. At Acland Burghley I was one of eight or nine probationers all starting together. There was a real feeling of working together – life was very hard. At first, you had to spend all your energy learning to survive. But it was fun. We all felt we were in it together. We all learnt together and developed a very close relationship. Some of the friends I made then are still my friends now. I taught French and a bit of PE. I slowly worked my way up the languages department becoming head of department, then senior teacher in charge of primary liaison. I did feel I had built up a really good department which offered French, Spanish and a bit of German. I loved the teaching. I always felt first and foremost that I had to build up a relationship with the children so they could trust me and understand my sense of humour. Once again I reverted to what I had learnt as a youth leader.

I worked for four heads. One a very quiet retiring man – a father figure; another was Sam Fisher. People in London would know of him and his wife – he was very influential; very good to me. When he fell ill I found myself running the Staff Association and that was when I woke up. I had to talk. Until then, I had never, ever spoken publicly. At first, running the Association nearly finished me. In the end I loved it and I realized I had something of a leader in me after all. At the same time I started taking children to France – at first the sixth form groups and later 150 first-years, every year for a week. We linked up with schools there. We taught Maths, History, PE – everything in French for a week. That was one of the things that kept me at that school for so long. I really enjoyed those school journeys.

Then I met the best head for whom I have ever worked – David Kelly. He is now head of a sixth form centre in Essex. He was everywhere at the same time. If, for example, you arrived late he always seemed to be at the entrance to meet you – and there were nine entrances! He listened to you – he always looked at you straight in the eye and you knew he was listening. He only stayed for a few years – but during that time he changed the school. I learnt a lot by watching him. He didn't speak a lot to me, but he greatly influenced me. I spent fourteen years at Acland Burghley and then suddenly, in the last year, I felt totally bored and I don't get bored easily. This was very upsetting. I was happy there – my friends were there and we had fun in spite of the hard work. I found this feeling of boredom very painful and I knew I had to go. I had to decide what to do next. Did I want to study or did I want to climb the career ladder? I didn't actually answer the question to myself, I just went for deputy headship. I knew I didn't really want to go back to university. I had my Masters degree and did not really want to start a doctorate. I got a deputy headship in Haringey, at Highgate Wood School – a predominantly boys' school at the time.

In Haringey there were ten, then nine, secondary schools and that was very important. The deputies of the nine schools formed a very close unit. I did not get on very well with my head and only stayed for four years. But I was very lucky because when I got there, there were these two wonderful deputies – both Welsh. They were huge men. The head took me on as a pastoral deputy; I loved that because there was that responsibility for the whole child which has always been so important to me. I still taught French and started teaching German for the first time. I was about three pages ahead of the children – but I enjoyed it. I had a very good head of department. And the deputy, with whom I worked closely, kept reminding me 'The single most important resource we have are staff. Your most important job is to look after the staff, they must be happy.' That has been the guiding light for me here. Two years later I became the curriculum deputy – I loved that. I wrote the timetable which I had never done before. A scientist showed me how he did it – on a piece of paper, no bigger than an exercise page. Wonderful. The timetable is such a powerful tool. It brought me in much closer contact with the staff. Why did I want to leave? Partly because I didn't get on with the head – but I wasn't at all bored. Part of it was an inner challenge – I have constantly to do something that frightens me. So I started to apply for headships.

I had always worked in mixed schools. I went for Hendon School, a big mixed school. I liked it because it was in those days a pretty downtrodden school. I remember seeing a greasy motor-mechanic area and thinking 'I must change this so that girls will like it. It is disgusting.' But I didn't change it because I did not get that job. I then thought that I would go for something totally different and so I applied for Enfield Boys' Grammar School. I went genuinely believing that a female could or should run a male secondary school.

PR: *I am not sure I can think of any who do. But there are a few men running girls' schools.*

HH: I don't know of any women heads of boys' schools either. Enfield is a beautiful school. I went through two or three rounds of interviews. After the final interview they took us into this most beautiful chapel and I fell about laughing because they had on the walls all these wonderful heads – with a sword and hilt under one breast – and I wondered if I get the job would I be expected to wear a sword and hilt? I got to the final interview. I think they felt they couldn't really appoint a female. A woman could not really be an appropriate role model for the boys.

PR: *Do you think they were right?*

HH: Not at all. But I can understand the view that boys want to see a male role model. In some ways girls want to see a female role model. In any case, from their point of view it did not seem the right time to have a female there. It is sad, boys' schools can be too macho, they need the female influence. I would never call the boys by their surnames ever. Then I applied for a job in Hertfordshire but withdrew at the last moment: something told me that the school would close and it did. After that I put in an application to my present school. I did not get shortlisted. Later, I received a telephone call from somebody who said he was very sorry that I had withdrawn from the other school, but was I aware that they were re-advertising at Watford Grammar? I said I didn't know anything about it, but that I hadn't been shortlisted. He said get your paper in tonight. I had to handwrite it and deliver it by hand. I did so not because I was passionate about a girls' school as such, but I did want this school. I knew the area I had driven around and spoken to shopkeepers and local people. The school had quite a good reputation but people in the area believed it could be even better. This time I was shortlisted – and after three interviews, was appointed.

PR: *Did you think you were going to get it?*

HH: I certainly didn't think I would after the first interview. It was very taxing. Lunch was excruciating – and we had two lunches over the two days. I kept thinking the only thing they are looking for are my table manners and nothing coherent came out of my mouth. I hated that. The other thing which worried me was that somebody from the school – the head of biology – was going for the job – that put me off. I had never been in that situation before. But at the end of the third interview, I felt that at least I had performed reasonably well.

PR: *That you were in with a real chance?*

HH: Yes, but you know you usually have to wait for the result – well I couldn't wait. I had to get to the Albert Hall to see Paul Simon with my daughters. There was no way I could disappoint my children on this. So I gave an excuse and left. I phoned the governors from a telephone booth outside the Albert Hall and was told I had got the job, and here I am.

PR: *Did you ever make a conscious decision to become a head?*

HH: I've talked to my husband about this – I'm always putting myself into a situation which is new and a challenge. I knew I had to try for the job. If I stayed too long as a deputy – I would begin to enjoy it too much. I love the challenge of focusing my ideas on an application form and trying to imagine what they would ask me. In preparation I wrote a side of A4 on every education issue I could find. That was a kind of preparation for headship. But I also went on a course which was called The Management of Change. It was run by someone who had brought about major change in industry – in ICL I think. After the course I realized I needed another challenge and that is why I applied for a headship. I did not begin by thinking overtly 'I am going to be a head' – I never thought that.

PR: *You did not overtly prepare yourself for a headship?*

HH: No – but I had this idea going during the third year of my deputy headship. I must have known then that I was going to look for headship. I began to think about the heads I had known. David Kelly was a positive role model. He spoke wonderfully to the children and staff. In the third year I started preparing my ideas. I could never just go anywhere without having prepared carefully. I can't ad-lib.

PR: *What about more formal preparation?*

HH: I wanted to go on a COSMOS course. I did go on one in Wales – it wasn't a true COSMOS course, but it was basically the same sort of thing. I enjoyed it immensely but not as much as the Management of Change course I told you about earlier.

PR: *Weindling and Earley suggest the early years of headship are often difficult. What were your first three years like? How well prepared did you feel? I remember you describing yourself as sweating blood when you walked in the door for the first time?*

HH: I was sweating blood and I sweated blood for more than three years. I was appointed in April, for September. I felt I knew absolutely nothing about my school and that all my previous experience was worth nothing. I was lucky because I was allowed to come every Wednesday and the two senior deputies were outstanding – they held my hand with everything. But I did everything their way and the way in which the school had always done things. I did two things immediately after I had met the staff in April. The first was to opt for compulsory Combined Science. I could see what was coming within the scientific world and the scientist who had first shown me how to timetable influenced this decision.

PR: *He was in favour of Combined Science?*

HH: Yes, and I was in favour of it for girls. I was desperately worried about the number of girls dropping Physics. Combined Science for all was essential. I also brought in a pastoral structure based on heads of year.

PR: *Had there been a house system before?*

HH: No, there wasn't anything.

PR: *So you introduced a new pastoral care structure?*

HH: Yes, and I made the head of biology who had not got the headship responsible for the pastoral system – she has subsequently become my deputy and is very close to me.

PR: *Was she very disappointed? It would have been a big jump. It was not uncommon twenty years ago. More recently, I know Peter Downes did it and my wife had one term as a deputy before becoming the head of a secondary school. But this is not common now.*

HH: I think she was disappointed and we did have some difficult moments for the first few years – but she is outstanding, she is a real problem-solver. We respect each other, so there isn't a problem. During the first year, because she had a new project to develop, she kind of kept out of my way for a little while which I thought was wise.

One of my most traumatic experiences was my first assembly. I had this wonderful reading which I have used subsequently – a part of Martin Luther King's speech 'I have a Dream'. I arrived on the stage and the girls stood and I realized that I didn't know how to make them sit down. I froze and was halfway through my reading, about two lines from the bottom, before I said 'I am sorry, please sit down – you've been standing for more than ten minutes.' They then sat down and as I reached the end of my reading I had to get them to stand up again for the prayer. This standing and sitting seemed to go on and on! For most of the first year not one girl looked me in the eye – I felt like a fish out of water. I was embarrassed by many things. Let me tell you about my first parents' meeting. It must have been in November – so what I knew about the school by then was more 'dangerous' than useful. I had taken away the little traditional hymn books which everybody had. I had plans to produce our own hymn book. But the parents really went for me. Amongst other things, they wanted to know whether I saw myself as the new broom. Some of the parents who went for me subsequently became governors and have become very good supporters – but they did teach me that every second word would have to be 'excellence'. So for the next two years all I did was talk 'excellence' until it got to the stage when my staff started teasing me and then I felt a little bit better – but they talk 'excellence' now.

Looking back, I could not say I enjoyed the first two or three years. I had made many of the changes I wanted – but I didn't feel confident enough to correct the staff. It probably took at least five years before I really felt the school was 'mine'. It may even have been seven years, by which time one whole cohort of girls had gone right through the school. Certainly, it took several years before I felt ready to introduce a new sixth form badge. Having a daughter at the school has been a great help. She tells me the truth – a critical friend.

PR: *It was her choice?*

HH: We gave her lots of options because we were still living far away. I have two daughters. The elder one went to school in London. I didn't like that school at all. It was a girls' school and I used that to exemplify certain things I didn't want in my own school. Having my younger daughter here has made me much more aware of what the girls' needs are. Also, if something is good enough for my daughter it must be good enough for all the girls here.

PR: *Your vision for Watford Grammar School for Girls is set out in detail in the prospectus. It has five main aspects including such traditional statements as 'The ethos of the school is based on traditional academic excellence – all girls are expected to work hard and develop to their full potential in all areas of the curriculum and in all areas of school life.' Even so the two statements which particularly struck me were:*
*   *The school should be a microcosm of what we would like society to be: a happy, caring collection of motivated and hardworking individuals, capable of living together harmoniously while recognising and respecting each other's differences.*
*   *Each girl should, while pursuing her own goals, never forget that service to others is of paramount involvement.*
What else might you add to that statement of vision?

HH: Well it does summarize my view. But there are other things I could add. One is that it must continue to be a respected place of learning and of academic achievement. That is what I inherited and that is what I see as my duty to perpetuate. That is what the parents want – high academic standards – they expect us to have high expectations of the girls in work and in life. Of equal importance to me is that the academic work takes place within a warm and caring environment. Our girls do have self-discipline and a sense of responsibility. I am glad to say that they develop confidence in themselves, in each other and in the school. If you walk around you will see that they feel that they can walk together arm in arm and they talk freely. Earlier this week I was with another member of staff and we saw two girls arm in arm and one of the two girls gave the other a big kiss on the cheek. My colleague asked 'What are you doing Alice?' I answered 'Well, they haven't seen each other all week – they are just saying hello', and I think that is wonderful.

One of my teachers at a Conference for Heads of Year in which the conversation had turned to the topic of physical contact between teachers and pupils was asked 'What would you do if you saw a child crying and very upset?' She answered 'I would go and put my arm around the child and give the child a hug.' Her questioner responded 'You must never do that, it is absolutely out of the question – what would your head say?' My colleague responded that 'If my head saw it she would give the child a hug before I had a chance to do so.' That is absolutely right. Even so, this is a girls' school and for obvious reasons, I could not extend the same privilege to the men unfortunately. But the school is a very warm and caring place and the girls feel that there are people here who love them. If there are teachers here who do not feel that, then they should not be here. So as far as the pupils are concerned I am trying to maintain a respected place of academic learning characterized by a warm and caring environment for the pupils.

PR: *What of the staff?*

HH: I respect my staff enormously. They know that and they know I trust them. They are the experts. We have moved a long way from the stage in which the head is expected to know it all. Let us consider the case of the National Curriculum. There was a time when I used to try to read everything in detail. I have come to see that this is neither possible nor sensible. So now I don't try to keep up with all the details. I trust my head of history to read the history documents with great care and, if there are changes to be made, to let me know what they are. The same is true of every other subject and department. My heads of department have a high degree of autonomy. They have their own budgets and they take their own curriculum decisions but they do so within the framework of the philosophy of the school. As staff, we are subject to the same ethic of service that we expect from the pupils. We are all serving the school and the wider community. Having said that, this is not a community school as such. Rather it is a regional school since many of our children come from outside the immediate area.

PR: *Given this scenario, do you think heads are necessary? Would it be possible to achieve the kinds of things you have been talking about in a more collegiate way?*

HH: We do work in a partly collegiate way. I have three deputies and a senior teacher whom I meet as individuals and as a group every week. I also meet the School Management Group every week – this is made up of the four senior staff plus a head of year and a head of department. All major decisions go though this group. I use this group, and my Curriculum Committee, as sounding boards and for advice. But in the end there are some decisions which if you don't take them they are not taken. When I was first appointed one of my junior history teachers said to me 'What I like about it here, is that you see yourself as a benevolent dictator.' I had not thought about that, now; 'benevolent' is not a term I am happy with. It sounds very patronizing. Nor would I glad to be thought of as a 'dictator'. But when necessary, I will take the decisions that must be made.

For the first three years I hardly took a major decision. I was so busy consulting that we went nowhere. I felt that I really needed to find something I could say 'No' to. But I did not find it and instead kept on saying 'Yes' to staff. It has taken me a long time to realize that staff do not make huge unreasonable requests. So I stopped consulting and asking for advice all the time. Instead, now I am much more likely to take quick and clear decisions. The staff don't say to me anymore 'I wish you or somebody, anybody, would take a decision.' In that sense I am not a 'benevolent dictator' anymore. Having said that, I find it difficult to say what kind of leader I am. But I do try to listen. This is crucial. In making decisions, I always try to use appropriate sounding boards – often my governors or one or both of the staff committees which I described earlier. And, of course, I am talking to my deputies and senior teachers all the time. But having heard what they all have to say, I then go away and think about it and tell them what I have decided.

PR: *You are clearly proud of your policy of trusting your heads of department. I once talked to another head who took a similar approach. In my judgement, and in that of the staff, this meant that there were some wonderful departments and some dire departments. How do you avoid the dire whilst enabling the excellent?*

HH: Heads of department do enjoy much autonomy, but in exercising their responsibilities they all feel they need somebody to talk to. One possibility is through the appraisal system but some believed that talking to their appraisers might unhelpfully influence their appraisal. Even so they did want somebody senior to talk to. So I have taken my Senior Management Team and divided the heads of department amongst them. This means, for example, that my curriculum deputy is responsible for seven heads of department and she meets with each of them once or twice every term. I occasionally put items on the agenda for their meetings, for example our OFSTED report, but otherwise they generate the agenda. For my own part I see the heads of department formally twice a year, in July and September. But, of course, I meet them often in the normal course of events and also there are regular middle management meetings. These are all ways in which we can monitor the ways they are working and I think they are pretty effective.

At the school management meeting which takes place each week, I table the minutes of meetings with departmental heads which have taken place. This process keeps the whole Board well informed about what is happening across the school. But if there are confidential issues they come and see me and I go directly to the head of department concerned. I am very pleased with this structure. It does mean that my deputies are overworked, but they also see the benefits of the arrangement. It means, for example, that the finance resources deputy is heavily involved with the curriculum because she is working with the heads of departments. That is how it should be. The pastoral deputy, who by the way is a man, also looks at curriculum matters. So there is a lot of cross-fertilization.

What is more difficult to achieve is to get the departments to work together. I've got the obvious ones working together but this is some way short of the collective effort I would like to see taking place. To try to make this possible we have tried something new. For some time we have had these awful middle management meetings with six heads of year and 20 heads of department – ghastly. So my pastoral deputy has suggested that we should take a specific problem to each meeting and divide them up into groups and get them to work together. We have had some very, very good feedback from this. For example, for some time we have been struggling with our grading system. Using the new approach enabled us to get some useful ideas and to ensure all those who carry a management responsibility felt consulted. Our middle management meetings will now be run like this – as a problem-solving exercise. I hope they feel it is worthwhile.

PR: *In what sense?*

HH: As opposed to coming to a meeting with 26 people in which all too often the assertive few or those with an axe to grind hold forth and the shyer people say nothing. I have never felt comfortable running that kind of meeting. Now I can make a short presentation – explain the problems, sometimes outline the options and sometimes not because sometimes they know more about it than I do. Using such an approach you get good and quick feedback.

PR: *All this seems an interesting way of improving your knowledge of what is happening within the departments but, to paraphrase what seems to be the key OFSTED question, how do you know about the quality of what goes on in your classrooms?*

HH: What I have done – not in the first three years – was to arrange to spend every half term with a new department. This has been wonderful. For example, I have just come out of Science. I make sure I see every teacher teaching and teaching in every year. So I have seen every single member of my staff teach and I have seen teaching within all the year groups. This means that I know what is going on in each department and year. I should stress that I am not attempting to monitor the teachers as an appraiser might. Rather, what I am looking at is the way the children are receiving the lesson. I sit with the children and if worksheets go round, I have a look at the worksheet. Not that I necessarily do it – with Maths, I don't think I could. [*At this point a girl came in and spoke to Mrs Hyde.*] That girl asked me if I would take her home. I take that as a real compliment. I don't know her very well. But I do know her father has a shop in the village where I live. I take that to be a real achievement. It shows the girls are not frightened of me. They can treat me 'like their Mums'. I can be a taxi driver like their mothers [*laughs*].

PR: *Who do you see as your managers? To whom are you accountable and how has that changed since going grant maintained?*

HH: First, I am accountable to myself. I set myself high standards and continually push myself. I have constantly to do better to make sure this is the best possible place for learning. Second, I am accountable to my staff. I have to ensure, and I suppose this is the answer to the questions you asked about leadership, that I am as effective a facilitator of their work as I can be. Staff have to be able to trust and rely on me as a real leader to represent and to guide and look after them. Third, and a close third, I am accountable to my pupils. They must be able to trust me; to respect my personal standards. I must be the best role model I can be. I have been here for eight years, and wore trousers for the first time last week! I have done this on purpose, because I believe the girls need to see me as a whole person, not only a person who wears a skirt. It has taken eight years – but I have finally done it.

Fourth, my governors and fifth the parents. I worry a bit about all the parent power – but they keep us on our toes and it's right I should be accountable to them – but they are only here for seven years. I do respect the parents and I have a lot of close contact with them – I attend every single school function. I make a point of talking to parents and to make them feel that I believe every child is important. But I will also stand my ground and I will be very cross with parents if they try to push me too far. Beyond that I cannot be accountable. I don't feel I am accountable to the wider community. I cannot cope with that idea anymore. While I was a deputy, I had this wonderful view that as a head I would carry a kind of general social responsibility. I do not believe it anymore. My job is here. It is an enormous and demanding job and I can't cope with anything more.

PR: *You are not a community leader, a social worker, a marriage guidance counsellor . . .*

HH: No I am not, although I do enough of those things – and I don't mind. I would try to help any parent that needs my help, but they would have to be a parent. I cannot do more than that.

PR: *What do you see as the function of the governors?*

HH: They are critical advisers – like a Board of Directors – what I like about my governors is they come with a wealth of experience and information from all sorts of places. They are always at the end of a telephone. If I have a major concern I can phone my chairman or the two chairs of the main sub-committees at any time and say – 'We've a meeting, can you come in half an hour earlier?' or 'I'm going to do such and such with a child – are you happy with this?' If they are not happy they will tell me and I'll think again. But I'll fight my corner if I still think I am right. They don't give me an easy time if they don't think I deserve it – but they trust me. My chairman is a very wise man and the fact that he trusts me makes me feel I have something very important to do here.

I haven't had the chance to stress the importance of humility. It is, in my view, an essential trait of effective leadership. I don't like to assume that I am an important and influential person. When people talk of me like that I don't think they are talking about me – they are talking about somebody down the road. If you lack humility you lose contact with what is really important and that is the children and the staff. Without humility you cannot get 'into their shoes'. If the child feels loved and respected then you can teach and you can push them hard. The staff and I do push hard togeth-er – without this you go nowhere. This school has proved that more than anything else to me.

PR: *Tolerance as well?*

HH: Tolerance and mutual respect.

PR: *Are these your key educational and managerial values?*

HH: Every school claims this but in my case I only got to know what tolerance, mutual respect and care in a school really meant once I got here. The teach-ing staff taught me this. They are a constant example to me. The way they nurture the girls but also the way in which they push them when they need this.

PR: *Do staff ever need pushing?*

HH: Everybody does. For me, this is the most difficult part of the job. The great majority of staff are fantastic and work as hard or even harder than duty requires. In pushing, I work initially through my heads of department – in any case they usually bring the problem to me. Then I try to work through the person who is supporting the head of department to work with the member of staff concerned. But appraisal can also help. I have talked to staff and I have said 'One thing I cannot abide is sarcasm to children – sixth formers you can joke with – but no sarcasm – the younger children are unable to understand it and they can take it very personally.' If I was in a classroom and witnessed it I would – at the end of the lesson – say to the teacher 'I really don't think that is the right way.' I would be glad to be able to change the way some staff talk to the children, but I don't always succeed.

PR: *You were appointed in 1987, just shortly before the 1988 Education Act. How do you regard the reforms it set in train and what have its consequences been for you as a head?*

HH: When the National Curriculum started it really didn't worry me at all. We had already begun to do many of the things it specified. For example, even before the documents on compulsory Modern Languages had been pro-duced we had already gone for this. Before the documents proposing 20 per cent or 12 per cent for Science we had already had compulsory 20 per cent Science. So the broad perspective of the National Curriculum did not have a major impact – we were already doing much that was proposed. The five cross-curricular themes were more problematic because we had only just set up a marvellous PSE programme designed to cover the first five years – we had not yet looked at the sixth form. What we had set up was coherent, it did the things which we thought were important. I sup-pose I should have said NO – after all many other schools did – but I was just too nervous to say NO to anything. So my heads of year put back into our PSE curriculum all the 'stuff' we had to do for the cross-curricular themes. After monitoring this for two/three years we realized that the girls had come to hate PSE. We had never had that before. Unfortunately in my monitoring of classroom work I did not go into PSE lessons. I much regret this. In the end a head of year came to see me and she was very disturbed – she said, 'I am really sorry, Helen but we have lost something important.' From there I took the decision that we were going back to where we had been. She was absolutely right. The heads of year re-wrote our PSE programme. From the National Curriculum themes we still have sex education, which we always had, and careers education. All the 'stuff' the children don't need until possibly the sixth form or later we dropped. We have done what we believe right. We should have done so in the first place. I had taken a silly decision and I did it because it was the law rather than because it was right – perhaps it is my South African upbringing? There, if the police tell you to do something you do it because you are too frightened to disobey.

Another silly decision, and one which was taken for much the same reason was related to Technology. On my desk landed a document which insisted that Technology was compulsory. I was anticipating an OFSTED inspection. We were going to be one of the first schools inspected nationally. I took one of the worst decisions I have ever taken. Again, it was because there was a law which seemed to require that there should be compulsory technology for all year 10 pupils. We looked at what impact this would have for the options which were available to the girls. I made the decision in spite of the fact that implementing the policy meant option choices were much restricted. You could still have a linguist doing two languages but you could not have History and Geography. I had a dilemma. Either the pupils would suffer because they couldn't have a broad curriculum in years 10 and 11 or they could follow what the law required. At the time we had a bid in to the DFE for a Technology block so I felt I had little choice. To this day I regret that decision deeply because the girls have followed a Technology syllabus which I can only describe as absolute garbage. Even now nobody knows what the GCSE is going to look like. I could have done what many other schools did at the time – ignore it. I'm quite good at doing this now. They tell me compulsory Technology will be coming back in 1996 – but it's not coming back here unless I am very sure of the educational content of the courses.

PR: *My wife believes Technology is not just a subject for boys. Because it was compulsory helped her to persuade staff they had to take it seriously, that it was something for all girls.*

HH: I couldn't agree more. I agree with the principle. All girls should be doing Sciences and Technology. But I am not happy that all girls should be doing Maths, Science, Technology for up to 35 per cent of their timetable if this means that everything else gets squeezed. Also whilst I agree that Technology is crucial for all girls, if the content being proposed is rubbish then you shouldn't be doing it.

PR: *What is your view on the National Curriculum? Is it appropriate for the Government to have a major say in determining it?*

HH: I think there should be a National Curriculum. Only then can you have some confidence in what any child might expect to get – an entitlement. It also enables greater co-operation between secondary schools and between primary and secondary schools. In any case, the existence of a National Curriculum does not mean that all flexibility has disappeared as far as the individual school is concerned. It does not mean that at all.

PR: *I was reading the Minutes of the Clarendon Commission of 1864 recently and was surprised to discover they suggest a curriculum very like the National Curriculum.*

HH: Even so, I think we do need a National Curriculum. I think it helps everybody. As we have it now, there is time to do things we want to do. There is lots of time within each subject to teach in very exciting ways. I still have worries. For example, in the lack of coursework in English – I think that is a bad mistake. Coursework can be extremely stretching – both for the able and less able child. It is possible for all pupils to show their worth in a nonthreatening way. Exams can be very stressful. That is not to say that I am opposed to exams. We have lots of them here, but we look very carefully at what we do. When we were told coursework was not stretching enough for the bright child – we sent examples of the GCSE coursework produced by our brightest pupils to the various people taking these decisions and described the circumstances under which it was produced. It was splendid work. But we got nowhere – I think this is the single biggest loss in the Dearing review.

PR: *What of assessment? Some argue the 1988 reforms did not set up a National Curriculum but imposed a very constraining national system of assessment instead.*

HH: I think that is probably true. I don't think the National Curriculum tests offer anything much at all. We are going to do them and package them off to whoever we are supposed to send them to, because we must. I think it is very sad that they have gone down that line. Assessment is a very difficult area. We are struggling in this school. For us, assessment should simply mean marking a child's work in such a way that the child is helped to develop and improve – nothing more important than that it must result in the child's further development. The purpose of the GCSE and 'A' level is different. But to enable the pupils to do as well as they might in these, you have to give them practice of such exams under exam conditions. In any case I think the 'A' level should be broader.

PR: *Can you say a bit more on that?*

HH: I think you need a broader 'A' level, not just specializing in three subjects. But I am not in favour of the Baccalaureate. Perhaps five subjects would do? In this school – pupils have to do English if they are not doing 'A' level English, and Maths if they are not doing 'A' level Maths. So we make sure the curriculum is broad. Picking up on assessment again, I don't believe in Records of Achievement. I do not allow my staff to get involved in them. We do summative sheets because that is unavoidable. At my previous school we did a lot of self-assessment. We followed our forms from year 1 to the sixth form. By the time I was doing self-assessment with my fifths they used to say 'We don't want to do it again. Photocopy what we said before and stick it on the sheet for us. We're bored with it. We hate it.'

The staff were supposed to spend time and negotiate what was to be recorded with each child. This meant that instead of having a form period where we could talk as a whole group, I had to let most of them get on with something else whilst I talked with each child. I was panicking all the time because I felt the rest of the children needed more – something more meaningful and structured. It was all just too time-consuming. We don't have the time for that. So when the wine covers came out (wonderful burgundy colour) in their thousands I said to my staff – 'I'm going to hold out as long as I can – you are not going to have to do them.' Instead we have a kind of record of achievement for the sixth form – a progress chart over the two years – and a careers progress chart for which some self-assessment is necessary for end of years 7, 9 and 11. When I interview children in the sixth form and they bring me these wonderful things – I have only 20 minutes to talk to them to hear their views and thoughts. I make the right sounds – but I don't look at it in detail – I talk to the girls – and then look at their results – so for me it is a waste of time. If I was in industry I'd have even less time.

PR: *What do you feel about the proposals for RE and for corporate acts of worship?*

HH: I had not been to a religious assembly since leaving my own secondary school. When I first came I used to take whole school assemblies but now the school is too big. I still take an assembly myself every day – if I'm not here then a deputy takes it. In the last three years I have come to realize how very important they are for me personally. I can see the whole school and I can talk to the girls – I can compliment them – amazingly for me I can sometimes even ad-lib. Today, for example, is Valentine's Day and I began to speak about the real meaning of love. In the end I started joking about it and the girls were laughing with me. On a personal level I am deeply religious. So collective worship is not a problem. I do not interpret it even vaguely as 'wholly and broadly Christian'. Being a religious Jewess and a theologian – 'wholly and broadly Christian' is, for me, based on the Hebrew Bible. I will not assign a special value to Jesus. I will not assign a special value to anybody but God. I don't insist that the girls pray. I say 'Will you stand for the prayer.' Those who wish to pray – pray. Those who don't – don't. The same goes for the hymn. Our senior assembly can be excruciatingly embarrassing because they don't sing – there is a tradition in the school that year 11 girls don't sing hymns, but everyone else does. I don't mind the tradition – in a way, it's maturing girls' exercising rights to do that sort of thing. The Junior assembly is lovely – the little ones do sing. My director of music has some lovely hymns – the Jewish girls skip over the words they don't want to say – the Moslem girls don't try to sing. It is not a problem and I just break the law. But I do have assembly every day and I would defy anybody to tell me there is not a spiritual attitude in the school. We will continue to have assemblies. They are an important part of the day. I think very deeply about what I am going to read. The prayer is usually about helping others, helping the less fortunate, thinking of others. At our Open Evening I tell the parents that when they choose this school, I will not allow withdrawal from assembly – in spite of the law – because it is appropriate to all girls and an important part of the life of our school.

Religious Studies is compulsory in every year except the sixth form, and even there it is included to some extent within General Studies – I would like it there as well. All years have two periods a week. It is a wonderful growing area for the girls. It is creative. There is a lot of discussion and acting. The girls love it. Our real problem is RE is such a popular subject – we have huge GCSE and 'A' level groups. 'A' level is not a problem, but the GCSE syllabus has become a serious problem. I am having a running battle with Dearing. If you wanted to divide the school population you can think of it as Jewish, Christian, Muslim and Hindu and others. It is a wonderfully rich community. In the past for GCSE we chose a syllabus dealing with Christianity, Judaism and Islam and for 'A' level – Christianity and Hinduism. The Government now tells me the syllabus deals with two religions only and I must make a choice. So we rotate – this year 40 or 50 GCSE girls are doing Christianity and Judaism and next year they are doing Christianity and Islam. They also suggest that I separate the girls by religion. This is ridiculous – it undermines everything we stand for.

PR: *It has been claimed that the introduction of site-based management in the wake of the 1988 Act has forced heads to spend much more time on budget and personnel management and that this has taken place at the expense of their role as curriculum managers. Do you share this view? How do you structure the management of the school?*

HH: I don't teach as much as I did – four or five lessons a week now. I have done my teaching. I know I can teach. I use my teaching to have a rest and because I love the girls. I have a wonderful time. And it helps me with appraisal and maintaining staff credibility. I don't spend more time than I want to on financial management. I have an outstanding deputy who looks after this. I meet her once a week. I like to keep in touch. I also have an outstanding pastoral deputy and another in charge of the curriculum/ staffing/sixth form and a senior mistress who is in charge of the daily organization.

I also have a bursar – not a posh bursar because I have my finance deputy – some agree with that and some don't. I am happy with that because I trust my deputy – we speak the same language. We learnt together. I am no mathematician and she showed me what I needed to know. At first, she used to tell me everything and we did everything together because I wanted to learn. We are now at a level where I don't need to do this. I have learnt the questions to ask. We still meet regularly but I am spending less time doing the trivial and preparatory things. We are working on a big issue at the moment. I have asked her to prepare the ground with me. There are other resource-related things to do. For example, I do need to see the site manager, but my deputy is in charge of him too. We have a lot of 8 a.m. meetings which relieve the pressures of the day a bit for me. We also have lots of evening meetings. I don't think I'm doing anything that I don't want to do. I do whatever is important for the school.

PR: *Talking about decisions that are important for the school, who took the decision to go GM?*

HH: We had two attempts at it. The Boys' School went GM first. They had a very experienced headmaster, Keith Turner. I came along as an 'innocent little girl' who didn't know what she was doing. My Union advised me to sit on the fence – don't say anything because you are not confident enough. I listened to them and didn't say a word. We were totally out-voted.

PR: *Even though you were in favour of it?*

HH: I didn't know what I wanted. I was terrified – the Boys had got it and seemed to be thriving in it. I have never not worked in an authority. When I was first appointed as head, the authority invited me up to Hertford, sat me in a big room with a huge table with all these advisers around it and told me about the school I was going to. I wrote everything down. They went through every department and criticized all aspects of the school. I kept thinking what have I taken on? I never ever got over that. It seemed that when the authority needed something they came to the school, otherwise we were the forgotten partners. I should say that Hertfordshire are good people to work for, they are not 'baddies' at all. But I felt we were not really welcome in Hertfordshire. We had to wait a year but then I went for it overtly. I called parents' meetings myself and spoke at nine in all. I believed that if we had stayed with the LEA we were going to lose a lot of money and that I would have to make two staff redundant. But more importantly, I went for grant maintained status because I valued the flexibility, the ability to make quick decisions which I thought it would offer. I wanted to be in a position that if we needed something important for this school, tarmac the drive, paint the school or whatever, we could get on with it. I pushed for it, but I had a wonderful parent group with me. They masterminded the meetings and got the parents there. They were a crucial source of support.

PR: *Why are you in favour of going GM for this school and what is your general attitude towards the idea of grant maintained status?*

HH: I saw it as ideal for this school, not least because the governors, the staff and parent body are very keyed in, they know what they want. We know where we are going. We are a very popular school with 180 places in year 7 and over 600 applicants. The parents want an academic school – it has been branded elitist but the parents are clear they want us to maintain our standards. The only way we could do that without having things constantly watered down was to be our own boss. I am purposely using 'our' to mean the governors/parents/staff. I have a real pride in my school now – because I know that what we have achieved we have done ourselves. I do not rely on Hertfordshire to come in and bail me out or to help me. I don't need that. I need the support of other heads, of course. I have this. We have never been isolated. The idea GM results in isolation is a total fallacy.

When we went GM there were four GM schools here. We have continued to work as a consortium. Our admissions are now organized within the consortium. But even when we were not in a consortium we had the support of other GM schools. The GM movement means you support each other. I can contact any GM head in the country and be confident they will help me. I noticed this when we were going GM and also when we were going through OFSTED. I found people were willing to fax examples of their policies on various things to me and I have done it for others. That is how it has been and is now. We support each other overtly – even if the philosophies of the school are different – so I don't feel we are isolated. Furthermore, take staff development – we have got the most outstanding choices – and the flexibility to accept or reject suggestions for in-school training. I welcome this. I like being independent. I would like all schools to experience the flexibility we have.

PR: *It is sometimes claimed that those who go GM commonly do so for the money?*

HH: It was good initially – but it is not good now. We were lucky to have been able to save funds for two major building projects. But Central Formula Funding (CFF) is going to work against us. We are going to have to be very very careful in terms of staff numbers. When we went GM, the only negative thing was that we had to take in another class group – another 30 children in spite of not having the space. That is going to work against us under the CFF figures. As it is, our funding has been going steadily down. We have also been paying back the central funding. That is not a problem. I think it right and proper we do so.

PR: *What do you mean?*

HH: We were funded at 15 per cent central funding to pay for things which the authority used to pay for. Now it is felt this was much too high and therefore we are paying back 10 per cent of this fund each year. We have budgeted for that. The argument on money is constantly thrown in our face. But the money and the decision to go GM do not go hand in hand. The philosophy is central and the key question should be 'Do you want independence or do you want to work as part of an authority? Do you want real flexibility working with your parents, your governors or do you want to work for the authority?'

PR: *What is your feeling about the publication of league tables?*

HH: I don't like it. It gives parents the wrong information. Perhaps not that but it doesn't tell the whole story. I'm lucky – we have outstanding exam results. That is important. It is the single most important thing as far as parents are concerned. But schools are very good at nurturing children in all kinds of ways. This is not recognized. I know what the Government is doing and I understand why they are doing it – but if schools are to continue to do their job and be respected by society for doing so – you can't just rely on league tables. Some have stressed the importance of judgements made on a value added basis. I wonder if the public will understand this. I noticed in a recent league table that those schools that had improved by x per cent on last year were identified in bold – but will this be understood? What people seem to want to know is are you in the top x per cent. If you are, then you are thought to be a good school. Parents are constantly saying that. If you go to my previous school, they do an outstanding job for their children, but they don't do well in the league tables. They are sending out children ready for the difficulties they are going to have to face in Haringey – surely this must be recognized. Even so, I think the league tables are here to stay.

PR: *What do you think will happen if there is a Labour Government?*

HH: I hope a Labour Government will look at what is good in GM and either extend it to all schools or give people the choice. You can go back to the LEA if you want, or you can stay out if you want. They could put two more locally elected governors on my governing body if they wished. That is not a problem. I don't want them to start treating me like a child again. I don't want that ever again. I hope a Labour Government will look at what is good in GM and build on that without making it threatening to GM or non-GM schools. GM schools have the parents behind them. I am apolitical – I think politicians are all the same – but I am totally in favour of GM because of the independence of thought it gives one. I think Labour believes in accountability and in locally managed schools. Locally managed schools have gone so far down the line that they could adopt the major aspects which GM status gives. I agree with equal funding. Some, in fact, LMS schools are better funded than GM schools now. I would go for a national funding formula for all schools. I think the Labour party are in support of that too.

PR: *Can we turn now to your OFSTED experience?*

HH: I have heard many heads being critical of OFSTED. I don't know why they are so critical. Our inspectors had some teething problems because it was the first inspection which they had ever done. In general terms I think that schools should be inspected.

PR: *You are in favour of regular cycles of inspection?*

HH: Yes, I am and for the publication of findings. I experienced a quinquennial inspection when I worked in London. It was very demanding and we produced the huge amounts of paper required and endured a week of disruption and all for a bland and anonymous HMI report. It was ridiculous. Our OFSTED inspection, however, made us do some very deep thinking and analysis. The preparation for the inspection was outstanding – every head of department was prepared properly. I had people that had trained as inspectors coming in and training my staff – getting them to the state where they were supposed to be. As a result we now have proper syllabuses, programmes of study, etc. I could not have achieved this on my own. In practice, the inspection was very traumatic for staff. When the report came out there were minor problems in the 'report back' but we clarified them in a very professional manner. The inspection identified key issues for action. There was some rubbish, of course, such as what they had to say on Collective Worship for all children every day. But many of the other things they identified were things we needed to work on. We are now a year ahead. We have tackled all the key areas for action and that is wonderful. More recently, we have undertaken a detailed analysis of the fine print. We did so by focusing on anything in the report that could be seen as critical. Everything is being worked on – that has got to be good for a school. I am in favour of what is happening. I wasn't in the beginning. But I am pleased we have gone through it and we'll be prepared for the next one when it comes round.

PR: *You have been a head now for eight years. Do you still enjoy it?*

HH: I'll read what I wrote in preparation for our meeting, 'I really love the job – I love coming to school – I love dealing with the personnel side – I like dealing with my staff – I like to feel I am helpful and I like to feel my school is achieving for the girls. I love the job – I really do.'

PR: *Is headship harder than it used to be? Does experience help?*

HH: I don't feel that I am all that experienced and I don't feel that I have all the answers. Even so, I don't feel it's more difficult than when I first started. The first three years were hard for me – I didn't know anything – I didn't know what I was doing – now at least I feel more confident in myself. I feel confident that if I've made a mistake I can admit to my staff/parents/anybody that I've made a mistake. There are exceptions to this. Technology is one. I've told my staff I feel terrible about the decision I made but I can't say anything to the parents yet because I feel this would be bad for the girls. But I am on a learning curve. I am creeping up – whereas I was probably going down during the first three years – now I can say I am learning again. I now know where I want my school to go. It has got easier in some senses and more stressful in others. I'm worried all the time about standards and expectations being lowered, that I might be becoming complacent. Fortunately, I have my deputies nagging me all the time.

PR: *What do you do when things go wrong?*

HH: I talk to my deputies first and then my senior team – I don't keep anything from them – and I really mean that. I talk to my chairman – and we solve problems together. I don't like having to reprimand staff, I absolutely hate it and it takes everything out of me – I usually do it first thing in the morning to get it over with otherwise the day is destroyed. I am grateful I don't have to do a lot of it because my staff are very good – but that is what I hate most in the job. Otherwise there is nothing in the job that I don't like doing.

PR: *You sound like many other heads I have talked to – you work all God's hours – how do you cope with that? With two daughters and a marriage how do you find time for another life?*

HH: My husband also works very hard – we like working in the evenings thank goodness, but I have always worked in the evenings. I don't know what I will do when I retire – probably study. So that is not a problem for me. I do work all the time but go to a gym at least three times a week – I'm going after this. I go to a Theology study group once a week. I sew – all the tapestries you see are mine. The busier you are the more you do. I can't sit doing nothing. I drive my husband absolutely batty. I can't be with people who sit doing nothing and then complain that they are very busy.

PR: *If a capable colleague comes and says I am thinking of headship what would you advise?*

HH: Shadow one of my deputies and then shadow all of them to get the breadth of understanding. If they were a head of department I would make sure they had a pastoral view too – you can't be a good head without a pastoral view and a pastoral feeling. After the 'shadowing' I would have another talk to them about the deputy's role – I do feel you need a few years being a deputy before headship and then I would advise them to apply for a deputy headship. If they can't cope with the multiplicity of roles and tasks which deputies face – they will never cope with a headship. I don't think courses are instrumental in whether you should go for a deputy headship. I would be frank – if I didn't think they were good teachers and didn't love children I would not advise them to go for a headship.

PR: *Did being a woman make it more difficult for you to get a headship?*

HH: I don't think being a woman was a problem. I did think what was difficult, you might think I'm paranoid, I was Jewish. Here I am the first married Jewish head – all my predecessors were single. I don't think getting the headship was a problem. The fact that I was a woman made no difference at all. When I first came to Hertfordshire, on occasions I was the only woman, but there are many more female heads now – which is wonderful.

PR: *Do women manage headship differently from men? If so in what way and why?*

HH: Definitely! Women are used to doing a million things at once – at home, etc., etc. They can cope with this. I'm not saying men can't cope, although perhaps I am, with deciding many different things all at once and doing all of them effectively. For many women organization is not a big deal. We are used to doing five things at once because we do it all the time. I also think that women deal with people differently. They can be overtly caring. They don't seem to have the same need for hierarchy in the same way that men often seem to. I can't say much more than that – every woman is different. Some women are very macho and others are not. But more women tend to have that element of humility than men do and I am attracted by that. Furthermore, men don't tend to be open and they are usually less ready to admit mistakes. I know you have told me of some exceptions to this rule and I know my colleague at the boys' school is not like that. We share everything and really talk about things to each other which is lovely. I have not come across many other male heads who share in that way – who are not afraid that they made 'a total mess of this or that' or who are willing to say 'I don't know how to do this.' Perhaps they are more willing to talk to you about such things then they are to me?

PR: *Are women more cautious?*

HH: Perhaps. I can walk into a room and people say 'Look, another confident female head'. But it's nonsense, I'm not, it's a big act. But I think women deal with their staff at a different level. I see the girls as my children. I'm not sure a man could or would say they 'are my children'. I don't really know. It is just my gut reaction. It is not based on rigorous evidence.

CHAPTER 8

Mary Marsh

In conversation with Janet Ouston

JO: *Could you describe your own education and say to what extent this has influenced you in what you've tried to achieve as a teacher and a headteacher?*

MM: I enjoyed my education, although I now realize that in parts it was limited. I went to an all-girls direct grant school which was therefore very academically focused. It was highly selective, and what now distresses me looking back was those of my peer group who felt that they weren't achieving and were failures when they were clearly some of the brightest and best of my generation. There's something wrong in that principle somewhere. But I enjoyed it because I came out in the right half of the year group and felt that I was successful and did achieve reasonably well academically. I enjoyed it and I went on straight from school to university – I didn't have any sort of a pause at that point.

As far as knowing what I wanted to do with my life I never planned to go into teaching. My mother used to encourage me to think teaching was a good profession for a woman – all those wonderful school holidays fitted in with your family, etc. She was a doctor and my father was a doctor. She had done her medical training but in fact has hardly worked. She worked for a little before her first child and thereafter very intermittently. Because she was way out of date when she went back to work it was clear for her the idea of doing a job you could do with a family was something she thought a good idea. I was adamant – I was not going to be a teacher. Having spent my education seeing teaching from the perspective of the learner in the classroom, I didn't see that it would be a particularly rewarding occupation.

I went to university and did my degree in geography. I had difficulty all the way through choosing what subjects to do because I have a fascination with quite a wide range of things. I wanted to study languages but was persuaded that was the wrong thing to do. I realized that my aptitude was in science but I wanted to be more in the middle and ended up with geography which certainly suited me very well. I like to know what's going on now and where things are going, rather than too much about where we've come from. I had a good degree at Nottingham – in the 1960s it was at the forefront of modern geography which was fascinating because it was challenging all the earlier assumptions about how geography should be studied, and it used lots of new techniques like modern maths and topology. That was a positive period and it was a good period for me personally.

When I left university I got married – I met my husband at Nottingham – and I still didn't know what I wanted to do. The university careers advisory people were useless – the only thing they came up with was a librarian and having a traditional view of what a librarian was I nearly died. I now see that there might have been something in it if they had presented it to me slightly differently but I certainly didn't explore that. So I applied for a job in market research and very nearly took a job as an industrial market researcher in London but my husband got a job first so then I knew where I had to live. It was in Luton. He was going to be in export and we planned to go and live abroad, so I thought what I ought to do was qualify as a teacher of English as a Foreign Language as this would be a useful thing to be able to do while we were abroad. The alternative that had been open to me was to go into academic research. I had decided that to do academic research would be self-indulgence. Certainly at that stage it wouldn't have qualified me to do anything later on, so perhaps I thought I ought to do something a bit more practical. I tried to go to the London Institute to do a PGCE in EFL. They were very nice about it but said 'You have no experience – go away and get some experience and come back next year.' Most people who do that PGCE have been abroad for a year but I couldn't do that. So I looked in Luton for a job as English as a Second Language teacher. Of course you couldn't get those without qualifications so I was a bit stuck. There was a shortage of teachers in the 1960s, and when I applied to Luton LEA for a job in ESL they called me for interview. But when I arrived they said 'Well, actually we've filled that post with somebody who's qualified but we have got a job in a comprehensive school where there's a unit attached where you could do some time.' I fell for it and thought 'It wouldn't do any harm to do this for a year and maybe it would give me a chance to try teaching some English.' So I found myself in an 11–16 comprehensive school teaching geography and to my amazement I absolutely loved it.

I was very fortunate, I think this is true of many who enter teaching successfully, that I had a very positive head of department who was extremely encouraging and very fair. But it was a school that I wasn't comfortable with. It had very rigid streaming – full streaming – but the head of department made sure that we all got a fair share across every age and the ability range in spite of the fact that I was very new. And there I was teaching geography without having done a PGCE at all because you could in those days – I only had my degree and they were so desperate for teachers they took me. But I was hooked, and I applied from there for a post at St Christopher because I was intrigued by the school. I hadn't been to it before, and found myself with only a year in teaching, and no PGCE, applying to be a head of geography in this small, progressive independent school. I got the job. That gave me a whole new dimension of experience very early on because I was running a small department and was part of a fascinating all-age school. It was alternative in many ways although not very radical in its curriculum – it was a bit stuck as far as curriculum development was concerned.

JO: *So were you at St Christopher twice?*

MM: Yes, my first incarnation at St Christopher was in the late 1960s and early 1970s, when I was head of geography, then my husband's job changed. We never ended up abroad – he travelled the world but I stayed at home. His company chose to send him on short, month-long, export sales trips rather than basing him abroad. When he changed jobs that moved us over to Essex from Hertfordshire and I accepted that it was going to be impossible to carry on at St Christopher. But in fact it coincided with the arrival of our first child. So I stopped teaching in the early 1970s and spent getting on for eight years in Essex bringing up my tribe of four sons which was a hugely important part of the experience that contributes to who I am. I really enjoyed it. It was very positive, extremely demanding, very rich and enlightening. I learned a lot. I really didn't know very much about bringing up small children – I thought I did but I didn't have a clue. But they were a wonderful crowd and I did a lot of it on my own because my husband was abroad so much. That's quite tough because I had no family nearby so it was pretty much full-time. I tried to do a PGCE – a distance one – but I just couldn't sustain it. There just wasn't the time to do it and there wasn't support that would release me to do it. I did some work teaching Asian women English in Barking which got me involved in the whole multicultural debate, and I worked with the Community Relations Council in Barking and I enjoyed that. You asked me earlier about my education – this is all my education – I've always gone on learning and there were more stages for my learning after that.

JO: *When you went back to teaching after the eight years where did you go back to?*

MM: Well, this is the most amazing part of my career I suppose. When our youngest child was just two weeks old and the oldest was 6, a letter landed on the doormat from St Christopher saying that the governors had met to discuss the fact that the deputy head would be retiring within a year. They had asked the head to approach me to see whether I was interested in the post. My husband had been looking for a way of not travelling the globe and if I was to work at St Christopher the boys would have a chance to go there too. This was something we were both very pleased to consider. We took a deep breath and accepted the fact that there would be quite a big drop in income, even with a deputy head's post, compared to what my husband was earning as an export executive, but we decided to go for it. So we moved to Letchworth, after he took redundancy from his job in Essex. We were in Letchworth for about nine months before I actually took up my post in 1980. So I went from my eight years of maternity leave, back into teaching as a deputy head. This was an unusual progression. And I think I found the one job in the country where the people appointing me placed great value on the fact that I had spent eight years at home bringing up my family and they saw that as adding significantly to what I could offer. They knew me from my previous time at St Christopher and they had identified that this was somebody they wanted to draw back in. I think it was quite a big risk on their part and it could have gone very badly wrong but I never thought about that at the time – it didn't occur to me. I just thought I'd grasp the opportunity for the family and myself.

JO: *So you stayed there for about ten years?*

MM: Yes, I was there about ten years. My family (who were less than 1 and 6 when I started) were all in their teens by the time I left. The eldest had left school and the youngest was at secondary level. While I'd been at St Christopher I did all sorts of different things. Within six months we took over a boarding house for 14–19 year olds – there were 120 of them in this huge boarding house which my husband and I ran for 18 months together with our young family who lived with us.

That was interesting – I learned a lot from doing that. After that I decided it was about time I got on with my own education – that I got some qualifications in education. Here I was in teaching having done a range of things but I still wasn't in any way qualified. And what was then Hatfield Poly – the University of Hertfordshire – had a diploma in education management and they were prepared to accept somebody with a degree but without a PGCE if they thought their experience warranted it. They accepted me so I did that for two years. It was a wonderful course. There were 15 of us on the course: five from each sector of mainstream education – so there were five primary, five secondary and five FE in the group. I think that was exceptional and I wish we did more training across educational sectors like that. I learned so much about current issues in FE and the primary level by being together with this group and obviously vice versa. It was brilliant. And it was particularly fortunate that there was this primary link because in the middle of my doing the course the head of the junior school at St Christopher left at short notice. It was decided that the head should be an internal management responsibility for a period to pull things together before the post was advertised. So I took it on initially for nine months but ended up doing it for nearly two years. So I've also run a junior school for two years at the same time as being deputy of the whole school.

JO: *So at St Christopher your responsibilities were mainly curriculum?*

MM: I was director of studies throughout my time as deputy there. I ran the curriculum and took over things like writing the timetable but I also took on other responsibilities. One of the interesting things, I think, is that St Christopher, being a smaller school, was almost a better preparation for headship than spending all your career in large schools. As a senior manager in a small school you do everything. So I was responsible for introducing the school's response to the 1981 Act on special educational needs. There are a number of special needs children at St Christopher so we took a lot of trouble to get that right. We worked with the educational psychologist who came into the school so I was very actively involved in establishing procedures for special needs in a more overt, explicit, way than had been traditional before. I took on the careers side and really enjoyed that. It's something I am very fascinated by – the whole issue of careers guidance. I think that's probably stayed with me in a number of different threads through my own career and I certainly say to my staff now that I regard all of them as careers advisers. I think it's a core responsibility, it's not something that just comes in at particular points in time and is only done by specialists. It's there all the time you're educating everybody. It's a very comprehensive picture that I have of careers guidance.

Now what about other mainstream responsibilities. Obviously I was dealing with the boarding side as well which is an unusual dimension. I did a bit on business links there but never really got them going as well as I would have liked to do. Then, of course, the very big thrust from the mid-1980s to the end of my time at St Christopher there was the Education 2000 Project which started in 1985. With that came IT, and that set me off on another wave of learning – my own development of my interest and competence in IT.

JO: *Now you did an MBA at some point?*
MM: I did, yes, after I'd completed my diploma at Hatfield. I thought I needed further management training and I looked around at the education Masters degrees. But even those called management Masters in the 1980s were rather soft. There were all the organization behaviour, human resource management, issues. None of the finance, marketing, strategy – none of those areas were there. So I realized that probably what I ought to do was an MBA but I wasn't quite sure where. I applied to a number of business schools and was completely taken by the particulars from the London Business School. This was particularly because their part-time programme had an element in it which meant that they wanted and expected people from the public and voluntary sector to apply. That's unusual so I went to an information session there and was utterly convinced that it was what I wanted to do. The governors at the time – 1985–86 – said that I should have the time released to do it, although they could see that the pressure would have been on me, but they said 'Not this year because we don't know what demands Education 2000 will make.' But the following year I was able to get agreement from them; some of the sponsorship for me to do it came from Education 2000. I applied to do it in 1987–89, and was delighted when I was accepted. I had to take a G-MAT exam in order to get on the course, which interestingly was done in the buildings just across the playing fields. I'd never been to Watford before in my life and I came to the American University which is now closed, next door to Queen's, and took

my four-hour G-MAT exam there. It was the first exam I had done for 20 years. That was really quite a salutary experience for somebody in the middle of their career as a teacher to suddenly have to sit timed exams. I was quite intrigued by the effect it had on me. I got a satisfactory G-MAT grade and got in.

JO: *And fairly soon after that you came here?*

MM: Yes, when I was completing my MBA – I finished at Christmas – I'd started thinking about what I should do next. I realized after being in one post for ten years – even though I'd done all these different things and it didn't feel like one post for ten years – that really I ought to move on and do something else, but I had a rather odd c.v. with an eight-year break in it and so much time at St Christopher that it didn't carry much weight or credibility for most people. But I applied for the post at Queen's and was appointed the same week as my MBA results came out in 1990.

JO: *So when you came here you had a lot of experience from a much smaller progressive school out of the maintained sector, and this was then an LEA school?*

MM: Yes.

JO: *So how did headship feel when you came into it?*

MM: Well, many people said to me 'How are you going to adjust to this very different kind of school?' but it was fascinating to see how many of the underlying issues were to do with people and they are the same almost wherever you go. Certainly schools have many strong common threads, and young people are fundamentally the same even if they are asked to look rather different in some schools. So I didn't find that transition anything like as difficult as many people thought that I might. The size didn't worry me because I was quite clear that if I was going to be in a comprehensive school – you needed a school of over 1000 to give you the scope to do what you needed to do. I definitely wanted a large mixed school so I was very happy that I had found that. I don't think I would have moved to a much smaller school. It wouldn't have achieved what I was looking for in terms of my long-term career at all.

I'd had a term at St Christopher being acting head before I came to Queen's so I suppose in that way I'd had some preparation for my first headship. Being an acting head isn't the same as being a head at all because you are a caretaker. You've got to be very careful, and you don't move anything. You don't rearrange the deckchairs even – never mind throwing them overboard – you've just got to keep things ticking over.

I suppose the thing that I found most extraordinary about headship – and I think it's an amazing statement of how I think things have moved on in the last five years, because I don't think it would happen to people taking up headships now – was the lack of induction. I asked the authority 'What are your arrangements for induction for heads?' and they somewhat shamefacedly told me that they didn't have them. Yes, they agreed that perhaps they ought to and they did invite me join some conferences – so I met some other heads – but that was about it. This was before LMS – we were a year behind – so the school still didn't have a delegated budget. When I arrived the governing body was gearing itself up for LMS but it hadn't got into the full flood of all those kinds of responsibilities. So they were quite used to leaving the day-to-day running of the school to the head and there was no thought from them that there should be any sort of involvement from them in my early days at all – I don't remember seeing them for several weeks of being here. But I do remember on my first day sitting down at my desk and finding all around me was just emptiness – I didn't even have pens or paper clips, or a pad of paper. It was very odd because it was not immediately evident what I was really supposed to do. There was no pressure on me to leap up and down and do it. I did set about meeting a lot of people. There was no agenda, there was only a limited schedule of meetings, there were no immediate decisions to be made and no outstanding matters to be resolved. There was a flow of paper from the authority and that seemed to be about it. So I set about creating my own agenda about how to move things forward.

JO: *And did you get any formal induction into headship?*

MM: None at all. I just don't believe that would happen now. I suppose possibly some schools might not prepare, but certainly if you wanted advice and training you could easily find it now – there are plenty of places you can go to get help if somebody doesn't lay it on – including all the mentoring that is in place now. I could really have done with that: somebody to speak to but there was nobody. Being a head is potentially a lonely position because people don't realize what your needs might be – your role is to support and encourage others rather than anyone thinking that you need support, encouragement and direction. To be fair the county area secondary adviser whom I'd met before – he did come in early on and had a discussion with me about what I was doing and what I was planning to do. He must have been reasonably satisfied with that because I suspect if he wasn't he'd have been back more frequently – so I suppose to that extent somebody did have an eye on what I was doing. Maybe when you look back it's a bit emptier than it really was at the time. But I do remember that I set about filling my diary with long meetings with every post-holder in the school, exploring issues and getting some sense of what the key priorities were and getting groups together to work on them. That was certainly how I set about it.

JO: *What were your priorities and your emerging vision for the school at that stage?*

MM: I found it very interesting trying to distinguish between the things which you should leave untouched regardless of whether, in the longer term, you thought they were right or not, and the things you felt that if you started to tackle them you would create all kinds of instabilities in things that were crucial to the school continuing to operate with confidence. Because the school was confident, it was over-subscribed, and it had good support from parents. There was every reason to think that this was a good school and there weren't major concerns about it. But in fact there were a number of areas where things had not been looked at critically for some time. I suppose my key priority was how to get a group of people who've operated very much in separate, fairly independent, department groups – to some extent almost at loggerheads with each other – to come together and work in some kind of coherent whole. Also to accept that reflection on what we were doing and deciding that some things were not quite right and that we needed to do things differently, and that this could be done in a way that didn't set off a wave of lack of confidence while maintaining the school's confident image outside. This was obviously important while all this reflection was going on.

If you ask the right questions you can begin to get the key answers and that's really what I set about doing. On the first training day I asked some very simple questions to start off discussion in cross-departmental and departmental groups. We used the feedback from that to decide the priorities by asking them 'What are the strengths of the school? What are its best achievements? What are the things that give you most concern? Where do you think the priorities should be? What are the key weaknesses?' Four or five simple questions and you very rapidly got a pretty comprehensive diagnosis of where the school was from the staff. They could get at it far quicker than I could. Then it was a question of steering the priorities. I could see that regular assessment and monitoring of learning, and actually ensuring that standards of achievement were of the best, was at the heart of it. But there were also a lot of organizational things – such as how to set the structures in the school so that this became more possible than it was – that I wanted to look at as well.

JO: *Did going grant maintained come up at that early stage?*

MM: No. That was later – that wasn't until 1992. We were firmly opposed to it right up to the general election in 1992. The governors had made a very clear decision about that, but after the 1992 election there already were grant maintained schools in the area, and it was clear there were going to be more. Once other schools in the area started to make moves to opt out the governors were determined that they were not going to be last. Their key concern was to protect the interests of the school. They saw that it needed the independence to manage its own affairs in this particular context. If we were going to do it we had to do it positively, which is certainly what we set about doing.

JO: *You said when you came here that it was a successful school and popular with parents. Has it changed since you've been here, in terms of its values, or its aims and priorities, or has what you have done been to implement things more effectively?*

MM: I think a lot of things are based on what was there before but the school didn't have a very sharply worded statement on what it was about. That was certainly one of the early issues. I found that whatever we set out to do – whether it was thinking about the prospectus which needed rewriting, or trying to get groups to grapple with issues of the curriculum – I kept realizing that until we'd had this debate about the aims and values of the school we really were in a vacuum. So we had a couple of very good meetings to look at that – 'What does Queen's School exist for?' It's these simple questions that are important – or perhaps it's a technique I use! You ask these simple questions and you wait for the responses, then you jumble them all up and you actually begin to get some strong, coherent messages coming through. You get some things that are extreme, but there are strong common things that come through.

Although the first responses to that question were all very exam result oriented, it very clearly became evident in the discussion that in fact people felt very strongly that Queen's was much more than that. So we came up with our simple threefold statement of what the school was about. Our by-line is 'Encouraging learning for life'. It took us a long time to get to that, we didn't realize it until the last eighteen months. The three core aims were largely being accepted as being right by the end of the spring term of my first year – within nine months. We agreed that the school was here to encourage effective learning, develop self-awareness and develop consideration for others. And they have stood up very well as the three aims around which everything else develops. Somebody said that we should start talking about preparing them for the future, but effectively if you get those three aims right you have prepared them for the future because that's about knowing who you are and what is important to you. Also we emphasized the importance of encouraging people to be different rather than having any kind of uniformity, and a view of an ideal outcome for all. We are into celebrating differences here rather than trying to be the same and recognizing that people have different potentials. The important thing is that they are as fully developed as possible. Obviously the whole 'consideration for others' aim is to do with community values, work in teams, and so on. You can see how it can be unpacked and at the heart of everything is the question of effective learning. We've used these as the touchstone for everything all the way through, and it's beginning to stick. I really do think people accept that learning is the most important issue in the school. What the school is trying to do is more clearly understood by everybody and this gave us a better sense of purpose about how things are done together.

I think the school is also much more inclined to look forward now rather than be complacent on the basis of where it's come from. I think we're very much readier now to be forward looking, to take stock of what we've achieved, and to ask questions about it confidently. I think that is quite a change – that sort of dialogue and debate and sharing of issues is something that was not so common when I came.

JO: *And that's come from your own leadership style, has it?*

MM: Yes, my predecessor was a very open warm person but his style was possibly less consultative. He probably delegated less than I do. But it's the nature of effective management that you have different styles for different contexts. He had run the school extraordinarily successfully for 17 years and it had had a long period of stability. Many things in the way in which the school operated probably hadn't changed in ten years, and there was no reason to, because it was fine. That hadn't been a problem, but we were moving into a rather different period, both in the way the school was run, and in the kinds of things we needed to do to face the future. Look at the National Curriculum – pre-1990 there was no National Curriculum, no LMS – now it's a different world.

JO: *Do you think it's harder to be an effective school leader than it used to be?*

MM: It's probably harder to feel satisfied that you are effective – to believe it yourself. I think that when the pace of life was a bit slower you could take longer over things. The range of demands was much smaller. As a head I think you could begin to feel that you were on top of the job, and be aware that you were, in a way that most heads now can't, unless they've got an extraordinarily strong and effective stable senior team they've worked with and developed themselves. But for most heads it's pretty hard to feel that you are doing everything you ought to be doing. Most weeks you don't do something you should have done that's quite big. And you've just got to cope with not having done it or find time to do it in the next week which is even worse than the last one. The pressures are from the range of things you need to be doing – it is impossible to do it all – so if you are at all self-critical, which you absolutely have to be to survive as a head, you are very aware of this. The loneliness you can experience sometimes is in terms of getting feedback – you have got to be the one judging things a lot of the time. If you are working in that way, to do that and to be very aware of what you're not doing, and yet say to yourself 'I am succeeding, I am an effective leader' is actually quite difficult. So I think you probably can be an effective head as much now as you ever could be, but to believe you are is probably more difficult.

JO: *Who manages you and to whom you are accountable? Is that a straightforward question?*

MM: Well, when I came here one of my MBA colleagues came to interview me because she was doing some work with a local authority as a consultant. She felt she needed to know something about schools, so she came to talk to me to give her some background. One of her first questions was 'Who is your line manager?' and I just said 'I don't have one.' She could not understand this. And you don't really have a line manager in a grant maintained school. Yes, clearly, you are appointed by the governors but as soon as you are appointed you are ex-officio a member of that governing body. So you're in it as well as without it as it were. You can say that for a grant maintained school head ultimately it's the Secretary of State you are accountable to but that's pretty far removed.

Certainly in a local authority school the relationship with the authority is one that is different in every local authority you go into. The degree to which that feels like a relationship in which you are managed, or one in which you are a partner in a joint enterprise, or that you're left to get on with it – there is every shade of this. In Hertfordshire it has certainly moved very rapidly to the partnership principle with the new Director of Education who arrived soon after I came. Hertfordshire has been very successful in changing the way the authority operates in relation to its schools in establishing that kind of way of working. While I was an LEA head I felt very comfortable with the relationship I had in terms of management. But when you come to be appraised the Hertfordshire model of appraisal was the secondary adviser and a local head, but nobody from the governing body was directly involved. But that may be different now. It is likely in this grant maintained school that the chairman of governors is going to want to be involved in my appraisal debriefing interview later this term. And I think that's probably quite right.

JO: *So how did that change in questions of accountability feel?*

MM: Well, you're even more on your own in a grant maintained school because your governing body, who now have these enormous responsibilities, aren't here because they are non-executive. They may be very supportive, they may be very ready to be here if you want them, but on a day-to-day basis they aren't the ones who are doing it. Certainly as we went grant maintained I made a very conscious decision to protect the school from the change as much as possible to reduce the turbulence within the school. I encouraged the deputies to continue as they were, running the school. It was myself and the governors who managed the transition. But that inevitably meant that too much was falling to me, and looking back on it we really ought to have had some extra help as other schools do. But I've only got two deputies and it would have distorted things to have taken one of them out of running the school in order to be more involved in the transition.

The nature of the responsibilities, in terms of your total operation as a financial and personnel unit, is quite considerable. I don't know whether people always appreciate the scale of these. In my post today there is advice about liability for corporation tax which is something I had just heard about somewhere else but it's the not the sort of thing that had even crossed people's minds until recently. They might think about liability for value added tax which could occur as in an LEA school, but corporation tax is something that people in education probably are a bit surprised to learn that this is a liability they might be running up now. So it's a very different world you're in when you're operating on your own as an independent charity.

JO: *Do you get support from the Grant Maintained Schools Centre?*

MM: You can buy in what you want, but it's very difficult to know what to choose. You want to be very sure that any advice you buy is good advice. I think when we went grant maintained the sector was still learning. My colleague heads were my best touchstone at that time. And the auditors we appointed are pretty important people in terms of the advice. We appointed our own solicitor, and I am very glad we did that. Again, that is something you wouldn't even have to think about as an LEA head. Our potential legal liabilities for example – the possibility that somebody might sue you about something – and the need to give the governors correct advice about matters like that. Obviously the headteacher associations can also support you, but the grant maintained sector is still relatively new. As often happens in new contexts the law won't be established until case law has established it. I think there are some difficulties to come that mercifully I haven't had to deal with yet. I've seen where they could be and that's an additional pressure. It takes your mind quite a long way off learning. Apart from my own learning – and I have I learnt so much!

JO: *What have you learnt?*

MM: Well, I knew all about the principles of accounting having studied it. I now have a much sharper understanding of what that actually means on the ground so that we implement it properly. A really rigorous attention to the separation of responsibilities, procedures and controls, and internal audit and all of that – things I knew in theory but when you actually come to do it, it's rather different – that's just an example.

JO: *A more difficult question – what do you see as your key educational and managerial values? What sort of a leader are you?*

MM: In terms of values I am passionately committed to openness and trust – and being direct. I think that's absolutely crucial. It's actually a very difficult thing to sustain because there are times when – for whatever reason – you've got to deal with something without necessarily explaining everything or preparing people for it. And I'm very aware of how vulnerable people's confidence, and their trust, actually is. You've got to live it and work it every day. It only takes one serious incident where people feel things were handled badly, or they felt that they weren't being consulted, for you to lose that. You know when you've got it – when you've been through one of those difficulties and you come out the other side, and you've still got everybody with you. But as you go through it you still feel very vulnerable. This is very important to me – I'm looking to do things with other people rather than to them or for them – that's fundamental.

I also believe in risk, and grasping opportunities and encouraging people to tackle things and see the potential that challenges bring. The upside of difficulties if you like. Also knowing how important it is that you try things even if it isn't what you end up wanting to do in the longer term. What you've learnt from trying is of benefit when you come to actually take matters forward. If you wait to arrive at the perfect solution by discussion, debate and somebody else to tell you, I think you make very slow progress. So I very much wanted to get on and do things, and try to make debate and discussion focused on particular issues in defined time spans to take things forward.

Where we haven't been able to do this is in the curriculum – I felt very trapped by the National Curriculum. There were all sorts of things I wanted to do with it, but I felt the whole thing was unstable, as indeed it has proved to be. I wasn't going to rush off reinventing something when the ground rules might be different before too long. So I've played that one pretty long while I've been here, and I think that will be a big issue for my successor. We haven't looked at things like the structure and balance of the school day. We've adjusted it, we've had a review of it, and we've agreed fundamental principles but the boxes that deliver the curriculum are still substantially the same as when I arrived. Nothing very dramatic has happened there.

My leadership is also pragmatic, because I will take advantage of whatever is there. I'm not (I hope I'm not!) over-ideological so that although I have things that I am more at home with personally, I accept other ways of doing things can actually be the right way to do them at a particular time or for other people. You've got to have a fair degree of drive to be effective because you've got to have the energy to sustain whatever you set off. If you aren't fairly determined sometimes things will come along and run you over or deflect you. So I recognize that presenting that drive to other people in a way that they think it's a good, not a threatening, thing is yet another problem. I think I'm very aware of timing (it's this pragmatic point), of when things happen, the manner in which they happen, and the pace at which you do things. These are all so crucial as to whether something works or not.

So what it is that you are trying to do often is much less important than how you're trying to do it, and that's the bit you need to get right. Yes, you've got to set very clear targets and objectives, but you shouldn't spend weeks developing elaborate ones. Keep it snappy, short, focused, and get on with it. Do it and review it. 'Is it working? No, it isn't. What do we do next?' So it's much more immediate and not so large-scale.

JO: *And is it still enjoyable being a head?*

MM: Oh, yes. I do enjoy it. I'm surprised I enjoy it as much I do, because when I was doing my MBA there were all sorts of other suggestions. 'Why – you're a teacher, why do you want to be a head? What are you in the LEA for? Why not do something else?' – a rather limited view of what the management challenges of being a head actually are. I also knew that I wouldn't want to be the head of just any school. I was going to be quite fussy. I am surprised that I've found a second headship that I'm equally excited and positive about as I was about this one when I came here.

JO: *What are you thinking about the new school?*

MM: It's a huge opportunity. The school has had a period when it has not moved forward. Certainly it has worked very hard to face up to some of the key issues in recent years. It's at the point where I think a great deal could be done to take advantage of this – if it's all handled in the right way, so that you build people's confidence. The trouble is that they've been subjected to, and taken part in, so much rigorous review and debate and inspection that they are at a point – and I don't think this is very different from other areas in the profession – where there is a lack of professional confidence to get on and do things. There is a sense of unease that I think pervades a lot of teachers because they have been made to feel so inadequate. I think there is a combination of that, and some continuing complacency about areas that do need to be addressed. Things need to come out into the open. I think being a bit more hard-edged about issues is something they haven't felt comfortable about. It's always this concern to be supportive and encouraging rather than challenging – I think that's where the emphasis needs shifting.

But it is a school with enormously strong roots in terms of its culture, and mutual respect between staff and students. The work the school does to support students with extraordinarily difficult backgrounds is good and they make great progress with them. There are some very precious things there that have got to be nurtured because you could easily trample all over them in trying to do other things. You could change it into another school, but it's got something of its own that I think ought to provide a special opportunity. I think we can get all the issues to do with learning and achievement right in the context which is Holland Park by the millennium. That's five years away and that's my initial time span. Some people will be looking for outcomes sooner than that and I'm sure we will deliver in some areas. But I think that the school is going to be more ready for the challenges of the twenty-first century than some others. I think it has the potential to be flexible, adaptable and conscious of the need to develop creative, non-conformist people, which is what the world needs. It's the way the world's going to be. Although school cultures are often very strong they are often very stuck and very hard to move.

I think it will be very exciting to be in a school which is very dynamic and alive and in touch with the world outside – it has the world outside in it – so the opportunities for action to start making those boundaries work are great. The community around it is so rich, too. I just think it's an amazing opportunity and it's a school environment that I feel very at home in.

Note: This interview was tape-recorded on 7 March 1995. It was then transcribed by Janet Ouston, and minor amendments were made to the transcript by Mary Marsh.

CHAPTER 9

Mick Brown

In conversation with Len Cantor

LC: *How would you describe your own education, and to what extent has this experience influenced what you have tried to achieve as a teacher and principal?*

MB: My education was somewhat unconventional. I attended a primary school which had an unorthodox approach to education, and as a consequence, very few passed the 11+ examination which was current at the time, and I, with the great majority went to a secondary modern school. Then, a few years later in 1964, selection was abandoned, and the higher streams in the secondary modern school – I was in one of them – were transferred to the grammar school. This was not very popular with the grammar school and we were made to feel somewhat unwelcome. The experience has left its mark on me and as a consequence, as a teacher, I've always been inclined to avoid the conventional wisdom to encourage critical examination of circumstances, and look beyond the orthodox.

I have carried this background and outlook into my own work as a teacher, and to an extent, as a principal. For example, this college does not subscribe to some of the conventional orthodoxies. We are one of a small minority who are not members of the College Employers' Forum. I describe myself still as 'principal' and not as 'chief executive'; my governors are still 'governors'; and we describe ourselves as a 'college' and not as a 'corporation'; and the non-teaching support staff are known as 'non-teaching support staff' and not as 'business support staff'.

But, to return to my school career, academically I did well at school and eventually went into the sixth form. I did not see myself as going to university at first and so went into banking for about four years, after which I did go to university and took a degree in Economics. I then trained as a teacher, and then obtained a job in further education. While at the bank I had been a part-time FE student, having taken an Institute of Bankers' qualification, and so I sought a job in further education. Then I moved through various stages in my career. I wanted to achieve a variety of ends in education and in order to do so had to assume leadership. On the other hand, I never had an ambition to move up the educational ladder for its own sake, and I became a head of department almost by accident. And then, vice-principal almost in a similar fashion. Having been a head of department in one college, I moved to another as vice-principal, where I spent three and a half almost idyllic years. The reason for moving from the first to the second college was that I didn't want to stay as head of department in the former, and in order to move up I more or less had to move out to a more senior job. I then came into my present post as principal, where I have been for four years. There is so much distance between the vice-principal and principal in one's ability to influence and shape the character of an institution, and because I wanted to shape a college of my own, I decided to apply for the principalship. I had been approached by the governors in the college in which I was vice-principal, to consider being principal when the current principal retired. However, I decided it would be more difficult to act effectively as principal in a college where I had been vice-principal than it would be in a new college, and so I decided on the latter.

LC: *How and why did you become a teacher and a principal?*

MB: Well, I think that question has effectively been answered by what I've just said.

LC: *How did you prepare yourself for becoming a principal?*

MB: I don't think I prepared myself at all. The local authority regime that operated when I was vice-principal was one I had been well exposed to and had had a good deal of experience of. I was a member of county-wide committees, I spent time at County Hall, I knew the system, the officers and the politicians well and was therefore well prepared for operating in a conventional role as an LEA principal. However, as the enormous changes which have taken place in education in the last few years took effect, I was not at all prepared for operating as principal under the structure that emerged following the creation of the Further Education Funding Council and the demolition of the Local Education Authority. We now operate under a system of Funding Council stewardship in which the sector is shaped by this body, whether or not that is the government's, or indeed the Funding Council's intention.

LC: *In your view, how has the Funding Council shaped the sector?*

MB: In a variety of ways. One way is through its funding methodology which favours the full-time learner, and takes less account of adults, or of programmes which are educationally desirable, but which may not have 'approved' outcomes. The mechanism, despite avowed intentions to become 'mode free' is still heavily loaded towards 'time-serving', that is, the retention of students on programmes, or in other words, of keeping bodies on courses. The Funding Council also exerts control through its audit service, and through its inspectorate, neither of which have any independence of the sector. The Funding Council also shapes the sector through its circulars, which, while they're issued for consultation, often contain a clear, preferred outcome. Certainly, I feel that in the eyes of the great majority of principals, it is the Funding Council which controls the sector.

LC: *How well prepared were you for your first principalship?*

MB: Well, as I've just explained, I was well prepared in the conventional sense, that's to say if we had remained a conventional college, but very ill prepared for what was to come after April 1993 when the colleges became corporations.

LC: *What is your vision for your college, and how do you go about trying to achieve it? And if I may ask a supplementary question: from what you said at the beginning – about describing your institution as a college and yourself as principal – that sounded like a traditional college approach: is that a fair description?*

MB: The college is traditional only in the sense that we are very much oriented to the local market. We are not a European college, for example, seeking students from the continent, still less from further afield. We see ourselves as providing programmes for the local market, which is an area where skilled workers are under-represented and which has pockets of high youth unemployment. Therefore, we adopt a traditional approach in terms of serving our local priorities, but not in the way in which we deliver our curriculum. We have always had a strong tradition of pastoral support for our students, and we have maintained and strengthened that support at a time when many others appear to have forgotten that it is desirable. At an early stage, we decided to take opportunities for learning out into the community, so that we treat the concept of 'the learning community' very seriously. As a result, we have developed very close links with local employers, 85 per cent of whom in this area employ fewer than 25 people. We are increasingly basing our curriculum delivery on electronic forms, in which we involve employers, many of whom, because of their small size, have never had any systematic involvement in training. In achieving, or trying to achieve, my vision for the college, I know that the principal plays a key role in determining the nature of the institution, along, of course, with the governing body, which examines and ultimately endorses the approach taken.

LC: *How big a part do the governors play in formulating policy in your college?*

MB: Given the prescriptive role of the FEFC, the local TECs, and others, governors' real authority is rather limited. They look to the college – that is to say the principal and the Senior Management Team and the Academic Board – to indicate the direction and to provide options. We work very hard to ensure good relations with our governors, though occasionally governors can feel they are merely 'rubber stamping'. To a degree this is inevitable, because they only meet once a term, as does the governing body's Finance and General Purpose Committee. As a consequence, they touch the organization in the college tangentially at points in the year. Their real strength, I think, is to review performance against college targets, and the direction they have been asked to endorse.

LC: *But while governors don't meet together often, presumably you see the chairman of the governors much more frequently, and, if he wishes, he could doubtless play a bigger role in influencing college policy?*

MB: Yes, he can, but the chair of the governors of this college is very busy. As a consequence, I see much less of him than I used to. This does not necessarily impair the efficiency of the governing body however, for example, we've had to convince the governors that certain financial economies have been necessary in the last few years, as a consequence of which a number of staff have taken either voluntary or involuntary severance. We've said to our governors 'This is what we've had to do' and asked them to endorse this. They are prepared to accept changes that have to be made, though, of course, not everyone is necessarily entirely happy about it. But to come back to my vision for the college: when I came here, it was heavily biased towards full-time 16- to 19-year-old students. What I've tried to do, supported by senior staff and governors, is to emphasize our role as bringing learning to the community, and to enable the community to access learning in the colleges, by whatever means are appropriate. As a consequence, numbers of full-time students have declined relatively and absolutely over the last few years, while part-time student numbers have increased very significantly, and those accessing college programmes 'flexibly' have also increased significantly, very significantly. By accessing college programmes flexibly, I mean those who attend our learning centres. The college is located on six sites, and we have learning centres on four of these . . . our next phase is to locate computers there, and to enable students to have access to a central learning facility. We hope also to extend this facility to local small- and medium-sized firms. We are pursuing this development in conjunction with two other colleges.

LC: *Where do you get the cash to do this?*

MB: The majority comes either from the FEFC capital (Hunter) allocations, or the fund which the 1994 'competitiveness' White Paper recommended. We put in a bid for the latter this year, and have been successful. In moving in this direction, I have been strongly supported by my Senior Management Team, which has changed almost completely in the four years since I've been here. I was at first unable to change the team which I had inherited, because under the local authority regime prior to April 1993, there was a policy of 'no redundancy' which effectively meant 'no severance under any conditions'. Since then, I have changed the personnel of the Senior Management Team through persuasion, through accident in the sense that one retired through ill-health and in one case through dismissal.

LC: *Given the entirely different financial regime which applied after April 1993, presumably you have had to appoint somebody with financial expertise?*

MB: Yes, we decided to appoint someone who was a chartered accountant, and he was appointed in October 1991. In addition, my deputy is a human resource specialist, experienced in personnel and industrial relations: he was appointed in 1995.

LC: *Are you going to continue in this general direction as far as college policy is concerned?*

MB: Yes. Up until now, all colleges have been chasing the same market, as have been the secondary schools. Now, everybody understands that the only possibility for expansion is to recruit more adults, both unemployed adults, plus the very much bigger market of those in full-time employment. The policy has been forced upon colleges by the need to increase student numbers in order to survive financially. Indeed, the financial position of all the colleges that I have some knowledge of is fragile. Part of the problem may lie in the insecurities of those now responsible for the sector, who may occasionally exhibit ignorance of the complexities and diversities of further education. As a result, every time there's any suggestion that things are not quite right, there is a tendency to respond in a disproportionately heavy-handed fashion. Since the Nolan report, there appears increased nervousness about the use to which public funds are put.

LC: *What are your key educational and managerial values? How successful are you at putting them into practice?*

MB: As far as educational values are concerned, as I've said, what underpins the work of this college is our policy of accessibility and opportunity; our notion of the 'learning community' in society enabling people to have access to learning without discrimination. As for my managerial values, I believe in the 'no blame' culture. This has two aspects: first, that staff with responsibility for various aspects of the college should both be able to admit mistakes and secondly, should put them right. This takes some time for individuals to learn that this is not an easy option, and that unless you admit your mistakes you make no progress. Certainly, it is asking a lot of individuals, particularly those who are not very secure, to admit that they are wrong on occasion. However, this policy is about commitment, rather than compliance, and about ensuring that individuals are aware that as long as they act in a proper and professional way in pursuing what are often risky ventures, they will not be 'jumped upon' when things go wrong.

LC: *How successful have you been about putting this policy into practice?*

MB: As for educational values, this has been OK, because the county council previously had an underlying framework of values, which staff understand and which are basically congruent with those which are held by me and my governors. Where managerial values are concerned, the difficulty is that when you reconstruct the management systems and appoint new people, they bring other values with them. As a result, this is proving more difficult, and there's an element of cultural change that will take some time to work through. All the Senior Management Team, apart from the chartered accountant, have been recruited from the traditional FE sector, and have adapted very well to the changing climate. Nowadays, individuals applying for senior posts in further education understand the sort of culture they're dealing with and the sort of priorities that face us, and, on the whole, they don't lament the passing of the local authority controlled system.

LC: *Do you lament its passing?*

MB: It depends on the local authority. I was not favourably disposed towards the incorporation of colleges. It wasn't thought through. It was a political act, and I'm not satisfied yet that the overall effect has been positive. On the other hand, staying with a local authority was not necessarily a better option, and we certainly haven't got it right yet. At present, there is no strategic national framework for colleges, although freedom from the local authority was, in some respects, desirable. The fact remains that colleges are struggling to survive.

LC: *How lonely do you feel? Are there informal networks of principals? Is there anyone you can turn to for help and advice?*

MB: Although we've lost the support networks provided by the local authority, unofficial ones are quite buoyant. I'm in contact with a number of principals across the country to discuss common problems. There is a great deal of informal networking, virtually on a national basis. Although the former regional meetings of principals have gone, other meetings have replaced them. I am a member of a group of principals, for example, who meet from time to time, to lobby against the demise of certain programmes, and there is a group of us planning a regional framework in South Derbyshire who meet regularly. But to answer your question: yes, principals have a greater propensity for loneliness than hitherto.

LC: *How do you manage people and resources?*

MB: As for managing people, I think that good teachers are themselves good managers. However, they require empathy, which is critically important. I require of them both honesty and commitment, but I do not define the latter as long hours spent at the work-place which I think can be self-defeating. Communication is absolutely vital, by which I mean keeping people informed about one's thinking and one's objectives. It comes back to the principle that if people are not prepared to sign up to the 'no blame culture', they have to be confronted. Ideally, we should have a group of highly committed people who do not require managing, but in its absence one has to be prepared to deal with those who under-perform.

LC: *What part do you play in enabling more effective teaching and learning?*

MB: Very little directly. My direct influence is at the strategic level, where our action plan contains proposals for teaching and learning styles and priorities. However, I try to ensure effective teaching and learning in various ways. For example, every year I produce a detailed annual report, part of which looks at outcomes such as examination results. As long as these continue to be very good and students are happy, then I'm reasonably content. Also, the Funding Council's inspectors' reports have continued to be good, and I am in the middle of negotiating a system of appraisal to include classroom observation of teaching staff by their immediate line managers. My influence is indirect therefore, and has much to do with personal style and stated priorities.

LC: *How do you manage external relations?*

MB: This is very much my personal role, which requires a great deal of local involvement. For example, there is the Erewash Partnership, which is a local private and public sector economic development company, of which I am a member of the board. I also run the Learning Community project, which has close links with local industrialists and employers, and meet heads of local schools at an informal level. We also have a formal marketing policy, which requires me to go out into the community. All this is very time-consuming but essential. If an employer has a training need, I want them to think first of this institution, which increasingly they do. When I came here, the college had virtually no presence in the outside community, and its employer links were very poor. Since then, we have put a great deal of effort into this area which is increasingly paying off.

LC: *Is it harder to be an effective principal than it used to be?*

MB: In some ways, incorporation has made it easier to be an effective principal because one is freer of local authority bureaucracy and restrictions. However, effectiveness depends on the Funding Council keeping its distance, which all too often it doesn't – it creates problems, because, for example, its audit requirements are heavy handed, its inspection regime is massively disruptive and its funding mechanism is very complex. I have to say that in my view the sector as a whole views the Funding Council negatively, and regards it as a major problem.

LC: *How do you manage others within the college you lead?*

MB: I've already answered that, I think. I use the same approach throughout. As far as senior managers are concerned, it is about good communication, and looking to them to manage. They have to develop a certain autonomy, but not an independence from the organization. And, as I've said, have to admit when mistakes have been made, and be prepared to take the necessary action to correct them.

LC: *What sort of leader are you?*

MB: I like to think of myself as consultative, participative, empathic and approachable, but inflexible where effort and commitment are lacking, and uncompromising where 'game-playing' occurs. There is no room for 'game-playing' in managing a complex organization like this, and managers have to be aware of it. I am more aware of it, I think, because it becomes easier to identify with experience.

LC: *Who manages you, and to whom are you accountable?*

MB: No one actually manages me day to day, or perhaps my deputy manages me to some extent! Certainly, the relationship between us is a key one, as far as the running of the college is concerned, and is, in some respects, more important than my relationship with the chair of the governors. However, a number of principals have dispensed with their vice-principals, which I find difficult to understand. I delegate to him a great deal of responsibility for smoothing the internal ripples of the institution, and here his industrial relations and personal experience have proved invaluable. The day-to-day running of the college is very much in the hands of the Senior Management Team. For example, for every session of the day and evening there is someone who is acting principal and is in the building. I myself am accountable to the governing body, who are accountable in financial terms to the Funding Council. Only the governors can remove me from my post, although the Secretary of State can remove the governors.

LC: *Is there a part of your role that you find especially difficult, and/or do not like?*

MB: Yes: the unhealthy obsession on the part of the Funding Council with public sector accountability, and its deep paranoia which gives it the impression of it not properly understanding the sector. There is an obsession with ethics and probity, especially following the Nolan enquiry, which makes it very difficult for principals, because the slightest hint of anything untoward – which in a very volatile sector is inevitable – in comes the Council in a heavy handed way. They have a lack of confidence in principals, and exhibit a lack of security themselves. As far as industrial relations in the college are concerned, we have no particular problems, nor have we had any great problem in negotiating new contracts with the staff. We consult very closely with the staff unions and have been able to keep things very stable. We are not members of the College Employers' Forum, and have negotiated new college contracts with 92 per cent of the staff. However, another major difficulty is the increasing 'screwing down' of public expenditure on further education, especially since last November's Public Expenditure Review. As a result, we have had to examine our future and are now engaged in something of a struggle to survive. Fortunately, the situation here, at least, looks relatively secure.

LC: *Do you still enjoy being a principal?*

MB: Yes. Provided that I continue working in the further education sector, there is no other post I would rather have. Having built up relationships with the local community, and having a Board of Governors I'm happy with, I am now more settled in my role after four years as principal. However, were I not to be principal, I think I should leave the college. From time to time I consider my future and I think that I shall want to work in the further education sector in some capacity or other, if not as principal.

LC: *Is the term 'principal' still an accurate description of what you expect of yourself and what others expect of you?*

MB: Yes. As I've said, I don't use the term 'chief executive', though indeed the principal is both the chief executive and the leading professional. It would be very difficult for someone to be appointed as principal from outside this sector, either to make sense of it or to be credible in the eyes of the staff, who are highly articulate and highly critical. Moreover, people in the local community with whom I interact, such as employers, expect me to be knowledgeable about further education.

CHAPTER 10

Kenneth Edwards

In conversation with Hugh Busher

HB: *You were at a county grammar school in Shropshire?*

KE: I went to a fairly small county grammar school with a small sixth form in a small country town. It was not particularly well equipped but had a very supportive and encouraging environment for someone who clearly had, I suppose, some academic potential. I'm not sure that I recognized that at the time, but my teachers did and so I got a lot of support. I found I enjoyed science and the enthusiastic attitude of my science teachers.

My parents were farmers and so I found the idea of agricultural science attracted me. My parents were keen to see me move into a 'profession', since they remembered very vividly the difficulties of running a small family farm in the depressed years of the 1930s – so they were accepting of the idea that a university was OK, given that I did not like their first choice, which was that I get a job in a bank! I was the first member of my family ever to go to university and I enormously enjoyed the experience. I thought that it was something to be greatly valued partly because before going to university I'd spent two years in the Air Force. Having that break out of education made me appreciate getting back.

After university I went straight on to do a Ph.D. in a research institute. It was something that appealed to me. Already by that stage I could envisage a research career or at least I hoped for a research career. Going to a research institute to do a Ph.D. rather than doing one in a department opened up a vista of research which I think suited me. After that and various fellowships in the States and so on, I went to Cambridge as a lecturer and became a College Fellow and eventually became a head of department. Now I suppose it's interesting why anybody becomes a head of department. I think in my case it was the old story of the alternative people were too awful to contemplate. I couldn't really bear the thought of any of my colleagues being head of department. Originally I was going to hold the post for a year. In fact everybody obviously felt that I was doing quite well so I continued after that and eventually became Chairman of the School of Biological Sciences in Cambridge. After that I had this rather peculiar job in Cambridge called Secretary General, a full-time senior academic administrative job. To some extent that sums up my own experience. My own education had been so enjoyable that I felt (a) I wanted to stay in that kind of work and (b) I felt I could contribute something back, or I hoped I could contribute something back to it.

HB: *You started off as a researcher but you now seem to have little time for research. How do you see that change in balance in your life, in activity?*

KE: Yes I did start off as a pure researcher. I was working in a research institute for the first few years. After my Ph.D. I went back to doing no teaching. Why did I change? What were the factors? What has happened to me? I discovered I think by chance that I had administrative skills. I'm not quite sure what they were but I found I was able to cope with those sorts of things, to make sensible decisions and to get things done. That in a university is not actually always a very common currency. So I find myself being asked to do all sorts of things because I could do them without too much fuss. While doing research I discovered that although it was fascinating it was a slightly lonely activity and a rather narrow activity. By performing administrative tasks which were involved with research not just paper shuffling tasks, I was able to relate to people that I wouldn't have done otherwise. Particularly being a head of department allowed me to be able to help, advise and act as a mentor to younger members of staff who were trying to make their way. To see some of these succeed was immensely satisfying. I suppose it went from there really. I miss research. It's a long time now since I did any active research. It was about ten years ago. I miss the atmosphere in the laboratory, you know, the very informal and at times highly creative atmosphere of a lecture.

HB: *What did being a head of department in Cambridge involve you in doing?*

KE: Cambridge is a very loosely organized university. Every academic regards themselves as being highly autonomous. I think they would see parallels between themselves and a general practice of doctors or a partnership of solicitors, i.e. they bring their professional skills. The value of the organization is that it allows them to share some of the overhead costs and it produces a range of expertise which attracts more clients. Therefore being a head of department certainly doesn't give one much power. I suppose that one thing I learned from holding the post was that the sometimes rather slow business of trying to persuade people to do things rather than directing them to do things was one that I could live with. It probably suited my personality. In fact it conditioned my approach to the jobs that I have had subsequently.

HB: *How did you persuade them? Where did you meet people to persuade, to talk with them?*

KE: Well working in an experimental science subject you see a lot of the people in the department because of necessity most of them are tied to laboratories to do their research and to teach. Being a laboratory scientist myself, I'm used to working alongside people in experimental work. The rest of the networking in Cambridge that leads to decisions about how your department fits in with other departments is partly through the college system which produces a lot of informal networks and partly through an extraordinarily cumbersome and arcane committee system with which obviously, as a head of department, you spend a lot of time being involved. The Chair of the School of Biological Sciences rotates around the heads of departments.

HB: *Did that involve you in a lot of negotiations?*

KE: Yes. The School of Biological Sciences was essentially a talk shop. It didn't have a budget of its own but it did realize that in order to try to get what it thought was a fair share of the university cake, they had to be co-ordinated and well organized to stand alongside the other groups, like the physical sciences, social sciences and humanities.

HB: *How did you learn about leadership in the context of what you were doing in Cambridge?*

KE: To answer the question how did I learn about leadership implies that I feel I know very much about leadership. I think I know a little bit about leadership but I wouldn't like to be too positive about that because it's something that you're constantly re-learning because it comes in such varied shapes. As a head of department I realized that getting decisions made when you had no or very little direct power was essentially a political process. I think leadership is a political process, with a small 'p', in that you have to try to create an atmosphere in which the people involved feel the solution which has been produced, gives something for everyone and that the total solution, the total benefits from that solution, are better than any alternative. First of all leadership involves analysis of a situation to try and identify what the options are.

Secondly it considers how these affect various interest groups of people. Thirdly it requires the leader actually to try and produce with the other people an acceptance of a particular strategy. Now that's one aspect of leadership. Another aspect is the direct impact a leader can have on people who for one reason or another are feeling disenchanted or disappointed or disillusioned. That aspect of leadership involves a much more direct one-to-one relationship with people. It's an important part of leadership. It's been a considerable fascination to me to realize how poor, actually, the university system has been in some ways at caring for its members. The sense that nobody, in some cases, has taken any interest in the career of an individual has been quite disillusioning for some people. On the other hand there is a need to respect somebody's particular skills, expertise and experience. It's a question of finding the appropriate balance between respecting people as professionals on the one hand and trying to help if they need help or being aware that perhaps there is a need for help. That concern for individuals is another side of leadership that I suppose I became aware of when I was head of department.

HB: *What experience have you had of being led?*

KE: Well there's the military kind of course when I was in the Air Force. That was a fairly simple business of being told what to do when the consequences of not doing it were fairly serious. That was direction rather than leadership. In a sense I think I owe a great deal to the professor of the relatively small department where I was an undergraduate in my last two years. He was somebody I respected and I felt drew me out and encouraged me enormously. The head of department where I went for my first teaching post was someone who took a great deal of interest in his new young members of staff and encouraged their teaching and was constructively critical. That's another important aspect of leadership. At times you have got to be critical, and to try and get to do so in an atmosphere where people realize that you are being constructive and not destructive.

HB: *Why did you choose to become a vice-chancellor?*

KE: I think one has to go back a little bit and ask why I chose to become a secretary general at Cambridge. I think I did that because I'd already been head of department in Cambridge and chairman of the School of Biological Sciences. The secretary general post was on a scale that fascinated me. It was a kind of senior civil servant job in a sense. I enjoyed the experience of getting involved in the whole range of academic activities across the university. At the same time I found it somewhat frustrating because I wasn't in charge. Cambridge is not the place in which anybody is in charge in any obvious way. When I was invited to see if I was interested in the post of vice-chancellor it seemed a natural next step to move to a position in which you could try to exercise leadership.

HB: *How did your time as secretary general help to prepare you as vice-chancellor?*

KE: It taught me a good deal about how universities work, even though Cambridge is different in its organization. It led me to experience a wide range of academic activities. It taught me something about managing academic budgets and about resource allocation and it taught me a good deal about the outside world: about the university grants committees and research councils and so on, which was clearly a valuable experience to bring to the position of vice-chancellor.

HB: *What kind of leader do you see yourself as?*

KE   This is an interesting question because whenever I'm considering candidates for a professorship, I put down that we expect academic leadership from them and ask them what kind of leader do they think they are. What kind of leader am I or what kind of leader do I think I am? I think I am a hands-on leader. I think that when I came here I got involved a great deal in all sorts of details that, I gather now, not every vice-chancellor does. That's partly because I felt I wouldn't be comfortable unless I understood a good deal of the mechanisms and the issues over which I was chairing groups of people that were making rather strategic decisions. I think I see my role, and therefore I suppose this is the way I see myself in leadership, as being a kind of focusing device or exercising leadership to focus the views of members of the institution. I see a university as a source of points of light, many points of light – the bright ideas and intellectual ideas and forms of analysis by people. Yet we've so many points of light in three-dimensional space it's not easy to grasp the shape of this. Indeed you may be rather dazzled by these many points. So I feel a necessity to focus these in some way, to produce an image, which the institution recognizes as something that it is aspiring to. To put it perhaps more simply and a little more crudely, I see my job as creating a sense of the vision for the institution. In the end this is dependent upon everybody but I think that the vice-chancellor, as leader, has a particular role to play in trying to help an institution to create a sense of vision, of what kind of organization it is.

HB: *What sort of vision do you have for the university?*

KE: The change in the higher education system in the whole of Britain of course has been enormous in the last few years and there's now a greater range of institutions which go under the title of university. The range of institutions is just as great as before, but now that there's a single mechanism, the search for the particular niche which an individual institution may occupy has become more acute. At the same time, of course, there has been much greater pressure for institutions to be accountable for the contribution which they make to society. Therefore the image that an institution presents to the outside world becomes very important as well. Because there is this greater diversity, because there is greater competition I think there's been a very substantial change in the way in which universities see themselves. When I was an undergraduate when there were only 26 universities in the UK, every university saw itself as a fairly modest variant on a common theme. The external examining system ensured a strong commonality and they were all attempting to be vaguely like Oxford and Cambridge. In the 1960s what were then the new universities were created, some of the former Colleges of Advanced Technology became universities and the polytechnics were created. Now the range of institutions is so diverse there is a necessity to have an image which is identifiably that of your institution rather than something that is identifiable with all the rest. Today, not attempting to do everything that every other university is doing, I think, is a considerable change from the past. The image that I have and I think this university has, is seen partly in its traditional activities and role, and partly in where it sees itself in this new and complex world which now includes so many other players in this particular game. The image largely holds on to traditional values: concentrating on fairly basic research in certain areas where we have our strength; recruiting largely from the traditional cohort of 18/19 year olds coming full-time; concentrating on advanced Masters courses. That is much more of a traditional role than this university has had.

HB: *You used the metaphor just now of being a focusing lens for creating a sense of mission for the university. What actually does that involve you doing? How do you go about creating that sense of mission?*

KE: In the end it's by a lot of talking, not necessarily in formal committees although there is some of that, but in networking. When you talk about how you actually arrange things this sort of grand idea of the metaphor rather breaks down. How you create that sort of mission image is in fact by creating networks so that ideas and information flow upwards and downwards and from side to side. Traditionally universities did this by very elaborate committee structures in which there was lots of representation on every committee and formal proposals bounced around between committees and up and down the hierarchies. Of course most of the time that worked well though sometimes it didn't because it became so tedious and slow. Then the notion that the process represented democracy was actually a bit of a myth. In fact it represented the influence of those people who were prepared to operate the system while a lot of people only wanted to get on and do their academic work. Although it usually worked quite well, it was too slow to operate in a world where the external factors are changing so quickly. So you're left with two alternatives, one is to have a highly centralized, highly directed system of decision-making in which the decisions percolate down. The other is to try and create a web of informal networks although they're formalized in the sense that you have to have a few structures by which information flows to operate it. That means extending your managerial network in to a series of layers all of which can pick up information and ideas and spread ideas and produce feedback. For example, I mentioned the idea of writing a mission statement. You can't afford not to have one, but on the other hand you want to have one to which people assent, not just on a piece of paper saying it's a mission statement. It had to be something that people actually recognized as being descriptive of the university. I could have asked all the faculties and halls and various other committees for their views but in fact I did it through a rather formal manner. The deans are critical players in this particular game, having good contacts. It is important that the deans get on well together, so they feel supported by me and by one another. Actually one of my deans today put it that, it is a position where you can get attacked from the centre and from other people in the department. A dean is someone who manages to score own goals at both ends.

HB: *This idea of informal networks and how you get colleagues at all levels to accept a mission statement is interesting. How did you get colleagues to accept that mission statement?*

KE: I wouldn't claim it was a perfect acceptance of a perfect notion. The six academic deans and their equivalents for academic services and administration and myself and the pro-vice-chancellors had an away-day which gave us a chance to knock ideas together and produce a document. The deans then took it and did a similar process with the heads of their departments. Then the heads of department took it away to the departments. From the ideas which flowed from all these meetings we then put the mission statement together. Now that I think is different from the way it would have gone had it formally gone to some committee or other and then been passed on to the faculty boards to be bounced around in that way. We were trying to do it in a way which actually gives people some sense of responsibility. A committee can be a very amorphous and rather aloof. It's very impersonal if everything's passed on to a member of the committee. The chairman might feel some responsibility, but sometimes they just seem to be someone who starts and finishes the meeting and tries to make sure in between something happens.

HB: *Why did you choose to use that method for getting acceptance of the mission statement?*

KE: I think it coincided with the early stages of moving from a fairly centralized decision-making process. It's really all about resource allocation. There used to be a system whereby a series of central committees and departments made bids for this. This was a move to a more devolved system. What we did was to devolve the two essentials, the budget and appointments to faculty posts, to the deans. Now that of course seems revolutionary. A lot of people didn't like it because some people had had a sort of direct access to certain committees where they lobbied. They had got used to a system that they felt they knew how to manipulate. Of course we were changing the system and they no longer felt they knew how to manipulate it. I was keen to use this new network to actually make people feel involved in trying to produce a mission statement. I mean, we talked at length about mission statements. I think they can be over-rated but one needs to go through the exercise every now and then, not too often, perhaps every four or five years. I think we're probably at a stage now where we ought to repeat the process and see how people feel about it.

HB: *You said you changed the system and people didn't like it because they no longer knew how to play. Was it a conscious decision of yours to change the system to knock out the old networks?*

KE: No it wasn't a conscious decision to do that. There were a number of reasons for doing it. One is that when you've got a highly centralized system people bid for money and lobby for money. If you've got increasing amounts of money you can always hand out a few more lollipops. It works quite well because people on the whole know they can have the odd lollipop now and then so nobody feels too hard done by. On the other hand if you haven't got many lollipops to hand out, you really need people to try to face up to the fact that with a limited amount of funding and other resources, their decisions are in their hands. They have to decide how best to use what resources they have and what they can try to do to try and increase them. It's the departments rather than any central committee who know more about whether they should have a technician in this subject or that or how many technicians compared to lecturers. So the process of devolution of responsibility was a very practically based decision to try to get departments to take these decisions. I hoped to get a better use of resources and a better acceptance of people actually making decisions over which they felt they had some real control.

HB   *How do you maintain staff morale at a time when there are shrinking resources?*

KE: There's no single easy answer to that. Part of it actually is for them to feel they do have some influence over their own fate. By devolving a big amount of budget control, they can see that if they take on certain activities, for example recruiting more overseas students, they will see some benefit to themselves. People can see some direct relationship between their decisions and the outcomes and the use of resources. People can see better that they've got some control over their own fate. It's not tied to some mysterious committee which they may or may not have been successful in lobbying. Part of trying to keep morale up at a time when the world seems to be getting worse generally – fewer resources, having to take more students, more legislation from government, you know the usual sort of litany of complaints – is to try to make all the decision-making as soon as possible. So I explain the situation to people although sometimes that can seem rather dispiriting, as you can spend a lot of time doing that and still have people saying why haven't you given me an extra computer or something. What is important is that if people think the place is being run in what seems to be a reasonable and fair way, you will get better morale. It's very difficult to say whether you're managing to achieve that sort of feeling of fairness around the place but explaining to people why it's not possible to do certain things or what the limitations are, does help. Spending time doing that is an important part of leadership, trying to perfect the morale.

HB: *Earlier on you talked about people who felt they knew the system and knew how to manipulate it. What sorts of resistance did you feel you met when you were bringing about these changes and how have you gone about overcoming those?*

KE: There were several levels of resistance. There were various heads of departments who'd been in those positions for quite a long time who felt they knew how to run the system. They knew where to go and they knew which part of the administration to contact, the vice-chancellor's office or the registrar or wherever. They knew which committees there were and which people to lobby on them. Those people actually felt very insecure and therefore were hostile to the changes. There were also, on the other side, part of that particular alliance if you like, parts of the administration who felt insecure about devolving control and decision-making to bunches of amateurs, which was how they saw the academics out there. The administrators were afraid the academics wouldn't be able to keep control of their money and so on. So there was some resistance on their part. That was partly, I think, a feeling of being threatened and partly a feeling that in difficult times you need some clear, strong central decision-making which to some extent can be imposed on people for their own good. I feel there's a real issue here. I think if you run a very tight centre of control you can certainly keep an institution afloat. You may even be better at keeping it afloat than if you have the crew making their own decisions about when they paddle and when they don't paddle. On the other hand if you devolve power down and can get the sort of voluntary co-operation of people rowing enthusiastically, then the ship will go faster. We still have a good deal of central control. We don't just take a decision and dole the money out here and dole the money out there, and then sit back and see what happens. How money is allocated is dependent on departments producing plans.

They know the plans have to have a good basis, like any holding company would require of a subsidiary company. You'd want to see what the business plan was like before the finance director would issue them with more funds for the next round of activity.

HB: *How did you resolve the conflict of values that you seemed to be talking about just now between yourself as the incoming vice-chancellor and existing members of your staff?*

KE: By chance, some of the most strongly opposed people were fairly near retirement. A few took retirement. Some people moved anyway. There was one issue which is perhaps worth mentioning to you because there was a crisis in the Arts Faculty. The Arts Faculty was in considerable disarray. It had about 80 members of staff who were organized in 13 departments some of which were actually tiny, two people, three people. There were only two professors amongst the staff of the faculty and they were all lobbying hard to get two or three extra posts. There was clearly no way in which those could be created. The issue was so major that it forced a crisis. Normally these things would have come up to the various committees allocating academic staff posts, non-academic staff posts and money for recurrent expenditure, three separate central committees. As there was an incoming dean who was fairly new to the university as well, I went and talked to the whole faculty on a number of occasions. I explained we had to sort out the problem, explained we couldn't create the posts but asked them to try to come up with some sort of solution themselves. What would they like to do? And after a bit of blood on the carpet and probably a good deal of iteration it was agreed that with certain people coming up to retirement and certain people willing to take early retirement and certain people who had arranged to move to other universities we could reduce the number of staff in the faculty and merge some departments. Now we've got virtually six departments with much more tightly knit staff and reasonable size. That solution was something that involved having to by-pass the existing structure.

HB: *So you had to restructure?*

KE: So that actually gave staff a faculty with a degree of influence over its own affairs and direct involvement in decision-making. OK they had to persuade me that that's what they wanted to do and I had to agree to it, but there was a direct interchange. I then saw the potential for using the faculties as units that could actually have a degree of involvement in the way in which they were run and so on.

HB: *How have you forced through some decisions?*

KE: Well, I think I haven't. The changes in the Art Faculty in the end were forced through. The staff didn't want to do any of this and I said 'Look you know either you come up with some ideas and we discuss them or I make the decision but the status quo is not an option.' I hoped that they would actively have a discussion process and in the end they would feel that they had some part to play in the decision. I mean the decisions that were made on our new structure, were not forced through against overwhelming votes in senate. That didn't happen. But I had to force them in the sense of pressing staff and spending a lot of time explaining, until in the end people were persuaded or gave way. Some were persuaded and some gave way. Modularization was another issue which we forced in the sense that if left to its own devices, it would never have happened. First there was a breakthrough, myself and the pro-vice-chancellors and getting the deans on-board and then a sort of networking.

HB: *How did you manage to get staff involved for modularization?*

KE: It's interesting to go back because I'm not sure that I was ever conscious at the time what persuaded them. There was a succession of arguments, one of which was that modularization was becoming the flavour of the month in the system; modular 'A' levels were developing; students would be used to having things in modules. Staff could see there were some positive advantages in that students get better feedback at various stages. The chemistry department had actually gone ahead and modularized itself and the students thought it was great and the staff thought it was great. If you can actually persuade some enthusiast to do certain things in a certain way and then use them as an example it helps encourage others. For with Enterprise in Higher Education, when the idea was first moved, many staff were sceptical and indeed I myself didn't think very much of it in its initial form. But there were some funds there and we could see some possible things. We got some departments who were enthusiastic and gradually it spread.

HB: *One of the things that seems to have been coming out of what you've been saying is the notion that you feel yourself accountable in a way to the faculties as well as presumably to other people. I wonder to whom you are accountable and how you feel managed?*

KE: The formal position of course is that I am accountable to the University Council and directly to the Chairman. As the accounting officer for the Higher Education Funding Council for the public money we get, I've got other responsibilities to say to the Council if they make decisions that I think are not in line with my responsibilities. I feel that I'm much more generally or much more profoundly, actually, accountable to the university. I mean I have this temporary trusteeship as it were for the university. It had existed for a long time before I came and hopefully will exist for a long time after I've gone. There is actually a limit to the things that one can do in seven, eight, nine, ten years or whatever in a job like this. I think I'm accountable, or to at least have a responsibility to people who are devoting their lives to this institution, whether it's the staff or, for a short time obviously, students. I can't be individually accountable to every one of them but to the collective. Now it's difficult to express this because it's much easier to explain the formal accounting procedures and say what you have to report and what you've done with the money and so on. It's much easier to do that than to talk in rather general terms about a sense of commitment or responsibility to certain people within the institution. I mean in one sense of course you could get into a position where the responsibility is mainly to keep the institution in being. In a great financial crisis then the responsibility would be to survive. You might then have to force through decisions which are really very unpleasant for quite a lot of people in the institution. People around the university used to quote examples of decisions in which they felt their qualifications would apply that I feel responsible for.

HB: *One of the things that seemed to come out of what you were saying earlier was your sense of accountability to the students too?*

KE: I mean we are accountable to the students, we have to be accountable. If they didn't come we would all be out of jobs. Again in the formal sense, the existence of students' charters is raising student awareness of their rights. Competition between universities and the league tables are beginning to make the students perhaps a little more conscious of the fact that they don't have to accept everything that happens. I think that's only marginal so far, but we're all concerned that it's going to become stronger. Beyond that, there is something that is, I think, quite remarkable. Through all the trials of the last six, seven years or so, a bit longer, I have been impressed with the commitment of so many of the teaching staff, despite the pressures, to doing a good job for their students.

HB: *Yes, but you seem to have a concern for the students that went beyond that sort of formal thing of students' charters.*

KE: It goes back perhaps to my own sense of huge enjoyment of my own student days and how much it mattered to me. Particularly coming from an entirely non-academic background, university opened up for me wonderful opportunities. I hope that we can do similar things for students now. They deserve the best that we can give them. I can't do very much myself, I don't teach any of them, though I have dealings with the Student Union leaders of course and occasionally with the worst of the miscreants. What I try to do is to encourage people to pay attention to their teaching and learning activities, to be good teachers. Students are important not just because they're there and our incomes depend on them but because there are a lot of individuals out there whose lives are shaping up while they are here as students.

HB: *What aspects of your role do you enjoy most?*

KE: I think I really enjoy the people issues most of all, particularly when you get energetic people, committed people, whether doing brilliant research activities, or new exciting courses that are generating interest or just setting up a new entrepreneurial activity and doing it with vigour and enthusiasm and a lot of skill. The opportunity to support them and make it clear that you appreciate it. Those are the most pleasant parts of the job.

HB: *How do you provide them with support when you see these interesting new initiatives?*

KE: Well we try to provide material and practical support. For example, if someone has got a new research programme and they need some start-up costs, you hope that you can give these to them. If it goes well of course the initiative should be able to pull money in from outside. It's not that I keep a pot of gold in my bottom drawer to hand out but it's actually trying to talk through the system with the budget centres and see this enthusiasm and commitment being infectious. Then people do appreciate it if the vice-chancellor is around and can say that's great stuff.

HB: *What parts of your role do you find particularly difficult or do you not particularly like?*

KE: I'm still not at ease with situations in which I have to be highly critical of somebody sitting in this room. I'd be much happier if I could say nice things to people and not be critical, but what I have realized actually is that as long as you are reasonable, that is to say you explain why you are saying certain things, although people may not readily accept that it's a fair criticism or whatever, they do actually appreciate, most of them, a straightforward description of why they've not got promoted or why they've not been appointed for this task or that. I think that's a very important part of my job. During the last two years, this is nearly the end of the second year now, I've been chairman of the National Committee of Vice-Chancellors. That has obviously taken me away from the university and so I have devolved a lot of things to pro-vice-chancellors, to administrators and so on. One of the things I try to maintain is a kind of open door policy. It doesn't mean anybody can come in at any time. Clearly not. But I've never had to put anyone off who wanted to see me for more than a few days. If it's very urgent then I see that I'm back here to see them. That's actually a very important issue. So for people who are not promoted, I will always see them and explain why, if they want to come and see me. A number do. Everybody who is up for a promotion for a readership or a chair, I will see and talk to them about the process and about their case and so on. I feel happier doing it that way and therefore I hope that the place is a bit better.

HB: *I was going to ask you why you thought it was important to see the person?*

KE: Because people's ambitions and people's hopes matter a huge amount to them. Also if people do get personal Chairs as a result of this exercise I've got to know them and that's another part of my network. We have about 90 professors in the university and well over 50, probably now approaching 60, have actually either been promoted or appointed since I arrived. Because of the nature of our interviewing procedures on external appointments and because I get involved personally with people when they're being considered for internal promotion, there is a very important network there. They become people I can go and talk to and who feel free to come and talk to me. Sometimes it's important to have people around who will come with not just their own worries but say things to me that reflect something that is not being perceived in the university well. They may personally feel that critical or not but they can convey that view. That's an important part of the decision-making process. As vice-chancellor it's very easy to get cut off. It's very easy to think that because on the whole the decisions that have been made since you arrived have been accepted and absorbed, that life is good really and you have no need to worry about how your next proposals or decisions are being perceived.

HB: *Why and how is it easy to get cut off?*

KE: I think it would be very easy to sit in this office and surround yourself with your PVCs and your senior administrators and make various decisions. Particularly when the world outside is changing so rapidly, you may have made perfectly reasonable decisions, there may be perfectly good justifications for them in the circumstances, but then once you've started the implementation process you're suddenly hit by the next change in. So you sit around again and you respond to that. Unfortunately there's a whole bunch of people out there to whom these changes seem to be arbitrary. So it's important for a leader to communicate with other people in an institution, hence the networks.

HB: *Do you think it's becoming more difficult to be an effective university leader than it used to be and if so what is causing that?*

KE: I'm not sure that it's harder to be as effective because the internal changes are now happening more rapidly. People accept that they're happening more rapidly. In that sense I think that the way that the world has changed has made it easier to be more effective. To the extent that we're struggling with what we see as adverse pressures from outside, in that sense we're actually becoming a really efficient and effective institution. It may not be quite so easy, it's certainly harder work, I must admit.

HB: *Do you see yourself now more as a chief executive or more as a practising academic or is there some kind of fusion between the two?*

KE: Well I'd like to think that there is some kind of fusion, but essentially I see myself as a chief executive, although I hope I am someone who is well aware of what makes academics tick because of my own experiences. I can't claim to be anything other than a chief executive with a responsibility for an organization which has £100 million turnover and 2500 employees and so on. You just have to be in that sense an executive. You have to turn your mind from tax law about some entrepreneurial activity one day, to equal opportunities legislation, to the rules for the new Students' Union or access payments or whatever, and keep an eye on those things. You can't really regard yourself as anything but a chief executive.

HB: *To be an effective chief executive, do you have to understand the academic job?*

KE: I find it very hard to imagine how one would do the job without that academic background but then that's the way I am. I know other people have been very effective without actually having been academics or at least have not been academics perhaps for a very long time. There are people who come in from quite different walks of life who do a good job. Any one individual cannot get rid of the baggage that they carry from their own past. That conditions how you think and it conditions how you feel about the job. You can't imagine yourself doing it without that particular past experience. I like to think that having been an academic for a long time I do appreciate how they tick and what matters to them.

HB: *I've been very interested in the way that you've been talking about your networking and the way that in a sense you keep yourself up-to-date with what is going on through it.*

KE: I enjoy it very much. I haven't been able to do as much for the last couple of years because of my national commitments. Going round departments and talking to people, perhaps going to the Economic and Social History Department and saying well how do you define economic and social history? What is at the core of the subject? Hearing differences of opinion because economic history has got a different emphasis to social history and so on. Asking them why they're doing particular research activities and what's exciting about those. Letting people talk about what's exciting for them I think helps people to feel involved and to feel that I'm involved. It also actually helps me to identify those individuals who have really got a bit of fire in their belly and yet are capable of handling this in a rational and convincing way. It's an important part for me to see where the real movers and shakers are.

HB: *Is there anything else that we ought to talk about?*

KE: Nothing that I can think of at the moment. I'm not aware of any sort of aspect of what I do that we haven't talked about. At least nothing that I think is important.

PART 3

Analysis

CHAPTER 11

Pathways to headship and principalship

Janet Ouston

Introduction

This chapter will focus on the professional formation of the nine educational leaders whose interviews are included in this book. It will explore the early influences on our interviewees and their professional experiences before they were appointed to headship. It will start by reviewing the influence of their education, and then move on to review their lives as teachers before they were appointed to their first headship.

Early lives and later careers?

As a developmental psychologist in origin, I tend to see educational leadership from the individual perspective, with the individual being located in the broader context of the family, the school, the LEA, and changing educational policy and values. The person is in the middle of his or her world surrounded by concentric circles of influence which move outwards from those areas that have a direct, daily influence on professional life to those which are indirect, and concerned with the wider society. These concentric circles roll forward though time, changing and interacting. For me one cannot fully understand the nature of leadership as described by our interviewees without understanding something about their own history, locating them not only in the current context, but also in the past. While this study does not focus extensively on the interrelationships between past experience and current behaviour, this has been the concern of psychoanalysts, who interpret adult behaviour in terms of childhood experiences. Storr (1989) has written an interesting critique of the theoretical assumptions that underpin many of these ideas, in particular the predominant role of interpersonal relationships in psychological development. More directly relevant to the management of schools are psychodynamic interpretations of organizational life. These concepts may have much to offer educational organizations and their leaders. Two recent publications are particularly of interest, by Hirschhorn (1988) and Obholzer and Roberts (1994).

Not all those who study teaching careers are interested in childhood. Evetts

(1994) for example, in her study of the careers of secondary headteachers, focuses entirely on the adult lives of her informants seeing her interviews as 'career history data'. She is, however, concerned with the interrelationships between the professional and the personal in adult life, reflecting her interest in gender issues in headship. In contrast, our own study has only a minor focus on the personal aspects of adult life but does explore the links between childhood and adulthood. One of the very striking things about our interviewees' lives is their diversity. These highly regarded leaders had very varied routes into teaching and headship. In a time of increasing formalization of the expectations and role of 'the headteacher' (through, for example, the new National Professional Qualification for Headship) it is important to document this diversity. Our study shows that good educational leaders emerge from a wide range of backgrounds and experience.

Theoretical approaches

Two contrasting theoretical perspectives are most directly relevant to this study: life-span developmental psychology (Sugarman, 1986) and from the contrasting perspective of life history and narrative (Hatch and Wisniewski, 1995a). As will be seen in the brief presentation of these approaches below, the life-span approach might be seen as essentially psychological. It focuses primarily on the individual and on processes which relate to the individual. The life history approach is sociological in that its analyses are concerned with using data from the individual to interpret larger contextual issues.

Most writers on life-span development focus on the development of particular psychological characteristics, and the entwining of nature, nurture and experience in their various theoretical approaches (Sugarman, 1986). Vondracek, Lerner and Schulenberg (1986) present a more focused life-span analysis of the interactions between experience, employment and the wider adult life. They support the importance of understanding the development of careers because of their significance in our lives:

> Today, work is viewed as an imperative not only for socio-economic well-being but also for physical and psychological well-being. Moreover, recent statistics suggest that in the United States individuals tend to make a more permanent commitment to their work than to their first marital partner. (Vondracek, Lerner and Schulenberg, 1986, p. 1)

Whether work will remain as important in the postmodern world, where it is argued that individuals will build a portfolio of many different types of work during their life span is debatable. (See Harvey, 1990 for a discussion of postmodernity, and Hargreaves, 1994 for an analysis of teachers' work in postmodernity.) It seems possible that people may respond to the demands of the flexible, postmodern world by either 'taking it on' with relish, or by actively creating a personal coherence within the apparently incoherent, or by downgrading the importance of work in their lives and replacing it with other, more personal, concerns such as family and non-work achievement. Leading a school staff would become a very different task in each of these scenarios.

Life-span approaches argue that a particular stage in development is not direct-ly predictable from the previous stage: each stage offers a range of possible consequences, so that 'lifelines' can be seen as loosely linked with each stage result-ing from previous stages and from current circumstances. Sugarman uses the metaphor of a river:

> A river, whilst having a force and momentum of its own, is also shaped and modified by the terrain over and through which it flows. In turn, the river exerts its own influence on its surroundings. Indeed, it is somewhat artifi-cial to separate the river from its habitat; a more accurate picture is obtained when they are considered as a single unit. None the less, for ease and clarity of conceptual analysis they may be treated as separate entities. The results of such investigation only reveal their full meaning, however, when returned to the wider perspective of the river + surroundings unit. So it is with the individual life course. We can concentrate our attention on either the person or the environment as the focus of the developmental dynamic. However, we will only gain an incomplete picture of life-span development unless we consider the interactions between the two. (Sugarman, 1986, pp. 6–7)

This 'interactional' view can be contrasted with the 'transactional' view of development:

> Person and the environment are assumed to be in continuous reciprocal relationship such that it is inappropriate to think of and study them as distinct entities. The transaction between the organism and the environ-ment is seen as the most appropriate unit of analysis. (Sugarman, 1986, pp. 8–9)

Life history and narrative approaches are seen more broadly as a qualitative method-ology for the social sciences:

> Life history and narrative offer exciting alternatives for connecting the lives and stories of individuals to the understanding of larger human and social phenomena. (Hatch and Wisniewski, 1995b, p. 113)

Munro (quoted in Hatch and Wisniewski, 1995b) makes this point even more strongly:

> The focus on the individual is to gain a deeper understanding of the complex relations between ideology and culture, self and society. Life his-tory needs to be situated in a historical, cultural, political and social context in order to avoid the romanticization of the individual, and thus

reproduction of the hero narrative which reifies humanist notions of the individual as autonomous and unitary. (p. 117)

The analysis of the early lives of our interviewees presented here clearly takes the life-span interactionist approach: here the focus in on the interactions of 'river and river-bank': of person and experience.

Methodological issues

There are several methodological issues that are of concern in this study. First, the nine interviews were undertaken by nine people. We have, therefore, a total confounding of interviews and interviewees. We will never be able to know whether the differences between interviewees is partly accounted for by each having a different interviewer. Second, the interviewers and interviewees were given an agreed interview outline. But in fact the interviews had rather different emphases, covered rather different areas and in different sequences. This is a particular problem for the analysis of the leaders' early influences. In some interviews this area is covered in depth and in others hardly at all. These differences probably reflect the values and interests of the interviewers at least as much as the importance of these early influences for the interviewees.

A central issue in all research on life-span development is the extent to which interpretations of childhood and early adulthood are influenced by current circumstances. We all have multiple current selves, and carry multiple children around within us. Most young people experience happiness, fulfilment, anxiety, depression and many other emotions depending upon age, temperament and circumstances. Memory of this period 30 years or more later will be interpreted through more recent experiences. It seems likely that successful adults will see their earlier years in quite a different way from those who perceive themselves to be unsuccessful in adult life.

Blumenfeld-Jones (1995) develops the concept 'fidelity' rather than 'truth' in narratives:

> I take truth to be 'what happened in a situation' (the truth of the matter) and fidelity to be 'what it means to the teller of the tale' (fidelity to what happened for that person). Truth treats a situation as an object while fidelity is subjective. (Author's parentheses, p. 26)

My concern is both with the relationship between fidelity and truth, and also with the selectivity that must enter accounts such as ours which link a brief investigation into early life with current circumstances. Doubtless each of us, if pressed, could provide very contradictory interpretations of our perceptions of positive and negative early influences on our lives as adults.

An additional important methodological issue is that of analysis. The methods most appropriate for the analysis of interview data such as we have here is by no means self-evident. Polkinghorne (1995) (quoting Van Maanen, 1988) said that in much early ethnographic research: 'little need was felt to do much more than gather and arrange the materials, for they would . . . speak for themselves' (p. 13).

Polkinghorne rejected this approach, and offered a more structured 'paradigmatic analysis' where the researcher attempts to identify common themes from several narratives. There are two alternative approaches that can be taken, either (i) the possible themes are selected from an external source – perhaps previous theory or research – or (ii) the themes are recorded from the data themselves. It is this second approach that has been taken here. All nine interviews were reviewed and the themes recorded. Each theme, even if it only occurred in one interview, was recorded. Each interview was then dissected, with all the relevant information on each theme recorded. This then became the raw material for the analysis, which in turn was summarized to draw out some tentative conclusions. Just as interviewees will create their own coherence and fidelity in telling their stories, the researcher has created her own coherence through the analysis.

Issues reviewed in this chapter

1   What influence did family, friends, early life, etc. have on their experiences and views of education?
2   How do they remember their own education and what influence did this have on their views as educators and managers?
3   The contribution of professional experience before headship.

The context

In considering the early influences on our interviewees one has to keep in mind both family and community influences, but also the society that they grew up in. With the exception of Keith Bovair, who was raised in the States, all our interviewees went to selective secondary schools. Married women often did not work, and it was very rare for women with small children to work. Thus parents were often ambivalent about higher education for their daughters as they may well have expected them to follow their own life-style and not work once they had children. Mary Marsh made the point that her mother 'worked for a little before she had her first child, but thereafter very intermittently', and 'she was way out of date when she went back to work'.

Selective secondary education was almost universal, and 'the 11+' was a central feature of the lives of all primary school children and their parents. The minority stayed at school to take 'O' levels: and research undertaken at that time showed that young people from working-class families tended to achieve less well in selective schools and leave at 16. The majority, however, left secondary modern school at 15 with no formal qualifications, to go into employment or apprenticeships.

There was virtually full employment for young people, whether they left school or college at 15, 16, 18, or 21. Far fewer young people went to university – under 10 per cent of the age group overall, and even fewer girls. Students got means-tested grants, and the full grant was just enough to live on. Vacation jobs were available for all who wanted them. Men had to do National Service for two years until the end of the 1950s. Some did it before going to university and others deferred until they had completed their degrees. Girls got married young, in their early- to mid-20s, and had families in the next few years. Many would have completed their families by their late 20s.

It was an exciting time. The narrowness of the post-war period was over, and new ideas were everywhere: in education, in popular culture and so on. But one has to remember that much of what we now think of as 'the 60s' didn't actually take place until the early 1970s. One also has to remember that the 60s happened mainly in cities. Small country towns were a long way from Carnaby Street!

The influence of parents, family and school

Parents and family

Parental influence is not evident in all our interviews. Roy Blatchford and Mary Marsh both mentioned specific parental influences, but with rather different outcomes. Roy's father was a teacher, who didn't want his son to be a teacher – 'whatever you do don't go into teaching.' Mary's mother was a doctor and wanted her to be a teacher because she liked – 'a job that you could do with a family'. But Mary was adamant – 'I was not going to be a teacher.' Both, of course, became teachers, but not as their first choice of careers.

The other interviewees do not report a powerful influence from their parents on their career choice, although Helen Hyde and Rosemary Whinn-Sladden were clearly very influenced by their fathers. Rosemary reports how she 'spent a lot of time with him on the docks going round the boats from a very early age and I loved it'. Helen was more influenced by her father – 'My father is a person dedicated to all he undertakes, I have inherited this from him'; and by her mother's organizational skills 'I am a very organized person, I get that from my mother.' But her mother thought of her as a person with no brains and was constantly surprised by her achievements. 'She never put pressure on me to do anything. I think the understanding was that you studied until you got married.'

Overall, one does not get a picture of a uniformly powerful parental influence acting directly on our leaders' choice of careers. But one must place this in context. Very few of the parent's generation had stayed at school beyond the school-leaving age and even fewer had gone to university. Many of our interviewees' generation were the first in their family to go to university and parents – while being very proud of their children's achievements – had little direct help or experience to offer. Ken Edwards said that it was his teacher who recognized his academic potential 'so I got a lot of support. I was the first member of my family ever to go to university and I enormously enjoyed the experience.' The majority of our interviewees seemed to be making up their own minds rather than having very strong guidance from their parents.

Other family and home influences were interesting and quite idiosyncratic.

Bernard Clarke talks powerfully about the impact of his brothers' failure and unhappiness at a private school and how he 'refused to go' because he was happy at the local grammar school. 'This caused a tremendous hoo-ha in the family . . . I suppose I was a bit pious but, even at that early age, I had this moral objection to the notion of private education and I saw that it didn't work for either of my brothers.'

Helen Hyde talked about a range of family influences: her Jewish culture and the Jewish youth group, her fluency in languages, and her life-long interest in Biblical Studies. 'Looking back, my parents have had a lasting influence. I'm sure it is at the back of my mind to make them proud of me.'

School

Here a much clearer pattern emerges. None of our interviewees were positive about their primary schooling, in fact most were rather negative. Bernard Clarke reports 'a hatred of primary school and [a] fear of primary school teachers'. Mary Gray said 'I don't remember being particularly happy at primary school' and for Rosemary Whinn-Sladden it was at best a mixed experience. She was ill, and got into trouble for 'not fitting in', but one teacher seems to have made a much more positive impact.

It is, perhaps, interesting to speculate why some of our interviewees were so negative about primary school. Were they rather more mature, or more intelligent, than most of their classmates? Perhaps their less than positive experiences led them to feel that they could 'do it better'. Unfortunately we have no evidence to support either of these proposals. Secondary school was a much more positive experience for all except Keith Bovair, who was in conflict with his school, and Mick Brown, who was transferred from a secondary modern to the grammar school as the Local Education Authority's policy on selection changed. This contrasts with the negative experiences of many of the heads interviewed by Ribbins and Marland (1994). Although Mick was unhappy at the grammar school 'I did well at school and eventually went into the sixth form.' The other seven interviewees educated in the UK speak very warmly about how 'they loved it'. Their schools were traditional, selective, schools with academic values and, on the whole, these interviewees flourished. Roy Blatchford was more influenced by the theatre and sport than by the formal curriculum, and Bernard Clarke reports being devastated when he failed his 'A' levels – 'I always wanted to be a teacher.' He tried to resit them, but became ill. Even Keith Bovair, who was expelled from his private Catholic high school, 'fell in with a couple of good teachers (in a state school) . . . they influenced me, got me interested in things'.

While these traditional secondary schools were a major influence on our interviewees, interestingly none of them ended up working in selective schools. Indeed, Mick Brown said:

> This experience [his secondary schooling] has left its mark on me, and as a consequence, as a teacher. I've always been inclined to avoid the

conventional wisdom to encourage critical examination of circumstances, and look behind the orthodox position.

As headteachers they all moved towards a more egalitarian approach, choosing to work in comprehensive schools and with children from across the ability range. We must, however, keep in mind the changing external context. Many of the schools of the kind that our interviewees attended became comprehensive in the 1960s, so that aspiring headteachers would probably see their own future in the comprehensive system.

Higher education

Their enthusiasm for secondary school did not, however, lead all of them directly to university. Keith Bovair and Ken Edwards went into the Air Force, and Bernard Clarke failed his 'A' levels and went to work in a bank. Mick Brown also left school to work in a bank and Rosemary Whinn-Sladden lost her confidence that teaching was the right career for her. Although she had always wanted to be a teacher she 'panicked. I suddenly had a vision of my never setting foot outside the one school' so she went into the Civil Service. The other four interviewees all went to university directly from school but only one – Mary Gray – had a clear intention to be a teacher.

Keith and Bernard both got into university later through unconventional routes: Keith through the Air Force and Bernard through the back door. Rosemary got a place at a college for mature students when she was 22 having realized that teaching was what she really wanted to do. Mick Brown worked in the bank for four years, taking Institute of Bankers qualifications at the local college, and then went to university. Ken Edwards went to university after completing his National Service and continued along the traditional academic path through post-graduate degrees and fellowships.

Once our interviewees got to university they were all successful and enjoyed the experience. Like secondary school it was a powerful influence in their lives. But it is very striking that only four – Mary Gray and Rosemary Whinn-Sladden (who had both gone to teacher training colleges), Ken Edwards (as an academic researcher), and Mick Brown (an FE college lecturer) – were on the career route they eventually followed.

The most unconventional path was taken by Keith Bovair (or perhaps it just looks more unconventional to an English reader) who came back into education through courses taken in the Air Force. He went to night school to study psychology:

> I got interested in psychology. I took night courses and I got the grades – found I had the ability. I'd never gone to university because of the service, and if it wasn't for the GI Bill I'd have missed out. I went to Michigan University because my grades at night school were good . . . it was not a university [where he took night school] that the good grades came from –

and all I said was – look I've just come out of the service and I got drafted because of this Vietnam thing and I'm coming over to talk to you. I think they thought I was going to arrive with bandoleers and guns blazing because I got out there and they had the application forms all ready for me.

He starting studying psychology and was influenced and encouraged by two university teachers to move towards working with young people with special educational needs. But 'I never thought I would be a teacher.' Bernard Clarke, too, came back into education via teaching for VSO, residential social work, a general degree in Applied Social Sciences and a Social Work qualification. Mary Marsh was still determined not to be a teacher, and was doing a degree in Geography and intending to go into market research, Roy Blatchford was headed for publishing, and Helen Hyde had taken a PGCE because 'I didn't know what else to do. I really didn't think that I'd ever teach. I had to do something – everybody else had got their degrees and were going places and doing things. I didn't know what else to do other than to study.' So she completed her PGCE and then returned to university to complete her Honours degree.

For many of our interviewees their choice of subjects at university appears to have been a compromise. Roy Blatchford 'ended up doing linguistics partly because I didn't know what it was' and Mary Marsh 'had difficulty all the way through choosing what subjects to do because I have a fascination with a wide range of things. I realized that my aptitude was in science but I wanted to be more in the middle and ended up with geography which certainly suited me very well.'

None except Mary Gray and Rosemary Whinn-Sladden seem to have had very clear intentions to go into teaching during their time in higher education. They didn't have clear career routes mapped out for themselves, for most one step led to the next. As Mick Brown said:

> I never had an ambition to move up the educational ladder for its own sake and I became a head of department almost by accident. The reason for moving from the first to the second college was that I didn't want to stay as head of department in the former, and in order to move out I more or less had to move up to a more senior job.

It is, perhaps, worthwhile reflecting at this point whether, in the very changed climate of the 1990s, so much flexibility in career planning is possible today. Do young people today have similar opportunities, and the space, to develop themselves? My perception is that they either get on a career track in their early 20s, straight from college, or spend several years in and out of work before settling into non-professional work or the 'postmodern portfolio career'.

Other activities

Several of the interviewees comment on the importance of activities that were not specifically to do with studying or their teaching. Roy Blatchford commented:

> it's the extra curricular I remember in the sense that this has always lived with me as a teacher. It was only later that I realized the richness of the experience. It's a case of university being wasted on the young.

For Bernard Clarke 'one of the most important parts of my training as a head-teacher was the training I received as a social worker'. Mary Marsh stopped teaching in the early 1970s to raise her family of four boys: 'which was a hugely important part of the experience that contributes to who I am. I really enjoyed it. It was very positive, extremely demanding. Very rich and enlightening. I learned a lot.' Mary also did some work 'teaching Asian women English in Barking which got me involved in the whole multicultural debate, and I worked with the Community Relations Council in Barking and enjoyed that. . . . This is all my education – I've always gone on learning.'

Mary Gray took the opposite approach to child-rearing:

> I didn't have the feeling that I was the kind of person who wanted to stay at home at that stage. Perhaps because we had the children so young, I wasn't ready to stop teaching and I didn't really fancy the ironing and the washing and everything else that went with it.

Both Ken Edwards and Keith Bovair see National Service as having a positive side: for Ken ' . . . the break out of education made me appreciate getting back' and Keith was running an office in his early 20s 'with fifty individuals, civilian and military'.

Helen Hyde reflected on her experience as a youth leader:

> I moved up through the age groups starting with the little ones and by the time I was doing my PGCE working with the older ones. I had taken them on camps, living with the whole child and this experience has affected me in anything I have done ever since.

Becoming a teacher

After university Mary Marsh, Mary Gray, Rosemary Whinn-Sladden, Mick Brown and Ken Edwards were launched as teachers or academics; the others left university doing a wide range of things. But Mary Gray was the only one who went straight from school to teacher training college and into teaching. Mary Marsh and Helen Hyde came into teaching somewhat reluctantly because it fitted their family situation at that time. Helen was in London without a job, and Mary thought that she might be going to live abroad. For both of them teaching was a means to an end, and seen as an appropriate way for a married woman to earn her living. Ken saw his future as a researcher, and was working in academic research.

Keith Bovair, Bernard Clarke and Roy Blatchford all came into education through being involved with social work in the broadest sense. Keith worked in intermediate treatment and then in special education. Roy was a volunteer at Brixton Prison:

> What I didn't like about publishing was being behind a desk five days a week. So I started truanting, taking long weekends (as one discovers some teachers do before they leave teaching), and then I started doing some voluntary work at Brixton Prison. I walked in there one day interested in adult literacy and they took me on. Then I decided to go down to the local comprehensive in Brixton and started supply teaching – and stayed!

He was also impressed with 'the richness of what the ILEA offered – whether it was music centres for youngsters or the English Centres for teachers'. Bernard Clarke trained as a social worker, then took his PGCE in his mid-20s. His first teaching job was as a half-time teacher and half-time counsellor and youth leader. Mary Marsh, too, had worked with an Asian women's group in East London. Bernard set out the importance of this for his future career:

> In hindsight one of the most important parts of my training as a head-teacher was the training I received as a social worker. In those days the work was very much related to the dynamics of individual and interpersonal behaviour, understanding what happens in groups, and when people talk, trying to locate what their real feelings are underneath the words they use.

Rosemary Whinn-Sladden worked in the youth service in 'a dockland area with a lot of problems. I did several nights a week working in the youth service and that was very helpful.'

Developing attitudes and values

Some of the attitudes and values have already been recorded, but it is clear that experiences from the ages of 18 to 24 made a major impact on our interviewees. Although they were not all teachers at this point they appear energetic, thoughtful and guided by a framework of values which informed their future.

Moving towards leadership

There were not many threads common to our interviewees' early years in teaching. Bernard Clarke and Helen Hyde stayed for several years in their first school, progressing to senior posts. Each then left to take up deputy headships elsewhere. Helen said:

> Why did I want to leave? Partly because I didn't get on with the head –
> but I wasn't at all bored. Part of it was an inner challenge – I have con-
> stantly to do something that frightens me. So I started to apply for
> headships.

For Bernard:

> The atmosphere at Filton was not one of experiment and trying new things.
> It was run as a tight ship, a very safe organization, and after 11 years there
> I felt rather constrained.

Rosemary Whinn-Sladden and Mary Marsh also disliked the style of their first
schools. Mary disagreed with the rigid streaming at her school and moved on very
quickly. In contrast, Ken Edwards moved from being a researcher to be head of
department because 'the alternative people were too awful to contemplate'. He
'learned from holding the post that sometimes the rather slow business of trying to
persuade people to do things, rather than directing them, was one that I could live
with'. He also learned that 'getting decisions made was essentially a political
process'.

Several of our heads took advanced courses at this stage: Mary Marsh an MBA,
Mary Gray an Advanced Diploma, Helen Hyde and Roy Blatchford Masters
degrees, and Ken Edwards a Ph.D.

Several of the interviewees stressed the importance of choosing the right school
to become a deputy head. Roy Blatchford deliberately moved to a very different
type of school from his previous experience, to 'a grammar school going comprehensive . . . so I did a deputy head's job there, very much as a change agent'. Mary
Marsh was the only one who continued as deputy in a school she had previously
taught in, but she took up the deputy headship after eight years at home raising
her children.

Deputy headship

This was clearly an influential time on our school-based interviewees. They all
comment on how they learned from their heads. Rosemary Whinn-Sladden:
'learned to curb my tongue which I am not naturally talented at. I learned to persuade people to do things that I wanted them to do in different ways.' For most it
was a more positive experience. Helen Hyde said:

> He listened to you – he always looked you straight in the eye and you knew
> he was listening. He only stayed a few years but during that time he
> changed the school. I learnt a lot by watching him. He didn't speak a lot
> to me, but he greatly influenced me.

Bernard Clarke commented on the powerful influence of his head: 'she was quite
outrageous, but her educational vision was absolutely wonderful . . . It was the most

brilliant experience working for her and it was all the things I had been longing for.' He also reports a very different experience with another head: 'My time with him helped me to clarify the sort of head I wasn't going to be.'

Several others mention the importance of their head in giving them confidence in doing a wide range of tasks. In her small all-age progressive private school Mary Marsh 'did all sorts of things', which included running a boarding house, and the junior school as well as being deputy head of the whole school with responsibility for the curriculum and careers: 'St Christopher, being a smaller school, was almost a better preparation for headship than spending your whole career in large schools.' Several had posts as acting heads for short periods, but as Mary pointed out this had its limitations as a training for headship:

> Being an acting head isn't the same thing as being a head at all because you are a caretaker. You've got to be very careful, and you don't move anything. You don't rearrange the deckchairs even – never mind throwing them overboard. You've just got to keep things ticking over.

Roy Blatchford made a similar point: 'It was keeping a well-oiled machine going. The staff were right behind me as long as they knew there were no new initiatives.' Mick Brown also saw that change could only be achieved by being the principal:

> There is so much distance between the vice-principal and the principal in terms of one's ability to influence and shape the character of an institution, and because I wanted to shape a college of my own, I decided to apply for the principalship. I had been approached by the governors in the college in which I was vice-principal, to consider the prospect of becoming principal when the current principal retired. However, I decided it would be more difficult to act effectively as principal in a college where I had been vice-principal than it would be in a new college, so I decided on the latter.

All our heads, however, were reflective about their experiences in middle and senior management, either learning from the good aspects of the school, or clearly reacting against it in their own headships.

Applying for headships

In different ways each of our interviewees report a sense of readiness – or even impatience – to lead. Helen Hyde expressed this by saying 'part of it was inner challenge' and Bernard Clarke talked of his sense of readiness for headship: 'I reached a point where I found myself feeling that I could have a go at most of the things Keith did, and that Joan had done.' Keith Bovair was more explicit saying that as a head he wanted to 'take things forward, to shape the dynamics for children to learn'.

Leadership in universities is different from schools. As Ken said: 'Cambridge is not a place in which anybody is in charge in any obvious way.' He saw the move to vice-chancellorship as 'a natural next step to move to a position in which you could try to exercise leadership'.

Conclusion

In conclusion, none of our educational leaders seems to have followed a planned path to headship: they did not 'plan their careers' in the currently favoured style. They took opportunities as they arose, becoming more aware as they became older that choices and decisions had to be made about the route they were to take. All of them set these decisions within a broad framework of educational values, knowing the kind of school they wanted to create and lead, and realizing that headship would give them possibilities of achieving this. Returning to the analogy of the river and its terrain, these nine leaders were strong, purposeful, fast-flowing rivers who cut their ways through the surrounding land shaping it, and being shaped by it.

References

Blumenfeld-Jones, D. (1995) 'Fidelity as a criterion for practising and evaluating narrative enquiry' in Hatch, J. and Wisniewski, R. (eds) *Life History and Narrative*, London: Falmer Press.

Evetts, J. (1994) *Becoming a Secondary Headteacher*, London: Cassell.

Hargreaves, A. (1994) *Changing Teachers, Changing Times: Teachers' Work and Culture in the Postmodern Age*, London: Cassell.

Harvey, D. (1990) *The Condition of Postmodernity*, Oxford: Blackwell.

Hatch, J. and Wisniewski, R. (eds) (1995a) *Life History and Narrative*, London: Falmer Press.

Hatch, J. and Wisniewski, R. (1995b) 'Life history and narrative: questions, issues and exemplary works' in Hatch, J. and Wisniewski, R. (eds) *Life History and Narrative*, London: Falmer Press.

Hirschhorn, L. (1988) *The Workplace Within: the Psychodynamics of Organizational Life*, Cambridge, MA: The MIT Press.

Obholzer, A. and Roberts, V. (1994) *The Unconscious at Work*, London: Routledge.

Polkinghorne, D. (1995) 'Narrative configuration in qualitative analysis' in Hatch, J. and Wisniewski, R. (eds) *Life History and Narrative*, London: Falmer Press.

Ribbins, P. and Marland, M. (1994) *Headship Matters*, London: Longman.

Storr, A. (1989) *Solitude*, London: Fontana.

Sugarman, L. (1986) *Life Span Development: Concepts, Theories and Interventions*, London: Methuen.

Vondracek, F., Lerner, R. and Schulenberg, J. (1986) *Career Development: A Life-Span Developmental Approach*, London: Lawrence Erlbaum Associates.

CHAPTER 12

Principals and headteachers as leading professionals

Viv Garrett

Introduction

It was Hughes (1975) who coined the term 'leading professional' in one of his first discussions of the 'professional-as-administrator'. He suggested that the 'profes-sional as administrator', or the headteacher, had dual sub-roles: those of leading professional and chief executive. He warned, however, that:

> Though they are useful as analytical and heuristic devices, it has to be rec-ognized that our . . . role models are but abstractions, which only partially reflect the reality. In seeking to develop a more unified role model it is there-fore salutary to recall that many heads to some extent, and some heads to a great extent, succeed in simultaneously activating and integrating the contrasting and potentially conflicting aspects of their total role. (p. 59)

This acknowledgement of the existence of the managerial role was the result of research into the role of the secondary school headteacher; he proposed, however, that the model is equally applicable at other levels and in other types of educational organization. Morgan *et al* (1983) carried out similar research into the 'managerial tasks' of the secondary head and identified more differentiation between the sub-roles, whilst recognizing a close relationship. It is significant that both these studies focused on the secondary school. With the introduction of com-prehensive education and the growth of the large school, so 'management' needed to play a much greater part in the life of the head and the newly formed 'senior management teams'. Grace (1995) refers to this period of the 1960s, 1970s and early 1980s as the social democratic management phase in English state school-ing. The transfer to the market management phase from the mid-1980s onwards is now part of the dominant market culture of the public services in Britain. The 'commodification' of education is epitomized by the local management of schools, league tables and the new language of customers and quality control. So, is it still possible that the sub-role of leading professional is integrated into professional leadership today?

In order to answer the question, I will first of all unpack the full meaning of the term 'leading professional', and suggest five dimensions on which our educational leaders can be examined. I will then consider how the interviews with nine principals of educational organizations reported in the second part of this book may give us some insight into this issue. After reflecting on the evidence we have from the interviews, I will consider whether our educational leaders still retain a leading professional aspect to their roles.

What is a leading professional?

Before examining the meaning of the term 'leading professional', it may first be helpful briefly to explain Hughes' (1975, 1985) chief executive (CE) role model. He perceives this as having two sectors: the internal and the external. The internal sector is concerned essentially with the division and allocation of work, and the co-ordination and control of organizational activity which would include staff supervision and the setting up of efficient management systems and procedures. The external is related to the level of status and autonomy granted to the head by an external body. Hughes discovered a positive inter-relationship between these two sectors, in that a head scoring high on the external sector is likely also to have a high score relating to the internal sector, and vice versa.

Hughes, drawing upon ideas from Gouldner (1957), suggests that the leading professional (LP) role model also has two dimensions: the traditional (or local) and the innovating (or cosmopolitan). The traditional dimension encompasses such activities as teaching and involvement with students, and relationships with staff; the innovating dimension incorporates an openness to external professional influences, involvement in educational activities outside school, finding time for personal study, and getting staff to try out new ideas.

Hughes (1975) argues that 'the executive and professional aspects of the heads' role, though analytically distinct, are closely inter-related'. He draws upon a series of remarks from the headteachers to whom he spoke to support his conclusion that 'a crude formulation of the professional–organizational dilemma in terms of the polar extremes of a single continuum would be singularly naive' (p.309). Nevertheless, as Ribbins (1993) has pointed out, there is an influential strand of contemporary thinking among some practitioners and educational commentators which takes the view that the orientation which heads bring to their work may be defined in terms of the response they make to the continuum of responsibility they face. In this model, towards one polar end, are located a set of administrative tasks (e.g. financial management, personnel management, site management, resource management, public relations and marketing, the management of boundaries, supporting and contributing to aspects of governance, income generation) and, at the other polar end, a set of curriculum duties (e.g. determining the nature and quality of teaching and learning within the school as this is enabled through all aspects of the curriculum, through pupil assessment, welfare, pastoral care, through extra-curricular activities and the hidden curriculum in all its aspects, and through the management of order and discipline). All this assumes as heads emphasize one dimension of their role they must do so at the expense of the other. On the basis of his research Ribbins (1993) suggests this view may be unduly restrictive. He proposes an alternative in which the two dimensions are largely independent of each other rather than antithetical aspects of the orientation which heads bring to their work. Such a model can be represented diagrammatically as follows:

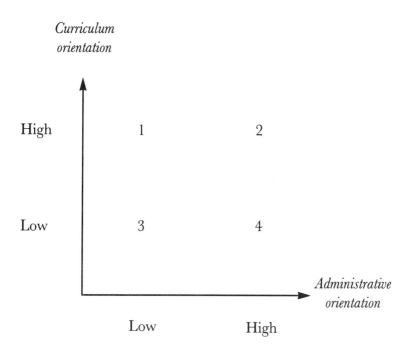

From this it is possible to derive four types of orientation to headship as follows – (i) *The Curriculum Chief* (above average on curriculum but below average in administration orientation); (ii) *The School Leader* (above average in curriculum and administration orientation); (iii) *The Abnegator* (below average in curriculum and administration orientation) and (iv) *The Chief Administrator* (above average in administration but below average in curriculum orientation). In his research, Ribbins has found few headteachers who see themselves, or their colleagues in any numbers, as Abnegators or as Chief Administrators and many who see themselves, and many of their colleagues as Curriculum Chiefs and even School Leaders as defined above (Ribbins, 1993). Whether they are justified in making such claims would, of course, require evidence of the kind which can be generated by the kind of level 2 and level 3 research described in the introduction to this book. To date, relatively little such research is available.

Much of the work discussed above has taken place in secondary education but the kinds of activities relating to these roles have been further developed by

Coulson (1986) in his study of the managerial work of primary heads and are summarized in the following table:

The managerial work of primary heads

Chief executive roles	*Leading professional roles*
Interpersonal roles	
Figurehead	Goal setter and evaluator
Leader/supervisor	Curriculum co-ordinator and developer
Liaison	Teacher
	Exemplar of professional values
Informational roles	
Monitor	
Disseminator	
Spokesperson	
Decisional roles	
Entrepreneur	
Disturbance handler	
Resource allocator	
Negotiator	

Source: Coulson (1986)

Coulson uses Mintzberg's terminology of interpersonal, informational and
decisional roles as dimensions of the CE aspect and allocates roles within them.
His identified LP roles were developed from Hughes' originals. It is recognized that
in Coulson's work the roles are essentially school-based. In the case of large organizations, and particularly in further and higher education, several of these
activities will be delegated. Within the LP dimension, the goal setter and evaluator role is concerned with determining the overall character of the school and
overseeing progress towards this in formulating the mission and aims of the school,
the shaping of the curriculum, and school self-evaluation. The curriculum
co-ordinator and developer relates to the organization and development of the
curriculum, the allocation of responsibilities and classroom supervision of teachers. The teacher role describes the head's time in classrooms either teaching
personally or working alongside teacher colleagues. The exemplar of professional
values is represented by high standards of professional conduct and a commitment
to both students and teachers. These classifications amply fulfil Hughes' traditional LP dimension, but Coulson could be criticized for not making the innovating
dimension more explicit.

While recognizing the inter-dependence of the two sub-roles of leading professional and chief executive, there will also be an inevitable tension between the two

as priorities become addressed. The combination of chief academic and chief administrator has been illustrated by Jarratt (1985):

> No one can doubt the need for the Vice-Chancellor to be recognized as the academic leader of his institution and in no way should other responsibilities be seen as diminishing this. But to enable the institution at least to survive and to seize the opportunities open to it in the future, the Vice-Chancellor will have to adopt a clear role as the executive leader as well – and have the necessary authority to carry it out. (p. 26)

Let us now attempt to combine these descriptions into the five dimensions of a leading professional. She or he will be one who:

- has undergone a lengthy period of professional training in a body of abstract knowledge (Goode, 1960; Coulson, 1986; Hughes, 1985), and who will have had experience in the relevant field, in most cases teaching;
- is controlled by a code of ethics and professional values (Barber, 1963, 1978; Coulson, 1986; Hughes, 1985);
- has a strong philosophy and clear vision (Hodgkinson, 1991; Coulson, 1986);
- is committed to the core business of the organization, i.e. the quality of student learning (Coulson, 1986);
- is politically adept and has an awareness of the external environment (Hughes, 1985).

So, how do our interviewees match up to these dimensions? I recognize that, in using nine different interviewers to interview nine different leaders, there will be different emphases and different interpretations given to the questions. However it is possible to develop a picture of each leader in their job. I will now, therefore, attempt to examine each of these pen portraits against each of my five dimensions of the leading professional role.

Professional training and experience

First, have all our interviewees undergone professional training? The interesting point here is that only one, Mary Gray, followed the traditional path of school, training college, then back to school as a teacher. Bernard Clarke, Rosemary Whinn-Sladden and Mick Brown all started other careers before deciding to take their teaching qualification. Keith Bovair won a university place after his period of service in the US Air Force, and then began his teaching career. Roy Blatchford, too, started in publishing after graduating, until he decided to forgo the deskbound life of the publisher for the challenges of teaching in Brixton Prison. Conversely, neither Helen Hyde nor Mary Marsh showed any great vocational enthusiasm for teaching: Helen completed a PGCE after her degree and only eventually started teaching when short of money, and Mary began as an untrained teacher when an anticipated move abroad with her new husband did not materialize. Ken Edwards envisaged a career in research until he moved to Cambridge as a lecturer. As Anderson (1995) points out, many of our leaders had an uncertain start to their careers in education, and very few expressed a vocational leaning towards education when early career decisions were being made. There is no doubt that these individuals can be termed 'professionals' but it is as much their ongoing experience in education, particularly the credibility gained in the actual task of teaching in the case of the headteachers, as it is their initial training that makes them deserving of this description.

This experience ranges from that of Helen Hyde and Bernard Clarke who both stayed in the schools of their first appointment for several years until they had attained senior roles, to that of Mary Gray who moved jobs a number of times to fit in with her husband's career. Clarke's apprenticeship as vice-principal at Burleigh Community College gave him the experience of working alongside 'two remarkable powerful people'. Roy Blatchford was particularly appreciative of the opportunities offered him in London. Not only was he able to continue with his interest in publishing, but 'there was always something to do if you wanted to be the extended professional'. That 'something to do' included being the chair of NAPCE (the National Association for Pastoral Care in Education), an external examiner and some part-time lecturing. For Mary Marsh, the eight years she spent out of teaching bringing up her four sons was 'a hugely important part of the experience that contributes to who I am'. She then obtained a deputy headship in a small progressive independent school, which she felt was the one job in the country where great value was placed on her time at home. Rosemary Whinn-Sladden speaks of a range of experience with different heads, all with very different personalities. She learnt from them as much what not to do, as what to do. Her period of deputy headship in a difficult school where she was responsible for everything helped her to 'learn how to walk on cracked eggs'. In addition, she learnt diplomacy, including a lot of useful skills such as how to curb her tongue. Whinn-Sladden also benefited from the experience of youth service work, as did Clarke and Blatchford.

The experiences of Mick Brown and Ken Edwards are, as might be expected, somewhat different. In Edwards' case, his professional credibility stems from laboratory research in his field of experimental science, through head of department and chair of school positions to a period as secretary general at Cambridge. This was a senior academic administrative post which involved him in a wide range of academic activities across the university; a position as vice-chancellor seemed a natural next step. Brown, on the other hand, says he never had an ambition to move up the educational ladder, and became a head of department 'almost by accident'. On deciding that he wanted to move to a different college, he 'more or less had to move up to a more senior job', i.e. vice-principal. He describes the great deal of experience he obtained of the local authority structures and systems, and felt well prepared for the traditional role of an LEA principal. However, by the time he gained his principalship, things had moved on and colleges had become corporations. He is honest enough to admit he was not at all prepared for operating under new structures, although I sense his previous experience stood him in good stead.

Code of ethics and professional values

Second, how do the issues of professional values and ethics affect our leaders? What makes them behave in the way that they do? Is it their role which dictates their behaviour, the rules affecting their sector, or their personal or professional ideologies? The overlap between personal and professional ideologies is a fascinating issue for those of us in education. If one examines the early lives of our leaders and their interpretation of events, one can get a feel for the forming of their professional ideologies. The amount of responsibility that an educational leader has for the development of those in their care makes the job a very special one and attracts those for whom personal values are important. This can be demonstrated by the fact that one of the strongest messages that came forth from the interviews was the feeling of accountability to the students in their care. Simkins (1992) identifies this as the professional model of accountability where individuals are granted autonomy while the professional ethic ensures that they act in the interests of their students. It is no surprise that all of our interviewees commented in some way upon the elements of this model, which they not only readily accepted but which related directly to their educational values and principles.

These beliefs can be demonstrated by the comments of Rosemary Whinn-Sladden, who feels a very strong accountability to the children in her school, and Ken Edwards, who has a responsibility to the 'people who are devoting their lives to this institution', whether staff or students, and states that 'they [students] deserve the best that we can give them'. Accountability to students was stated or implied in nearly all the interviews; Bernard Clarke had the added dimension of his own children being pupils at his school and was therefore subject to 'endless feedback'. Helen Hyde felt that she was first of all accountable to herself and the high standards she set herself. In common with the others, she then included staff and students as high priorities. 'Staff have to be able to trust and rely on me as a real leader to represent and to guide and look after them.' She also states the importance of being a good role model for students, 'I must be the best role model I can be', in which trust and respect play a big part. The same could be true for Keith Bovair. The special position of a headteacher in special education means that relationships with the child and the parents are crucial.

This accountability is also evident in the three central educational values held by all of our leaders: (i) a desire to provide high quality learning experiences for their students; (ii) a belief that students should be treated with respect as individuals; and (iii) the belief that individuals in their organizations should be treated with care (McMahon, 1995). As one reads through the interviews, one is struck by this commitment to students and their development. Hodgkinson (1991) would recognize this as representing the moral conscience of their organizations. Bernard Clarke's comment, 'All the time, the bottom line for me is the motivation, the expectation and the achievements of the students', clearly demonstrates the professional values underpinning most of his decision-making.

Strong philosophy and clear vision

Third, the leading professional has a strong philosophy and clear vision. What evidence of this do we have from our leaders? Rayner (1995) stresses the importance of leaders having 'the vision thing': a very strong mental image of the organization which they are trying to build (Holmes, 1993, p. 16). Bernard Clarke describes this well: 'My vision of leadership . . . is being responsible for creating the climate in which young people and adults can do their best.' He then goes on to say that his view of headship is of 'somebody who tries to articulate a set of principles, persuades people of those principles and then puts them into practice'. He cites his Code of Conduct as an example. Mary Gray's vision is 'creating the best working atmosphere I can for the children and offering them values where they will appreciate other people, recognize the contributions they can make both within the school and hopefully, as they get older, within the community'. Mary Marsh realized very early on in her headship, that 'whatever we set out to do – whether it was thinking about the prospectus which needed rewriting, or trying to get groups to grapple with issues of the curriculum – I kept realizing that until we'd had this debate about the aims and values of the school we really were in a vacuum'.

Rosemary Whinn-Sladden has a very strong philosophy to do the best for her children. She emphasizes fairness, respect and equality and stresses the importance of quality teaching in order to bring about quality learning: 'children deserve the best and I think that's what I get paid for'. Ken Edwards echoes this from the university sector ' . . . they [students] deserve the best that we can give them . . . what I try and do is to encourage people to pay attention to their teaching and learning activities, to be good teachers'. He creates this sense of a mission by 'a lot of talking' and creating networks, both formal and informal, 'so that ideas and information flow upwards and downwards and from side to side'.

Mick Brown's notions of accessibility and opportunity in post-16 education are further exemplified by his 'no blame' culture where his staff are encouraged to admit their mistakes and learn from them. Roy Blatchford cites self-criticism as one of his strategies for achieving his vision of high achievement, high expectations and the widening of horizons. Other strategies he includes are: a hands-on approach to his job; putting in the time; appointing the right people; and communicating his vision to everyone. Rayner (1995) sums this up neatly in his description of the VIP (Visionary, Implementer, Practitioner) role requirement facing a manager in special education, which can be said to mirror the management demands of every other phase of education. She or he should be a visionary, and know what they want and where it lies; she or he should be an implementer, in that they should know what they are going to move and in what direction; and she or he should be a practitioner, and lead by professional example. Coulson would add one further stage to this: that of evaluator.

Commitment to the core business

Fourth, the commitment to the core business of the organization, i.e. the quality of student learning. As can be seen above, and in the interviews, virtually all of our leaders professed commitment to the underpinning activity of their organization, i.e. teaching and learning. This commitment to the core activity is one that has put educational leaders under most stress in the last few years. For the traditional head-teacher in the primary school, the priority was the quality of the interactions in the classroom. It is no surprise then that studies of headteacher stress (e.g. Ostell and Oakland, 1992) frequently refer to the role changes of the last few years as a cause of considerable anxiety. Ostell and Oakland's research in a number of primary and middle schools in Bradford identify some of the implications of the role changes brought about by the 1988 Education Reform Act as: lack of managerial training, increased workload, diminishing teaching duties, bureaucratic frustrations and the sheer rapidity of changes. Stephen Ball (1994) refers to these tensions when he talks about 'new headship' in his book on education reform. He looks at the changes brought about by the 1988 Act and questions whether they articulate headship 'in terms of a new flexibility and autonomy or whether they actually construct a new but less obvious and immediate set of constraints upon headship' (p. 85). These constraints are well documented by our leaders and illustrate the tensions between the chief executive and leading professional roles.

The pressures and demands of an increased workload since the 1988 Act mean 'duplication of work' for Mary Gray particularly in regard to formal procedures of accountability. She admits that being the curriculum leader is now only one strand of her role as head. Mary Marsh too feels the pressure from the 'range of things you need to be doing', and admits that 'most weeks you don't do something you should have done that's quite big'. Rosemary Whinn-Sladden contributes to this by describing how she seemed to have a lot more time in her first headship. Her frustrations with bureaucracy lead her to admit to being 'not the most efficient paperwork person' in dealing with a now 'phenomenal' workload. She believes that the amount of work that takes her away from managing the curriculum is 'to the detriment of education'. 'A lot of heads try and do more teaching because that's their way, but I don't see myself as achieving progress through more teaching . . . it's in my management of their [teachers'] work, that I think I can make a difference.' Roy Blatchford, on the other hand, teaches for a third of the week. He feels that teaching is personally quite important for him and believes that this is the most effective way he can achieve his vision, by making sure he is 'in and amongst the children and teaching them'. He regularly attends football and rugby matches on Saturday mornings and is very sure of the way he wants to spend his time. 'I shall continue as a headteacher as long as I choose at lunchtimes to watch children rehearsing for a pantomime or "Blind Date" rather than sitting in the office looking at the latest budget cuts.'

It is interesting to note that the emphasis of OFSTED on the teaching and learning process is encouraging headteachers to move back into the classrooms to monitor what is going on. Although Helen Hyde teaches for only a small proportion of the week, she spends every half term with a new department so that she sees 'every teacher teaching and teaching in every year'. Salmons *et al* (1995), in their report for OFSTED, identify professional leadership as one of the eleven key factors in their review of research into effective schools. Within this category, they actually use the phrase 'leading professional' implying involvement in and knowledge about what goes on in the classroom (p. 10).

The interviews with Mick Brown and Ken Edwards very much reflect the different culture in which they work. While they both acknowledge the centrality of the teaching and learning process, their priorities lie in the task of managing a large institution in a volatile market culture. In that respect, their involvement in ensuring the quality of teaching and learning is at the strategic level, rather than in the classroom, the laboratory or the lecture theatre.

Political skills and external awareness

The fifth dimension of a leading professional embraces political sensitivity and skills and an awareness of the external environment. Several of our educational leaders have had a range of previous experience outside education which gives them a wider view of the world outside their institution. It is noticeable how many believe that they have a commitment to the wider community and demonstrate this by their involvement in working parties, committees and membership of various groups. It is their breadth of experience which gives them the necessary level of political skills. Ken Edwards is very open about the 'political business' of leadership, in that 'you have to try to create an atmosphere in which the people involved feel that the solution which has been produced gives something for everyone and that the total solution, the total benefits from that solution, are better than any alternative'. He is not the only one who uses a web of informal networks, in his case 'a series of layers all of which can pick up information and ideas and spread ideas and produce feedback'. Mick Brown receives support from informal networks of principals, and Rosemary Whinn-Sladden speaks of the 'Goole Mafia': a group of headteachers set up to tackle the local authority on contentious issues. Will the Goole Mafia now be part of history along with the county of Humberside? Representation on external bodies has been an important part of the development of our leaders. Mary Gray was a member of the NAHT executive, and Rosemary Whinn-Sladden was her area NUT secretary. Her experience of taking part in formal negotiations for re-organization was instrumental in raising her self-esteem and broadening her view of education. Mick Brown sees representation very much as his role: involvement in the community is a crucial part of his marketing strategy.

The use of political skills, however, cannot be interpreted without an understanding of the personal and educational values which these leaders represent. This can be demonstrated by the work of Baddeley and James (1987) who use the dimensions of the skills of reading the politics of a situation together with those an individual is carrying into a situation, to produce an analogy of four types of behaviour: the clever fox, the wise owl, the innocent sheep and the inept donkey. The owl and sheep may both act with integrity but one is politically aware and the other unaware. Helen Hyde openly charts her political learning in the process of going grant maintained from being perceived as 'an innocent little girl' who didn't know what she was doing, to taking the initiative a year later and 'pushing for it'. Mary Gray's values shine through in her story about thanking the mums who had been digging all day planting trees: 'anybody who is willing to help is welcome'. She may or may not feel she is politically aware but the outcomes of her behaviour ensure that there are always those around her willing to help. The wisest owl may be Bernard Clarke whose own children have attended his school. Maybe Hodgkinson's words of standing or falling by one's values were never truer; indeed, none of our leaders could be deemed to be 'value-neutered public servants' (Hodgkinson, 1991).

Leading professional or chief executive

There is ample evidence here to show that all of our leaders can be termed leading professionals. The question left to answer is how much are they leading professionals and how much chief executives? Do they have to prioritize one over the other?

There is no argument that the external environment has changed for heads and principals during the last ten years. The growth of the market culture and the emphasis on output and results has led to a re-examination of Grace's (1995) 'modern professionalism' when school organization and administration was 'a necessary, second-order activity to the prime purpose of educating children and young people' (p. 31). Now there is a need for that traditional approach to be complemented by a 'more explicit and critical consideration of the relationships between educational institutions and those whom they serve' (Simkins *et al*, 1992, p. 295). In short, the client in the market place is a critical factor in the equation of what contributes towards a successful school, college or university. All of our interviewees bear this out. This market orientation, or 'image and impression management' (Ball, 1994) could lead to conflicts in values between those leading the organization and teachers whose leanings are towards teaching and learning and the needs of students. Ball warns of an increasing gap between heads and teachers; this view is supported by Evetts (1994) who feels that 'heads are no longer educational leaders; the gulf between heads and their teacher colleagues is growing' (p. 37). We certainly have no evidence from our interviews to suggest that this is true, although we only have the heads' perspectives.

The orientation towards the market is one of the tensions affecting the leading professional role. Another has been the imposition of the National Curriculum and testing. Heads can be said now to be managing an imposed curriculum rather than acting as Coulson's (1986) Curriculum Co-ordinator and Developer and shaping a curriculum pertinent to the needs of the school. Both of these major changes need to be considered in the context of a third: that of the local management of schools. Ball (1994) argues that self-management gives an 'illusion of autonomy and flexibility for the manager' (p. 66), quoting Kickert's (1991) theory of 'steering at a distance', i.e. the market providing a control to management but giving the appearance of autonomy. I would argue that, in each of these cases, it will be the manner of the heads' leadership rather than the actual activity which determines their attitudes towards autonomy and control. Those heads who accept the CE aspect of their role but none the less feel that the LP dimension should underpin any decision-making will be the ones who find the space to be the autonomous professional leader rather than the controlled manager.

The chief executive aspect to the educational leader's role cannot be denied. In post-16 and higher education leadership, it has been apparent for many years. The collegial culture of the professionals is being replaced by more hierarchical forms of management. Simkins *et al* (1992) warned us of this,

> Senior staff . . . need to consider how far they are leading professionals aspiring to develop a shared educational enterprise through building collegial relationships with colleagues, and how far they are executives managing the human and other resources of the institution towards organisational goals established at the top of the institution or outside it'. (p. 296)

It is clearly evident that this accountability to the world outside has expanded considerably in all sectors of education over recent years. From the autonomous professional's inbuilt sense of responsibility and commitment to what is 'best' for the student, additional elements have been introduced as part of the so-called process of improvement for education. Whatever one may personally feel about reforms which emphasize the market element, they have brought about a significant culture change across all sectors of education. Bowe *et al* (1992) refer to the 'new management (which) is oriented towards and constructed within a discourse of cost, income, efficiency, financial planning, image presentation and enterprise and modelled on the practices of business' (p. 145).

There is no doubt that this new management is very much part of our educational leaders' agenda. There is evidence, particularly from those in the primary sector, that they resent the amount of time it takes them away from the classroom and the students. It is in the prioritizing of the activities of headship and principalship that we can begin to examine the relative importance of the leading professional role. Laws and Dennison's (1991) review of the use of headteachers' time concludes that heads spend the greatest part of their time on activities which can be classified as chief executive. 'Their professional leadership actions, which occupy less than half their working week, could assume still lower significance' (p. 57). Although the highest percentage of time spent on an LP activity was on teaching, it is noted that heads' expertise in pedagogical issues is in danger of declining as other tasks take precedence. The underdeveloped LP activities were those of goal setting and evaluation. Evetts' (1994) study of secondary heads supports this conclusion, 'The new headteacher is a corporate manager first; aspects of educational leadership have diminished dramatically in the work culture of headship' (p. 46). And Grace (1995) is in no doubt that 'the position of the headteacher is itself in radical transformation as executive, entrepreneurial and managerial functions become constructed as the prime responsibilities of the role' (p. 43).

It is in the balancing of the two dimensions of chief executive and leading professional that the key skills of educational leaders lie. The dimensions are undoubtedly inter-related and inter-dependent. In their observation of the tasks of six primary heads, Laws and Dennison (1991) confirmed the inter-relationship of the LP and CE roles in noting that they often acted in both roles simultaneously. While it is crucial that leaders have 'knowledge of their product' (*Harvard Business Review*, 1992), and retain the credibility and support of their stakeholders, they owe it to those very stakeholders, including their students, to make a success of their institutions and maintain their viability. We do have evidence that students are still the most important factor in the lives of our leaders; that decisions are taken for the benefit of those who work in their institution, staff and students alike; and that parents too are an important factor, but then were they not always?

One, perhaps unexpected, external factor helping to keep the balance of chief executive and leading professional is the influence of OFSTED. Its emphasis upon the centrality of the teaching and learning process has forced a re-examination of what is important in schools and development planning, monitoring and reporting now play much more of a central role in the new managerial culture. Although Ball (1994) points out that 'Teachers' work is . . . increasingly viewed and evaluated solely in terms of output measures (test scores and examination performance) set against cost (subject time, class size, resource requirements)' (p. 51), our leaders give a far more positive perspective to the raising of performance for students and teachers. It is the key values which remain all-important, and for as long as leaders can maintain their underpinning professional values and develop a commitment to them from every part of the school, college or university community, we can be assured that educational leadership will still retain the dimension of the leading professional. Bernard Clarke sums this up succinctly: 'We still believe in equal opportunities, we still believe in the value of every student, we still believe in all those key principles and yet we've enabled youngsters, and their teachers, to raise their performance, and all being well, that will continue. So that's the buzz.'

That 'buzz' is a privilege which is felt by all our leaders. They are aware of the special position of a principal, who is able to influence the education, and future lives, of all the students in their care. As Rosemary Whinn-Sladden says 'Where else can you have a job where, whatever you do, a little wave just gets bigger?'

References

Anderson, L. (1995) *The early careers of leaders.* Unpublished theme paper for BEMAS Annual Conference 1995, 23–25 September, Oxford.

Baddeley, S. and James, K. (1987) 'Owl, fox, donkey or sheep: political skills for managers' *Management Education and Development*, 18 (1), 3–19.

Ball, S. (1994) *Education Reform: A Critical and Post-Structural Approach*, Buckingham: Open University Press.

Barber, B. (1963) 'Some problems in the sociology of the professions' *Daedalus*, 92, 669–688.

Barber, B. (1978) 'Control and responsibility in the powerful professions' *Political Science Quarterly*, 93, 599–615.

Bowe, R., Ball, S. and Gold, A. (1992) *Reforming Education and Changing Schools*, London, Routledge.

Coulson, A. (1986) 'The Managerial Work of Primary Headteachers', Sheffield: *Sheffield Papers in Education Management*, 48, Sheffield Hallam University.

Evetts, J. (1994) 'The new headteacher: the changing work culture of secondary headship' *School Organisation*, 14 (1), 37–47.

Goode, W (1960) 'Encroachment, charlatanism and the emerging professions: psychology, sociology and medicine' *American Sociological Review*, 25, 902–913.

Gouldner, A. (1957) 'Cosmopolitans and locals: towards an analysis of latent social roles', *Administrative Science Quarterly*, 2, 281–306, 448–480.

Grace, G. (1995) *School Leadership: Beyond Education Management*, London: Falmer.

Harvard Business Review (1992) 'Leaders on Leadership', Boston: Harvard Business School

Hodgkinson, C. (1991) *Educational Leadership: The Moral Art*, New York: SUNY.

Holmes, G. (1993) *Essential School Leadership: Developing Vision and Purpose in Management*, London: Kogan Page.

Hughes, M. (1975) 'The professional-as-administrator: the case of the secondary school head' in Houghton, V., McHugh, R. and Morgan, C. (eds) *Management in Education: The Management of Organizations and Individuals*, London: Open University Press.

Hughes, M. (1985) 'Leadership in professionally staffed organisations' in Hughes, M., Ribbins, P. and Thomas, H. (eds) *Managing Education: The System and the Institution*, Eastbourne: Holt, Rinehart and Winston.

Jarratt, A. (Chairman) (1985) *Report of the Steering Committee for Efficiency Studies in Universities*, London: Committee of Vice Chancellors and Principals.

Kickert, W. (1991) *Steering at a distance: a new paradigm of public governance in Dutch higher education*. Paper for the European Consortium for Political Research, March 1991, University of Essex.

Laws, J. and Dennison, W. (1991) 'The use of headteachers' time: leading professional or chief executive?' *Education 3–13*, June, 47–53.

McMahon, A. (1995) *The educational and managerial values of leaders*. Unpublished theme paper for the BEMAS Annual Conference 1995, 23–25 September, Oxford.

Morgan, C., Hall, V. and Mackay, H. (1983) *The Selection of Secondary School Headteachers*, Milton Keynes, Open University Press.

Ostell, A. and Oakland, S. (1992) *Headteacher Stress, Coping and Health*, Bradford: University of Bradford Management Centre.

Rayner, S. (1995) *Vision in educational leadership*. Unpublished theme paper for the BEMAS Annual Conference 1995, 23–25 September, Oxford.

Ribbins, P. (1993) 'Telling tales of secondary heads' in Chitty, C. (ed) *The National Curriculum: Is it Working?*, London: Longman.

Salmons, P., Hillman, J. and Mortimore, P. (1995) *Key Characteristics of Effective Schools*, London: Institute of Education, University of London, for OFSTED.

Simkins, T. (1992) 'Policy, accountability and management: perspectives on the implementation of reform' in Simkins, T., Ellison, L. and Garrett, V. (eds) *Implementing Education Reform: The Early Lessons*, Harlow: Longman, in association with BEMAS.

Simkins, T., Ellison, L. and Garrett, V. (1992) 'Beyond markets and managerialism: education management in a new context' in Simkins, T., Ellison, L. and Garrett, V. (eds) *Implementing Education Reform: The Early Lessons*, Harlow: Longman, in association with BEMAS.

CHAPTER 13

Principals and headteachers as chief executives

Hugh Busher

Introduction

Hughes (1973) first suggested that headteachers' (principals') roles could be conceptualized as both leading professional and chief executive. The latter role was given greater prominence by changes in society and by legislation in the 1980s in the UK. The role of leading professional was conceptualized collegially, mainly concerned with curriculum matters and pastoral care, although also responsible for providing an effective administrative framework within which teachers could work with considerable autonomy in the classroom. The role of chief executive is seen more in administrative terms, being concerned with managing a school as an organization, directing, planning and co-ordinating its resources and activities in a coherent manner.

The moves to local autonomy for schools which have occurred in the UK and elsewhere during the 1980s and 1990s have, perhaps, enhanced this shift in the principal's role, putting greater emphasis on the chief executive aspects than formerly. Some of the educational leaders reported in these chapters describe themselves as chief executives (Kenneth Edwards) or managing directors (Mary Gray). Similarly, Keith Bovair saw himself as a 'co-ordinator of other people's work'. Similar statements can be found in other texts. Valerie Bragg, for example, in Ribbins and Marland (1994), characterizes herself as 'chief executive'. Evetts (1994), in her study of headteachers in the Midlands in the UK, commented on the extent to which secondary school principals had become corporate managers. Alongside the greater autonomy given to schools under LMS (Local Management of Schools) since 1988 has been imposed the greater accountability of headteachers since 1986 in England and Wales to restructured and greatly empowered school governing bodies (Ribbins, 1989). This accountability has been tightened by the inauguration of regular OFSTED inspections since 1992.

The emergence of the school principal as a chief executive raises questions about the extent to which they remain school leaders, whether leading professionals or corporate bosses. The distinction between the functions of leading and managing is an important one conceptually even if, as Bryman (1992) points out, it is difficult to sustain the distinction in practice when observing people at work. Leaders have an important function in influencing events (Hunt, 1991), whether using their authority of office or the informal micro-political processes (Blase and Blase, 1995) that are embedded in the interpersonal dynamics of organizations. Bolman and Deal (1994) suggest that this influence occurs through the creation of shared meaning for the people with whom a leader works. Manipulating the symbols of an organization to create a coherent vision of purpose for a school, then, may be central to the work of leaders. How they manipulate these symbols gives rise to the styles of leadership people use, of which there have been numerous attempted categorizations (e.g. Kakabadse and Parker, 1984; Handy, 1985; Heller, 1985), some of which offer illuminating descriptions rather than critical analytical frameworks.

There have also been attempts to dichotomize the approaches to leadership which place central emphasis on vision and symbols from those which focus on leaders directing and gaining compliance from their followers, one form being categorized as transformational leadership, the other as transactional leadership (e.g. Bass, 1985; Bryman, 1992). Gronn (1995) amongst others doubts the substantive quality of this distinction, pointing out that it mirrors the more global differences between leadership (creating visions) and management. The latter can be described as a succession of transactional relationships with other people to direct, plan, co-ordinate, and evaluate their activities. In this framework, administration is the co-ordinating function of management. In practice, too, it is hard to find examples of the distinctions which such casuistry invents. Whether defined as leading professionals or chief executives, school principals have to manipulate symbols to help give schools an identity and coherence, and have to engage in managerial/administrative activity to co-ordinate a school's functioning. What tends most obviously to distinguish the one role from the other are the symbols manipulated and, in particular, the language which is used to help people frame meanings for their actions. Within this language are embedded values which convey messages about the purposes of an organization, how actions within in it are to be construed and how people are to be perceived.

In focusing on leaders and leadership, as Gronn (1995) points out, the role of followers is revealed. Leaders manipulate organizational symbols not only to give meaning to their own work but also to help the other people, with whom they work, to give meaning to their engagements with an organization. In the context of a school these other people include teaching and non-teaching staff, pupils (students), parents, and perhaps school governors, too, although the last group could be conceived of as the intended vision givers in the context of locally managed schools with powerful governing bodies. However, followers have to give willing credence to the activities of a leader if a leader's functioning is not to decline into mere headship. Gibb (1947) perceives the latter as holding titular office without either having the power to act effectively or knowing how to use the power available to act effectively.

A micro-political perspective provides an antidote to the charismatic view of leadership that agency is all important. It helps to avoid the unbalanced perception that somehow followers' roles are of less value than those of leaders in the effective functioning of a school, showing how a leader's influence is institutionally located, rather than inherent in their personality, and dependent on their interpersonal skills in bargaining and negotiation with other people over resources. Not surprisingly, then, Huckman and Hill (1994) found that their headteachers chose to work within staff preference for the distribution of salary increments rather than implement performance related pay, the latter being perceived as undermining teacher professionality and collegiality, whatever its claimed merits as a mechanism for distributing scarce resources to more effective practitioners.

A micro-political perspective also disabuses the managerial view of leadership that implementing structures which are said to be effective will necessarily create effective institutions. On the other hand it does not negate the need for schools to create effective organizational structures which allow the creative interplay of personalities, interests and beliefs. It is these last which Gronn (1986) suggested lay at the heart of leading and managing schools. However, it does suggest that processes of school improvement involve more than simply imposing on schools a blueprint derived from factors known to be associated with effective schools. Leaders have a key role in building coalitions of staff who can help to take the work of a school forward. To do this leaders not only have to negotiate transactionally but also to create a vision inspirationally that will help to define the quality and purposes of interpersonal relationships within a school.

This intertwining of transactional and inspirational leader processes to influence individuals and groups of people in organizations suggests that the leadership and management given by school principals should be considered as two inter-related functions. As chief executives, principals not only have to co-ordinate the work of teachers and others for whom they are accountable but they also have to play a facilitating role in inspiring a school's personnel, whether staff or pupils, to meet the demands which they face from the external environment.

The core qualities and abilities of principals as school leaders is variously defined in the literature. Charismatic explanations emphasize the importance of vision and values. For example, Bolman and Deal (1991) thought that although leaders needed to have flexible strategies to cope with changing environments, they also had to develop and sustain core values and beliefs which, Bennis and Nannus (1985) argued, then needed to be translated, through effective communications, into clear meanings for followers. These meanings, they suggested, came from manipulating symbols, that is, managing the culture of an organization (Bolman and Deal, 1994; Gronn, 1995) to help it meet the challenges of its environment.

Managing symbols in a consistent manner creates trust in leaders amongst their followers. However, if leaders try to change the culture of a school by using symbols from a different culture, even when that culture is the dominant socio-political perspective, such as the attempted imposition of a market culture on schools in the UK in the late 1980s and 1990s, they are likely to arouse suspicion and hostility amongst followers who hold different sets of values. Locke (1992) and Busher and Saran (1995) perceived trust as the key to effective leadership and management in schools, arguing that leaders and followers had to develop mutual trust through working together collegially. Leaders develop and indicate their trust of colleagues through consulting with them and delegating responsibility to them whenever possible. The sustaining of a vision helps a team to believe it has a firm sense of purpose. It is this approach to leadership which some writers have called transformational leadership.

Consistency of managing symbols and beliefs, however, may not be sufficient to ensure effective leadership. Indeed it may lead to rigidity in meeting the challenges of the environment and in taking account of the social needs of leaders' colleagues, an important facet of leadership according to Hoyle (1986) when negotiating the micro-political process in organizations. Bolman and Deal (1991) circumvent this problem by arguing the need for leaders to be flexible in developing strategies to meet the challenges of their tasks while sustaining core beliefs. In a rational–technical model this distinction would appear as that between aims, the core beliefs and objectives. Such flexibility allows leaders to take account of other people's interests and concerns when meeting the changes in the environment so encouraging those people to feel part of a team.

A bureaucratic view of the key qualities of the effective principal may well look somewhat different. Hodgkinson (1991), for example, claimed principals needed to have knowledge of the task facing them, knowledge of the situation in which a task was being undertaken, knowledge of the people who were or might be engaged in particular tasks and situations, and knowledge of themselves. The last included the capacity to evaluate critically their own actions. There is not enough space here to debate the quality of that knowledge or whether it includes knowledge through experience as well as knowledge through study and reflection.

A more detailed version of this bureaucratic paradigm emerged in the UK in 1995 when the Teacher Training Agency (TTA), a quango of central government linked to the Department for Education and Employment, specified the skills and abilities which heads (principals) needed to acquire. To embed this definition within the education system, the TTA used it as the basis on which to decide whether or not to license some people and institutions to be providers of training for newly appointed headteachers. Where a provider became so registered, headteachers attending relevant training courses with it had their costs reimbursed by the TTA up to £2500. Headteachers on at least one such training course found that the list of skills and abilities created a useful and all embracing structural framework within which to consider their practices as school leaders and managers.

The rest of this chapter pursues the bureaucratic paradigm, exploring the views of nine leaders of educational institutions on their roles as chief executives. The questions addressed are: what are their educational and leadership values; what is their leadership style; how do they manage people and resources; what is their notion of accountability. Of the leaders, four were female and five were male; four came from secondary schools, two from primary schools, and one each from special schools, higher education, and further education. Seven of the nine institutions represented come from an area south of the river Trent and east of the river Severn. With such an eclectic sample, it would be foolish to attempt even to develop grounded theory, let alone derive generalizations. It will be sufficient to report participants' views grouped according to the following four questions:

1   What are their educational and leadership values?
2   What is their leadership style?
3   How do they manage people and resources?
4   How do they understand their accountability?

What are their educational and leadership values?

Many of the principals interviewed thought that values were at the heart of their leadership. As Blatchford puts it 'The importance of values permeate everything you do as senior managers.' If these values were not in place then a school would lack a sense of purpose and people in it would not know what they were trying to achieve. As Mary Marsh explained: 'I kept realizing that until we'd had this debate about the aims and values of the school we really were in a vacuum.'

However, having a mission was not just parroting fine-sounding statements but enacting those values through the work undertaken in schools and colleges. In this way principals were able to make effective and visible their vision for their institution. Thus, for Keith Bovair 'Enacting the headteacher's vision through projects helps the students and staff begin to share that vision.'

The nine principals interviewed showed some degree of commonality over what that vision might be, surprisingly, given the diversity of their institutions. Several considered it important to have high expectations of their students and to expect the students to have high expectations for themselves: 'I certainly have a vision for raising children's self-expectations – my core vision if you like' (Blatchford). Others stressed the need to help students have such expectations and, in doing so, principals emphasized the importance of 'Creating a climate in which young people and adults can do their best' (Clarke). In this context, Mary Gray talked about 'creating the best working atmosphere I can for the children and offering them values where they will appreciate other people [and] recognize the contributions they can make both within the school . . . [and] within the community'.

Part of that vision was raising teachers' expectations of what children could achieve, according to Roy Blatchford: 'a teacher should be about widening those horizons for young people . . . clearly any vision for a school is about raising achievement'. This focus on student achievement manifested itself in the commitment to students which leaders claimed for themselves and for their staff: 'I have been impressed with the commitment of so many of the teaching staff, despite the pressures, to doing a good job for their students' (Edwards).

This commitment seemed to be based more on moral grounds of responsibility than on the commercial concerns of attracting large numbers of students, though the latter was not absent. Ken Edwards pointed out that without students he and his colleagues would be out of business. However, his main concern was for his accountability to students. He felt that 'They deserve the best that we can give them' and recalled, by way of a probable explanation for why he now held this view, how much value he had been given as a student.

Part of this commitment was to students' personal development as well as to their academic performance. Not surprisingly this showed up most clearly in the special school:

> [It is] important to have a depth of understanding of the dynamics of individuals when dealing with children with emotional difficulties because you need to handle the situation, the other people around the child, as well as the students themselves. (Bovair)

Facilitating such development involved creating an appropriate climate in a school, returning once again to the theme of what principals held as their core values. Rosemary Whinn-Sladden thought 'fairness is a key value to students and staff. I don't like having children picked on by teachers. If a child is having problems, teachers need to solve the problem not go on scolding the child.' While Bernard Clarke thought 'schools should be full of second chances for people because students don't usually get it right first time'.

The concern which principals showed for students as individuals found an echo in their attitudes to staff, where they emphasized the importance of caring for individuals, accepting differences of opinion but respecting views. In this person-centred culture of leadership, that strongly resembles the descriptions of transformational leadership considered earlier, several principals commented on their enjoyment at seeing others develop. As Mary Gray puts it 'Personally I enjoy seeing people blossom. The headteacher is a facilitator of opportunities for both staff and students.'

Within this paradigm, staff development was seen to be for all staff, and went beyond a crude instrumentality of human resources management of just trying to fit staff to the purposes of an institution:

> the importance of Investors in People as a means of promoting staff development – it helps all staff, teaching and non-teaching. . . . Staff development must not only emphasize promotion because this can be crushing on those staff who stay in the classroom. (Whinn-Sladden)

The means of fostering this support for staff lay in the development of groups of people working in teams and sharing purposes and values. Such teams had a tough dynamic rather than a woolly cosiness in private. As Roy Blatchford explained 'a team is more than a group of people: team members are publicly loyal to each other, however much they argue in private'. The development of such teams was of considerable importance to many of the nine principals interviewed, since as Bernard Clarke noted: 'It seems to me as a headteacher you can't do much, you can only achieve with the people you have around you, working with you.' Mary Gray also felt it necessary to 'promote collegiality among staff – giving people confidence by praise, by asking them to share ideas with other people' as a means of helping staff to improve their performances. Improving the quality of staff performance was seen as a crucial means of improving the quality of the teaching and learning experiences offered to students.

For some of the principals, delegation of responsibility was one of the key processes for promoting this improvement. As such 'It is important to be hands-off and to trust people. People are paid salaries for their responsibilities. People respond well to delegation' (Blatchford). To achieve this, however, principals needed to become adept in the micro-political processes of schools, 'as a headteacher you've got to be out there wheeling and dealing, making people feel that what they're involved with is worthwhile and is of value' (Bovair). This entailed being skilled in listening as well as talking, according to Helen Hyde, and adroit at diplomacy, 'learning to walk on cracked eggs', as Rosemary Whinn-Sladden put it.

Several principals expressed joy in the work they did. They liked working with other people to make things happen, although this was not an easy row to hoe. Several principals commented on the need for determination if they were to succeed in bringing about change: 'headteachers need to be brave to carry through what they believe to be worthwhile' (Whinn-Sladden). Bennis and Nannus (1985) also noted the need for leaders to be self-confident if they were to be successful. The enthusiasm which several principals claimed for their approach to their job was, perhaps, infectious to other staff. Mary Gray thought it important to act as you would like others to act. Roy Blatchford emphasized 'the importance of a leader leading by example by getting involved with a wide range of school activities'.

What is their leadership style?

The preceding section raises questions on the style of leadership interviewees espouse. There is no evidence available of what styles they actually used in different situations since members of their role sets were not interviewed. This is a key question for the culture and management of institutions since the impact of leaders on their institutions is well known. The influence of a leader entails 'a significant effect on an individual or group's well-being, interests, policies or behaviour and . . . is usually thought of as legitimate by those subjected to it' (Gronn, 1995, p. 3). As Mary Gray explained 'the headteacher is head of everything, not just the teachers . . . and sets the right atmosphere'.

The style of leadership which all the principals interviewed claimed to espouse was what might be described loosely as consultative or facilitative leadership, broadly meeting the definitions of transformational leadership discussed earlier in this chapter. Such a style was far removed from an abdication of leadership. 'Basically I am a managing director and the curriculum leader who identifies [a problem/opportunity] and delegates [responsibility for it]' (Gray). As Clarke explained, 'It is important to involve people in decision-making but part of your judgement as leader is knowing who to involve on which occasions. Not everybody wants to be involved in all decisions – they haven't time.'

Mary Gray perceived her style as benevolent and assertive. It involved putting strategies in place to achieve collegiality, e.g. staff meetings. Keith Bovair offered a similar view of being a supportive but ultimately directive co-ordinator of other people's work in which 'I don't try to manipulate or coerce staff, but I try to give them experiences which will carry them along.' To such principals, the hallmark of their styles was to 'Delegate responsibility. . . . Give [staff] autonomy, with departments controlling their own budgets and curriculum decisions within the framework of the philosophy of the school' (Hyde). But it was the principals who retained the key levers of power and developed the framework of philosophy and the structures of organizational practice in collaboration with their senior management teams (Hyde). Ken Edwards described this as 'creating a managerial network in a series of layers all of which can pick up information and ideas and spread ideas and produce feedback'.

The collegiality these principals established was, at best, bounded ('partial collegiality', as Helen Hyde described it). They developed it by trying to motivate and support people, staff as well as students (Blatchford; Hyde), as well as by delegating responsibility. Mary Gray said an important aspect of this process was 'giving people confidence by praise, by asking them to share ideas with other people'. Finally, Keith Bovair pointed to 'the importance of teamwork, collaboration by staff on projects, but also between staff and students in business enterprise, such as running a market stall'.

Another important aspect was trying to ensure both that people were fairly treated and that they felt themselves to be so. This means, for Clarke, that 'The school's code of conduct for students and staff is reviewed each year. It sets out people's rights and responsibilities. . . . Teachers need to treat each other and students with respect.' And for Marsh: 'Openness and trust are key managerial values, but they need working at each day, because people only need to feel badly handled once, or insufficiently consulted, for the headteacher to lose their trust.' A similar view led Helen Hyde, among others, to suggest that principals needed to be good listeners as well as enthusiastic and tenacious implementers of actions.

The workload of many of these principals was phenomenal (Whinn-Sladden), not only because of the amount of teaching which a few of them continued to do, but because of what was involved in managing a school. One principal talked about the necessity of breakfast meetings with her caretakers, this being the only time during the day when she and they could meet. Such hours of work are not uncommon according the School Teachers' Review Body Report (1994). It is not known how their staffs perceived such examples of dedicated professionalism, nor the extent to which hardworking principals expected the same level of dedication from their staff and what impact this had on the cultures of the institutions.

Despite the emphasis on collegial styles of working, democracy did not seem to be even on the agenda, except as a rhetoric for indicating that people with interests in situations would be consulted. This was most clearly expressed by Bernard Clarke who said

> I want to say I'm all the nice words like democrat, benign and so on. I suppose I would aim towards those characteristics . . . . [because] as a headteacher you can't do much, you can only achieve with the people you have around you . . . but people don't want to be involved in every decision. They haven't got time . . . and they may not be particularly interested.

Helen Hyde thought that there were some decisions which if she as principal did not make them would never be made. She claimed one of her junior staff had described her as a benevolent dictator, not an epithet of which she was particularly proud.

Whatever might be their appreciation of the merits of collegial styles of managing institutions, the nature of the principals' institutional structures ensured that they could never be completely democratic. Apart from the legal requirements on them to be accountable for the performances of the people in their institutions, as Ken Edwards, principal of the largest institution included in the interviews, pointed out 'with a responsibility for an organization which has £100 million turnover and 2500 employees . . . you can't really regard yourself as anything but a chief executive'.

The appeal, then, for leaders to be democratic in hierarchical organizations, such as that made by Davies (1995), perhaps has to be seen in terms not of its actual implementation but in terms of the manipulation of a powerful symbol from Western societies which associates involvement in decision-making, at least through consultation, with part ownership of the process and empowerment of those consulted. Consultation does not, however, even guarantee the influence of those consulted over the outcomes of decision-making, although there is evidence that where headteachers persistently use consultation in an insincere manner teachers quickly become aware of the sham (Busher and Saran, 1992). It may be this disjunction between the rhetoric and practice of consultation that in part leads to the suggestion of Sinclair (1995) that participative approaches to management can lead to lower employee satisfaction and consequently the need for teams to have leaders to be effective. Hargreaves (1990) describes such insincere uses of consultation as contrived collegiality.

How do they manage people and resources?

In their interviews principals acknowledged the administrative and financial loads which they carried, particularly since the 1988 Education Reform Act. As Sue Benton, quoted in a related study, has acknowledged, she had found this aspect of her work 'quite difficult at first' (Ribbins and Marland, 1994). As she explained: 'I did not come into headships expecting to carry out the detailed financial, staffing, marketing and other administrative responsibilities I am now expected to exercise.' Rosemary Whinn-Sladden thought the range of managerial responsibilities she had to undertake took her away from the curriculum, to the detriment of education. Similarly, Brian Sherratt, head of the largest school in the UK, suggests that some headteachers preferred to retreat into their administrative work because achieving a worthwhile curriculum was very difficult in the UK in the mid-1990s, but he thought this to be the road to isolation for headteachers from their staff (quoted in Ribbins and Marland, 1994).

In talking about their management of educational institutions, principals gave much greater emphasis to and detailed comments on the management of people than on the management of physical and financial resources. This reflects, perhaps, the recognition in education service industries of the centrality of people and their relationship to the effective provision of those services. It is reflected in the balance of material in this section.

In reflecting on the management of people, many principals made reference to how this grew from and was informed by the culture of a school, an aspect discussed earlier in this chapter under the educational and managerial values of leaders. Several principals commented on the need to manage themselves as one of those people. Discussion of this aspect has been included in the section on principals' leadership styles since style in part includes how people manage themselves in relation to other people and to the tasks which they face.

Several principals suggested or implied that there were or ought to be commonalties between the way in which staff were managed and the way in which other people – students and parents, not least – were managed. Such common aspects would be reflected in how people were treated as individuals as an enactment of a school's culture; how the interactions of gender and status were handled; how conflict was handled; how decisions were taken and implemented; how staff development was fostered; effective networking with parents, governors and the local community. These were set in the context of how principals managed the changes in the socio-political environment of education and the delegation of funding to their institutions.

Gender, status and respect for individuals

Principals tended to be concerned to encourage people 'to develop themselves as fully as possible; to learn for life and to be different' (Hyde). This required principals 'to trust staff and to encourage people to take risks and challenges' (Marsh). To 'promote that sense of challenge several principals talked about trying to delegate decision-making to staff whenever possible or explaining decisions openly' (Marsh). It led Rosemary Whinn-Sladden to consider 'fairness . . . a key value to managing staff and children and the non-teaching staff'.

Principals claimed that they demonstrated respect for people through 'a deep commitment to equal opportunities . . . that we are all in this together' (Clarke) which meant that 'Non-teaching staff must be considered equal with other staff, e.g. all staff come to staff meetings and all are listened to if they wish to contribute' (Whinn-Sladden). It also meant that 'equal opportunities should permeate everything you do, even if there is no explicit policy' (Blatchford) and this should be revealed through the curriculum, too. For example, there should be 'a concern to give girls equal opportunities especially in sciences' (Hyde).

How conflict was handled

Many of the principals interviewed claimed to want to diffuse tension whenever possible, although this did not inhibit them from taking tough action when necessary.

> The changes in the Arts Faculty in the end were forced through. The staff didn't want to do any of this but I said 'look you either come up with some ideas and we discuss them or I make the decision, but the status quo is not an option. (Edwards)

Changes in funding meant that the numbers of staff had to be reduced and the faculty restructured into a more effective shape.

Mary Gray felt good relations amongst staff were maintained by sustaining the self-esteem of staff, praising them when they did good work, encouraging them to take as much responsibility as they could (Hyde), and supporting staff when they faced problems (Whinn-Sladden). In addition the maintenance of agreed institutional values (Marsh), policies and practices (Whinn-Sladden; Marsh) were perceived as ways of preventing a build-up of tension, as was taking action quickly, if quietly, when things went wrong (Clarke; Gray). Finding out what people wanted from situations (Hyde) also helped, as did reducing people's anxiety (Hyde) about what might happen, sometimes by helping people to face situations which were inevitable (Clarke; Edwards).

This approach required principals to listen to what staff were saying to them: 'being aware of what is going on in every classroom and making time to talk with the teachers about it' (Whinn-Sladden). This could happen through formal processes of appraisal, through asking questions when there seemed to be a sense of unease amongst staff (Marsh), as well as through listening to grumbles. Keith Bovair thought that staff needed 'to sound-off occasionally, to have the opportunity to complain and grumble in a staff meeting. Then they are happy that the headteacher has listened.' Several principals emphasized that the way to handle conflict when it occurred was to be open with the protagonists but to see them quietly, away from a public arena: 'speaking with staff who are in conflict with you quietly and directly, explain that you can understand them but for the good of the school things have to be otherwise' (Gray). They also thought it important to reduce collateral damage from conflicts by being open about decisions. This reduced the degree of speculation amongst staff about what had been decided and the reasons for a decision. In turn this reduced the tendency for coalitions to form to support one or both camps in a conflict (Gray).

In routine cases of conflict, staff under-performance, for example, it was thought to be more effective to work through existing staff structures, within the framework of existing policy, than for a principal to intervene directly (Clarke; Edwards).

How decisions were taken and implemented

Although several principals perceived themselves as chief executives who had to take decisions and make judgements (Bovair), they also acknowledged that they had to have 'a well-oiled machine for running a school' (Blatchford). Ken Edwards thought it necessary to use 'a managerial network in a series of layers all of which can pick up information and ideas and spread ideas and produce feedback'. He believed the culture of universities precluded authoritarian leadership, a view which was echoed for schools by Brian Sherratt (Ribbins and Marland, 1994).

Several of the nine principals emphasized the importance of a collaborative approach to decision-making, pointing out that consultation (Clarke; Bovair; Hyde) and working alongside other people (Whinn-Sladden) were key means of developing teams of people who could take decisions in particular aspects of an institution's management: 'As a headteacher you can't do much on your own. You can only achieve things with people working around you' (Clarke). On the other hand 'delegating responsibility is difficult because you have to accept that staff will do the best they can although that may not be how you would have done it' (Gray), and there was a risk that action would not be taken or not be taken in time. To lessen the risks Mary Gray set clear datelines for tasks and offered support to those people who were struggling with them.

How staff development was fostered

Helen Hyde, among other principals, thought her most important job was to look after staff. Keith Bovair thought his school should apply its philosophy of empowering people consistently, equally to staff and to students. But other principals acknowledged the importance of appointing the right people in the first place (Blatchford; Whinn-Sladden) and then keeping in touch with their development (Edwards; Blatchford).

Effective staff development required principals to help people make the best use of the strengths they had at whatever point in their careers they found themselves (Bovair), although this sometimes meant helping them to face up to unpalatable choices (Edwards). Where staff development focused on preparing people for promotion, principals suggested a range of possibilities: 'work shadowing, working alongside more senior staff' (Hyde); 'being involved in conversations about decision-making particularly when there is conflict' (Clarke).

Delegation was also an important means of helping competent staff to develop because it gave them a chance to meet a school's needs creatively (Clarke). For senior staff it gave them a real opportunity to work with and support other staff. For heads of department and non-promoted teachers it gave them the opportunity to focus on particular tasks and take decisions in particular areas which were their delegated responsibilities (Hyde).

To promote staff development Roy Blatchford emphasized the importance of giving staff time when they needed it and of providing them with institutional support, though often that support would be to help them meet the school's needs (Whinn-Sladden) rather than, necessarily, their own idiosyncratic interests. Several principals thought training should be available for all staff, although there are problems in financing it for non-teaching staff in schools.

Effective networking with parents, governors and the local community

Principals placed considerable emphasis on the importance of helping parents and governors to share the values espoused by the schools. Helen Hyde described this as the need to talk excellence to parents. Rosemary Whinn-Sladden and Mary Gray stressed the importance of welcoming parents into schools and encouraging them to make a contribution to the pupils' education either by helping with the pedagogy or with the administration. She saw her school as part of a greater community and gave an example of parents helping the children plant trees to improve the environment. To recognize the help the parents gave, the school bought each a small plant. The importance of parental involvement to student educational development, particularly for younger pupils, is well attested. In turn this required principals to listen to what parents had to say about education (Bovair) and to allow them to influence the core values of a school (Hyde) developed by senior staff and governors (Bovair; Blatchford).

The benefits of collaboration with the civic community were seen to accrue to the students (Gray) who profited from good publicity. She also suggested that it reduced the level of vandalism to a school and the level of stress experienced by a headteacher. Schools gained positively from having greater access to resources to support the curriculum (Bovair) either from parents or from the local business community. Whinn-Sladden comments that 'We have a thriving education-business partnership which brings support and resources into the school. We are hoping to persuade the TEC to fund our use of GNVQs to develop non-teaching staff training.'

Roy Blatchford, amongst others, pointed out the value of a school having good professional links with other educational institutions to resolve problems and offer opportunities to students and also, perhaps, to staff. Rosemary Whinn-Sladden was rather less complimentary about her local professional networks of headteachers! Helen Hyde said that these networks offered her school considerable support, a view borne out by all the headteachers in a recent study of school networks by Busher and Hodgkinson (1996) in the midlands of the UK.

Managing resources in the changed socio-political environment of education

How senior staff managed the other people involved with their organizations was circumscribed by their administrative and financial responsibilities. These have been greatly increased in the UK in schools since the passing of the Education Reform Act (1988). Several principals commented on the long hours they worked, as was discussed earlier in this chapter, and that they worked most if not every evening of the week. Keith Bovair talked about needing to have help with the budget from two deputy heads, as well as making a great deal of use of computers in administration. Helen Hyde noted that despite the involvement of a deputy head and a bursar to help her she still had to have some meetings at 8 a.m. (with the site supervisor) to avoid interrupting people's work. Mortimore and Mortimore with Thomas (1994) noted the emergence of bursars as commonplace in maintained schools since 1990, and the School Teachers' Review Body (1995) noted a 30 per cent increase in non-teaching staff between 1989 and 1994 at a time when the employment of full-time teaching staff increased at a rate less than that of pupils in schools (2 per cent). Qualitative data from the east midlands of the UK suggests that much of this increase has been focused on clerical duties and posts to cope with the management of finance and personnel now undertaken by schools but previously carried out in maintained schools by LEAs. This suggests that the delegation of funding to school organizations has taken resources away from the core purposes of schools, students and the curriculum, into administration, of necessity to meet schools' new and increased administrative and financial responsibilities.

Although the delegation of funding 'had increased teachers' workloads, especially the amount of paperwork. The latter prevents headteachers being involved with teaching and learning' (Whinn-Sladden), several principals saw an advantage in the management of staff in the delegation of funding to schools. Mary Gray thought that in sharing school budget implications with staff it helped them to realize the problems the school faced in ensuring there were adequate resources available to meet the needs of pupils (Bovair). Helen Hyde and Roy Blatchford perceived it as a vehicle for giving staff increased autonomy within a whole-school framework, a view echoed by Ken Edwards in a university. On the other hand 'cut-backs in resources provided by the LEA have made it difficult to put in place ideas which will maximize existing resources. No sooner have you developed these than they are overtaken by another round of cuts' (Bovair).

How do they understand their accountability?

Simkins (1992) offers four main models of accountability for teachers and schools, first a professional model in which a licensed person is granted autonomy to act within a socially legitimated code, and then three other forms which represent various types of control by some people over the actions of others. These are a managerial model in which control is exercised through bureaucratic structures and power derives from the authority of office of the most senior person in an organization; a political model in which power derives from election to office; and a market model in which power is derived from consumer choice.

It is useful for purposes of analysis to recognize that teachers are called to account in a variety of ways, but more useful if those categories can be clearly distinguished. The East Sussex Accountability Project (1979) produced a threefold typology of responsiveness by teachers to their environment which offers such clarity. They suggested that one form of accountability was genuine, i.e. people could be called to account for their actions within an hierarchical process. If a person failed to carry out their prescribed duties they could be coerced and, ultimately, deprived of office. As power is hierarchically located in this model, it does not matter whether power derives from political election/acclamation or from the authority vested in a senior position in a bureaucracy. In this view political and managerial accountability are two closely related versions of the same model. Examples of such accountability by some of the principals who were interviewed are discussed below.

A second form, answerability, poses rather more problems since the location of power is not bureaucratically connected to the actor. Therefore the means of exercising that power are indirect. Indeed, power could be said to have become transmuted to influence, i.e. actors are open to various sorts of pressure, but not to legitimate coercion. It might be said, for example, that teachers are answerable to parents. In this case principals can feel they are obliged to respond to parental views about a school, as Mary Marsh indicated she felt she did. Were a principal not to respond, the parents would have to acquire political power through, say, joining the school governing body or influencing people already on that body, before they would have the right to coerce the principal into doing what they wanted. In doing so, of course, parents would move into an hierarchical relationship with the principal, activating the genuine or bureaucratic model of accountability.

Without recourse to a model of genuine (bureaucratic) accountability, were the parents so minded, they could exert influence over the principal in various ways, for example, by threatening or actually withdrawing their children from the school. The notion of answerability, then, fits comfortably with Simkins' (1992) notion of market accountability but has the advantage of keeping the term 'accountability' for one particular (bureaucratic) model of relationship between a professional worker and the stakeholders in an organization.

This leaves the model of professional 'accountability', which can, perhaps best be described as responsibility. In this, people may be said to be answerable for what they do, or morally accountable for their actions, though it is difficult to see how any pressure can be brought to bear through this model on a person for the quality of their work, apart from through the moral suasion of colleagues and others and the internalized values of the actor. It is in this sense, perhaps, that both Rosemary Whinn-Sladden and Ken Edwards acknowledge their accountability to their students and the *people who are devoting their lives to this institution* (Edwards). Such professional responsibility easily encompasses Helen Hyde's view that she set herself high standards of performance because '*staff have to be able to trust and rely on me as a real leader to represent and to guide and look after them [and] . . . I must be the best role model I can for the [students]*'. This sense of professional responsibility includes a professional ethic of how a person ought to behave. In other professions such ethics have been enshrined – the word is used deliberately – in professional codes of practice. These allow a bureaucratic accountability ultimately to be imposed on those practitioners who fail to implement sufficiently rigorously the work values which they are supposed to have internalized during their induction into a profession.

Within this framework of three types of responsiveness by principals to the stakeholders in their educational institutions, Rosemary Whinn-Sladden suggests there is a bureaucratic relationship of accountability between principals and their governors: 'They have got to be involved in those [school] decisions and not just ratify something that I say. . . . They have been known to give me a hard time over things, but that is fair because I give them a hard time over things and we work together'. Being accountable, as this suggests, also implies that the people with the greater power have responsibilities to those with the lesser. We begin to close on Salisbury's notions of the ideal relationship between the classes in mid-nineteenth-century England, where although the rich had privileges, they also had responsibilities to the poor, not least to ensure social chaos did not develop. In this vein some principals, such as Keith Bovair, recognized their accountability to the LEA, acknowledging that they still had to keep its officers informed. In return they looked for what support they could from the more slimly proportioned LEAs of the 1990s. Those principals in non-LEA institutions claimed no such obvious chain of accountability beyond their own governing bodies, though one exists for GM schools to the Grant Maintained Schools Centre and to the Funding Agency for Schools which was established in 1993.

The emergence of parent charters and student charters (Edwards) can be viewed as an attempt to give answerability an edge of bureaucracy, i.e. to begin to move the relationship between students, parents and principals into a mode of account-ability rather than answerability. In this context it is curious that Roy Blatchford does not perceive himself as accountable to, or at least through, the school inspec-tors who work for OFSTED, although he acknowledges they are an important part of the system. They clearly seem to be agents through which schools are held accountable to the state, i.e. bring about a genuine (bureaucratic) accountability of schools to some of those who wield power in the education system – central gov-ernment. The current inspectoral system with its central state control shows, perhaps, the extent to which the power of the Secretary of State reaches out to the periphery of the education system despite the rhetoric and the reality of the devo-lution of power to educational institutions and their governing bodies.

At any one time principals of educational institutions are likely to feel themselves engaged in all three types of responsiveness to different groups of stakeholders in their institutions. In the busy press of organizational life the principals in this study drew a crude distinction between formal accountability (genuine accountability and answerability) and their sense of professional responsibility for the quality of what they did. This is, perhaps, sufficient rational typology for processes which are essentially flows of power with particular strengths or valencies depending on the sources from which they emanate. More important in the future, perhaps, than further sophisticated casuistry in the naming of accountable parts is to understand the dynamics of how principals handle the ebb and flow of political, micro-political and moral influences in their relationships with those who have a stake in their institutions.

References

Bass, B. (1985) *Leadership and Performance Beyond Expectations*, New York: Free Press.

Bennis, W. and Nannus, B. (1985) *Leaders: The Strategies for Taking Charge*, London: Harper.

Blase, J. and Blase, J.(1995) 'The micropolitical orientation of facilitative school principals and its effects on teachers' sense of empowerment', paper given at the American Educational Research Association (AERA) Conference, San Francisco: April.

Bolman, L. and Deal, T. (1991) *Reframing Organisations*, Oxford: Jossey Bass.

Bolman, L. and Deal, T. (1994) 'Looking for leadership: Another search party's report' *Educational Administrative Quarterly* 30 (1) 77–96.

Bryman, A. (1992) *Charisma and Leadership in Organisations*, London: Sage.

Busher, H. and Hodgkinson, K. (1996) 'Co-operation and tension between autonomous schools: a study of inter-school networking' *Educational Review* 48 (1) 55–64.

Busher, H. and Saran, R. (1992) *Teachers and their conditions of employment*, Bedford Way series, London: Kogan Page in association with the London Institute of Education.

Busher, H. and Saran, R. (1995) 'Managing staff professionally' in Busher, H. and Saran, R. (eds) (1995) *Managing Teachers as Professionals in Schools*, London: Kogan Page.

Davies, L (1995) *Who needs Headteachers?* Keynote paper given at the BEMAS Annual Conference 1995, 23–25 September, Oxford, UK.

East Sussex Accountability Project (1979) 'Accountability in the middle years of schooling', University of Sussex mimeo in McCormick, R. (ed.) (1982) *Calling Education to Account*, London: Heinemann Educational.

Evetts, J. (1994) 'The new headteacher: the changing work culture of secondary headship' *School Organization*, 14 (1) 37–47.

Gibb, C. (1947) 'The principles and traits of leadership' in Gibb, C. (ed) *Leadership*, Harmondsworth: Penguin.

Gronn, P. (1986) 'Politics, power and the management of schools' in Hoyle, E. and McMahon, A. (eds) *The Management of Schools*, London: Kogan Page.

Gronn, P. (1996) 'From transactions to transformations: A new world order in the study of leadership' *Educational Management and Administration*, 24 (1) (Keynote paper given at the BEMAS Annual Conference 1995, 23–25 September, Oxford, UK).

Handy, C. (1991) *Gods of Management*, London: Business Books.

Hargreaves, A. (1990) 'Contrived collegiality: The micro-politics of teacher collaboration' in Blase, J. (ed) *The Politics of School Life*, New York: Sage.

Heller, H. (1985) *Helping Schools Change: A Handbook for Leaders in Education*, York: Centre for the Study of Comprehensive Schools.

Hodgkinson, C. (1991) *Educational Leadership: the Moral Art*, New York: SUNY Press.

Hoyle, E. (1986) *The Politics of School Management*, London: Hodder & Stoughton.

Huckman, L. and Hill, T. (1994) 'Local Management of Schools: rationality and decision-making in the employment of teachers' *Oxford Review of Education* 20 (2) 185–197.

Hughes, M. (1973) 'The professional-as-administrator: the case of the secondary school Head' *Educational Administration Bulletin*, 2 (1) 11–23.

Hunt, J. (1991) *Leadership: A new synthesis*, Newbury Park: Sage.

Locke, M. (1992) 'The application of trust in the management of institutions' paper given at the BEMAS Annual Conference, 12–13 September, Bristol.

Mortimore, P. and Mortimore, J. with Thomas, H. (1994) *Managing Associate Staff: Innovation in Primary and Secondary Schools*, London: Chapman.

Ribbins, P. and Marland, M. (1994) *Headship Matters: Conversations with Seven Secondary Headteachers*, London: Longman.

Ribbins, P. (1989) 'Managing secondary schools after the Act: Participation and Partnership?' in Lowe, R. (ed.) *The Changing Secondary School*, Lewes: Falmer.

School Teachers' Review Body (1995) *Fourth Report* CM 2765, London: HMSO.

Simkins, T. (1992) 'Policy, Accountability and management perspectives on the implementation of reform' in Simkins, T., Ellison, L. and Garrett, V. (1992) *Implementing Educational Reform: The Early Lessons,* Harlow: Longman in association with BEMAS.

Sinclair, A. (1995) 'The seduction of the self-managed team and the reinvention of the team as a group' *Leading and Managing* 1 (1) 44–63.

Index